Praise For
DANCE WHILE THE FIRE BURNS

"Deborah Ann Lucas sensitively explores the wild self yearning for art, recognition and connection, and how she grew to define herself as sister, wife and woman, and ultimately reclaim her artistic self. With humor, pathos and well-drawn characters, we see her family—both human and horse—as clearly as we see her art. A beautiful excursion into memoir from a driven artist triumphing over chronic pain and sharing the wisdom gained along the way."

— Allison K. Williams, author of *Seven Drafts*

"…Lucas pens her story in heart-warming transparency, exploring family bonds…she learns to embrace her unique path, particularly after meeting Greg—whose steady, loving presence grounds her and inspires pursuit of her artistic dreams….As Lucas builds a secure self-identity, readers will be moved by her touching story of found family and the unwavering love between siblings…."

— BookLife Review

"…her relationship with her brother is honest and raw, and though readers know the outcome from the beginning, the ending packs a punch. A heartfelt, often engaging exploration of messy family dynamics, grief, and healing."

— Kirkus Review

Lucas's story is a testament to perseverance, as she navigates obstacle after obstacle with unwavering determination. With skillful pacing and vivid descriptions, the author puts us right in the saddle, experiencing every triumph and heartache of her wild ride.

—Joan Fernandez, author of *Saving Vincent*

"I couldn't put the book down. Deborah pulled me into her world and didn't let go. Reading her memoir *Dance While The Fire Burns* is like

watching a movie....Fast paced and at times breathless, she tells her story with an unflinching look back on the first forty years of her life."
— Michaela von Schweinitz, writer, editor, and book coach

"when an author manages to pull you in so completely and you feel you stand with her in the story of her family and her life, you know you've got something special in your hands."
— Sandra Postma, writer, editor, and book coach

"Deborah Ann Lucas's decades-spanning memoir *Dance While the Fire Burns* is a bold and beautiful tale of an extraordinary life. Lucas's love for her family, her art, and the many animals that come into her life, is palpable and richly told."
— Jennifer Landau, writer, editor, and book coach

"*Dance While the Fire Burns* is a masterful weaving of the threads of the author's life—horses, art, and her family—all coming together in a way that couldn't be more compelling. It has inspired me to adhere to my dreams no matter what challenges may appear."
— Mary Yero Bernstein, book coach, editor, and writer

This memoir was engaging from the first page. I couldn't put it down....To read of Deborah's bravery and tenacity through her life's many challenges, of her healing by and of horses, of her true and enduring call as an artist and her refusal to deny what was calling her--this is all so inspiring and calls for self reflection by the reader. Dance While the Fire Burns is a book of hope for writer and reader.
— Karen, Goodreads review

"Deborah Ann Lucas' memoir is a captivating tapestry woven from threads of resilience, creativity, and healing that invites readers to embark on their own transformative journeys. ...I find myself enchanted by her ability to turn calamity into opportunities for growth and empowerment."
— Catherine L. Goodreads review

DANCE WHILE
THE FIRE BURNS

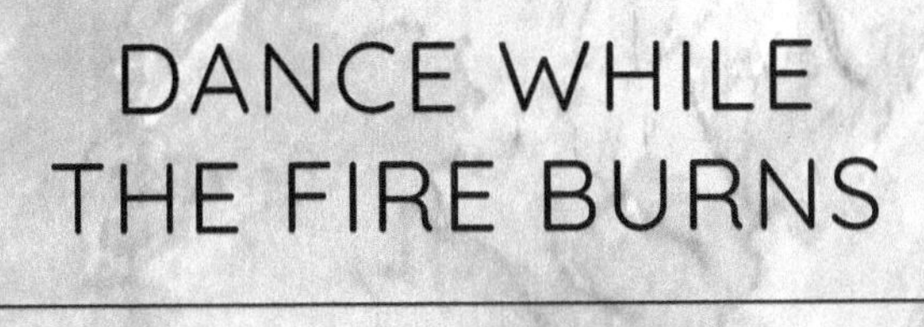

DANCE WHILE
THE FIRE BURNS

FAMILY, IDENTITY, AND DREAMS

DEBORAH ANN LUCAS

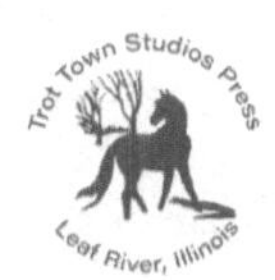

For Greg

My partner who makes all things possible.

The future belongs to those who

believe in the beauty of their dreams.

— ELEANOR ROOSEVELT

CONTENTS

PART 3

HEALING WITH HORSES

AUTHOR'S NOTE

With all my immediate family gone, I am unable to check my memories against theirs. But I believe they would be delighted to know their stories have been written and, even though told through my voice and perspective, are safe from the disintegration of time.

My intention has always been to tell the best truth, including my fear, regret, hope, and vision of the future, flawed as it may be. In each chapter, I write as if I am in that moment of time, without the benefit of reflection and insight that comes with aging.

This story is true, but to protect the privacy of some individuals, I have changed their names.

PART 1

SEARCHING FOR HOME

*Hope begins in the dark, the stubborn hope that
if you just show up and try to do the right thing, the dawn will come.
You wait and watch and work: you don't give up.*

— ANNE LAMOTT

CHAPTER ONE

THE CALL 1995

The August sun beats down on my back as I drag my feet across the limestone gravel drive to the barn. Cracks zigzag across the pasture; patches of thirsty brown blades, like me, plead for relief. I catch sight of our horses deep in the woods with heads lowered and tails swishing, grazing on grass, still green in the shade.

A thousand miles away, my brother Chuck lies in a bed at the Sarah House in Santa Barbara, where I moved him from the Van Nuys hospital three weeks ago. Before flying home, I hung my impressionist cafe scene, a lithograph he'd always wanted, above his Kachina collection in his room. A sweet aroma from the community garden outside his door comforts him, like the scent of roses he once tended at a home he no longer owns.

We both have red hair and brown eyes, like Mom. People often mistake us for twins, even though he is four years older than I am. Our family moved nearly every year when we were kids, leaving me lost in an endless stream of strangers, changed routines, and unfamiliar surroundings. When my loneliness became unbearable and our oldest brother, Mike, was off with his friends, Chuck spent time with me and my stuffed animals. Now, he needs me.

I slide open a heavy door to the old slumped-back barn, then pull a bale of hay from an unstable stack of forty-pound bales, the best my husband Greg and I could find when we arrived in the Midwest six months ago. I lift the misshapen bale by its loose strings, praying it holds together. But just outside the door in the pasture, the hay breaks out of its two-twine confinement, and the flakes fall to the ground. I wish I could fall apart too.

I pick up four flakes from the hay I dropped and carry them to the flat area south of the barn, adjacent to the old-growth forest. I shake one flake into a loose pile, then move six feet—longer than the body of a horse—to create the next pile.

Greg calls out, "Deborah! You have a phone call."

I twist in slow motion toward Greg on the porch, his hand bracing the glass storm door, unaware of the flies surely racing past him into our kitchen. I bite back my usual rebuke. What's a few more flies in that mess of a house from half-done renovations and repairs?

Greg says, softer than before, "I think it's time."

His words carry over the lawn, down the cement wall, across the yellow stone lane to the pasture where I stand clutching flakes of hay to my chest.

Shit. I'm not ready.

Not ready to leave Greg and the horses again after only a few weeks home. Not ready to squeeze my overweight body into a crammed airplane and disembark into a family drama with intolerable choices. I need more time. To rest. To recover my strength. To regain some level of emotional equilibrium. To cope with the strain of overseeing Chuck's care, knowing I will lose him no matter what I do.

I raise my voice. "I need to finish feeding the horses first."

For me, as much as for them.

Greg nods and disappears inside the house.

In a blur, the horses emerge from the shadows of the shagbark hickory and ancient burr oak as if the trees themselves have come to life. The herd, now six with the new foal, bursts out of the trees, their hooves pounding the dry earth. Ka-pa-lunk, ka-pa-lunk, ka-pa-lunk.

Lance, my seventeen-hand Thoroughbred and the head of the herd, draws near to where I am working. I hurry to retrieve the remainder of the bale and finish the circle. He slows to a trot, then to a walk to sample each pile. I step back to watch the rest of the herd arrive. Each claims a mound of hay, and their ritual begins. Lance pushes Sonia off her hay, so she tosses her head at Ben and takes his. And around they go, stopping for a few bites until chased off to find an unclaimed spot around the circle, like a game of musical chairs. Sometimes, Lance hoards two piles, stretching his long body between them, protecting one with the threat of his teeth, the other with a kick. I drop an extra flake or two, expanding the circle to minimize any conflict that might cause injuries.

When the game slows to a stop, I loop one hand under Lance's neck. With the other, I smooth out knots along his shoulder using the flat of my fist, then shift to work my fingers along his back.

I rest my forehead on Lance's flanks to inhale his sweet sweat. Nestling my fingers into his coat, I massage a tight muscle until I feel it release. Lance cradles me in an embrace, swinging his head around my back. This majestic gelding is my confidant. Chuck helped me buy him when I didn't have enough money of my own.

I don't know if I'm prepared to be Chuck's caretaker. You'd think my family, living within a few hours of Chuck, wouldn't need my help. But they do. Chuck, an RN, doesn't accept help easily. Mom tries. But with her inherited anxiety, amplified by another verbally abusive husband, she gets overwhelmed.

Our dad, married to someone else, has been absent. Mike drives into the city for a higher wage to make a better life for his kids. During his off time, he helps Chuck. I get anxious like Mom, scared I'll make the wrong choice, like pushing him too much or in the wrong direction, or if I give up too soon when he resists. Chuck is the best of our family; his humor lifts us up when times are tough.

He's been in and out of the hospital for the past ten years. When the doctors gave up on him, he fought his way back. Will he prove them wrong again? His partner Don died seven years ago, exhausted by the same battle. Maybe this time Chuck will give in too. Then we can all rest...but I'm ashamed for thinking it.

Tree leaves rustle. I lift my chin in the abusive heat to feel the light breeze pass over my skin, carrying away the dampness as it does the moisture from the broad hickory leaves. I slip my hand between Lance's front legs to gauge his body temperature, remembering the time we'd almost lost him to colic from the California desert heat.

"You doin' all right, boy?"

His left ear perks to my whisper. Lance drops his head and licks his lips. He's talking to me, and I know how to listen. His chest isn't hot, so I don't need to worry about him colicking—at least not today. But if I fly to LA, the horses will need close supervision to keep them cool and hydrated. Greg will need to do it all. That's what I'll be asking of him.

He steps out onto the covered porch. "Deborah! Are you coming?" His voice echoes across the expanse like the beating of a drum, summoning me for duty.

"Okay, okay." I look back at the hose. Taking the time to watch the fifty-gallon tank fill would be pleasant, to lose myself in the flow of the water, remembering how I dove into the lake when we were kids, the water streaming through my red hair and across my pale skin. How I swam out to meet my brothers, relaxing on the raft with Chuck in the warm sun, watching Mike practice jackknife dives.

Lance perks his ears toward the house, but I don't look. When I hear the screen door snap shut, I know Greg has gone back inside. Lance twitches, then drops his head. His dark eyes meet mine, soft like he understands, forgiving me for leaving again. He snorts toward the herd as they return to the woods to graze. I nod to send him on his way, and watch him lope over the dry packed earth, throwing clumps in the air when he bucks mid-stride.

Ducking under the hot-wire fence to take a shortcut back to the house, I get zapped for my carelessness. I knock the dirt off my broken-down Adidas on the concrete blocks that serve as steps, then hang onto the doorframe to steady my balance. Inside, I kick off my shoes in the mudroom, leaving me in stocking feet on the vinyl floor someone installed using staples along the edges.

The kitchen is how we found it eight months ago. Shelf paper, marred by rips, rubs, and digs, covers plywood countertops. One cabinet, not yet attached to the wall, rocks when I lean on it. We were crazy to have bought this house. But from the first time I stepped inside, I knew this was where I belonged. I see not a shambles, but what it *can* be. Anyway, it's the best we can afford.

I rinse the dirt off my hands and forearms over a sink full of dishes, clean up the splashes with a paper towel, then leave the rest for Greg. He may grumble a bit, but no matter how much I ask of him, he gets it done.

I reach for the phone, drop into the nearest chair, and punch in the numbers for the Sarah House. Debbie, the director, answers. "You need to come now."

CHAPTER TWO

UPSIDE DOWN 1964-1965

After three years in a Catholic school, with nothing but classwork and attending mass, I'm finally a freshman in the public high school where my brothers graduated. I've joined the theater makeup crew and the debate club, even tried out for the dance team.

Mashing potatoes at the sink, Mom asks, "So, how did it go?"

"I got nervous when my shorts rode up on my fat thighs and blew it in the final round." A burning smell wafts over from the stove.

"Mom, the peas are boiling." She rushes over to twist the heat off and removes the pan from the red-hot electric heat coil. My brothers used to tease her every time she boiled the peas, but with Mike in the army reserves, Chuck away in college, and Dad working late, dinners are often only Mom and me. I cut a serving of meatloaf, plop it on my plate next to the mashed potatoes, and reach for the catsup when Dad strides in the front door, all puffed up with a big grin.

"We're moving to Australia." He's beaming with pride, chosen out of all the GM automotive engineers for a special three-year troubleshooting assignment with the Holden division.

Sure, Australia is exciting, but I don't want to go. Arguing with Dad won't help. At 14, I have no choice but to submit.

This move, more than any of the others, will turn my life upside down. I guess by going *down under,* it will, literally. *That's funny.* Too bad I don't feel like sharing the pun.

After Dad leaves the table to watch the news, I ask Mom, "Can I take Tina on the plane?" She's my Scottish Terrier.

Mom's face drops. "We can't take her. The UK and Australia both have quarantine laws. That's a year before she'd be allowed in the country. She'd never survive it."

"Can't Dad figure out a way for her to come?"

Mom shakes her head.

I slump into my chair with arms crossed. I'll be miserable without Tina, but I won't make her suffer through quarantine. I can't stay here, so I shut down and do what I'm told.

When he comes home for Thanksgiving, Chuck says, "Maybe Dad will buy me a ticket so I can come visit."

Since Chuck doesn't write letters and we can't afford long-distance calls, I'll be on my own. Dad leaves Sunday night for Detroit to receive special training. The next day, the movers arrive to pack and crate our belongings. Mom helps me pack Grandma's old suitcase, then we join Dad at the Detroit hotel. The furniture needs more than a month's head start to cross the Pacific by ship before we can depart for Melbourne.

In late January I blow out candles in the restaurant of our hotel in downtown Detroit while I pretend to enjoy celebrating my fifteenth birthday. Dad presents me with my first watch, and Mom says, "We're going shopping. Debby and I need new luggage." She smiles at me. "You can choose any color you like." I'm thinking about red when Chuck gives me a hug from behind. "I need to get back to school and it's a long drive to Kalamazoo. Have a good flight. I'll see you next summer."

At Hudson's department store the next day, Mom says, "We'll buy all American Tourister. They make the best suitcases." I pick out a huge one in white and a smaller circular one to match. To add a bit of flair, I add a red over-the-shoulder bag for my cosmetics. Mom nods her approval. "Now, we're ready to travel around the world."

After staying a month in the hotel, Dad's training extends our stay into February. I'm going stir-crazy and sneak out to wander the city streets. When I return two hours later, Mom says, "You had me worried sick. Don't leave the hotel again."

Just before dawn, Mom drags me through the airport, my eyes out of focus, my senses numb. On the plane, I'm strapped in a seat with a view of cornfields and mountains, arriving on the west coast in a mere three hours. We're hustled onto a second plane, more crowded than the first, that will take us across the Pacific with a stopover in Hawaii.

I stare out the round window through parting clouds at the vast ocean below. When the hostess in her navy uniform serves me champagne and kangaroo-tail soup, I get a nod from Mom to drink the champagne. The soup is strange but eatable. I imagine a life jetting around the globe. But the ache from abandoning my dog drowns out my enthusiasm for traveling. She was my constant companion for three years. I fed her, learned to groom her wiry coat, and walked her before breakfast, dinner, and bedtime. When I attended Girl Scout camp one summer, I wrote her a postcard every day. Now, she is Grandma's dog.

The day we arrive in Melbourne, instead of the expected sunshine, it's raining. To make things worse, we learn dock strikes are delaying our furniture. We'll be living out of suitcases like vagabonds for another three months. To cheer me up, Mom takes me across a busy street to a beauty shop where I get a pixie haircut like hers. I love my new look!

The next day, the sun comes out, and the hotel pool, a luxury after a long winter back home, entices me in. I dive into the deep end and swim to the far edge, when I see the watch Dad gave me for my birthday on my wrist. *Shit! I forgot to take it off.*

"Dad, how do I get water out of my watch crystal?" I ask him that evening.

"I thought you'd take better care of it," he says in his gruff voice.

Disappointing him is worse than getting yelled at. He never fixes my watch. *I didn't really want a watch, anyway. It made my skin itch.*

"I don't want to go to an all-girls school." I'm wringing my hands in the backseat of a taxi with Mom while Dad's in front next to the driver.

Mom says, "You'll be fine. Just think of it as another adventure."

I hate when she says that. It just means me coping with the chaos of another move.

"Why can't I go to the coed public school?"

Dad says, "The tuition is too high."

I'm wearing a green and white checked dress, the required summer uniform. I did wear a Girl Scouts uniform in sixth grade. On those days, after school, I walked for miles with other girls to the meeting held in a church basement. Along the way, I spotted a barn from the road and ventured down a short lane to visit two horses. I'd been on pony rides at the fair, but never up close with a big horse, loose in a corral. The owner, a single woman about Mom's age, taught me to brush them, put hay in their manger, and muck out their stalls, but never how to ride. Petting them and smelling their sweet smell was like living in a dream. *Maybe I'll find a horse here.*

Mom opens her wallet. "You'll need money to ride the tram home. How many shillings are in a pound?"

"Twenty," I reply.

"Charlie, why couldn't you get me the new money?"

Dad glances back at us.

Mom stares steely-eyed at him. She shakes her head and fans the bills. I point out a colorful one with *Two Dollars* on the back and she hands it to me.

We turn into a gate between ten-foot-high walls with spikes and embedded broken glass. *It's like a prison.*

We meet with Mother Superior, then another sister leads me away through an open courtyard to a class among a long row of rooms. Unfamiliar with the accent, I understand half of what anyone is saying. This is ten times worse than being the new kid—I'm the only American.

At lunchtime, I'm directed to a room with long tables and benches. Some girls from my morning class wave me over. Most have dark hair twisted into one or two braids and all wear dresses identical to my uniform, only mine gaps over my bust. I reach into my pocket for a safety pin but come up empty.

The girl with horned-rimmed glasses out of the 40s blurts out, "How can you Yanks stand eating peanut butter and jelly sandwiches?" I can barely understand her accent.

"What? That's my favorite." I look at her with my head cocked to one side like my dog Tina used to do. *How I miss her.*

"We eat jelly with whipped cream or plain with a spoon. But never on bread! My favorite's lime."

I scrunch my brow. "Lime jelly?"

"You know," retro-glasses girl says, "you make it from a jelly packet: mix the powder with water in a bowl and put it in the fridge until it gets all wiggly." Several girls nod in agreement.

"We call that Jell-O." Their heads shake. *How do I explain?* "What do you call a fruit spread for toast that's smooth with no lumpy fruit in it?"

"Jam," three of the girls say in unison.

"That's jelly to us. No wonder you're confused." I laugh. The girls laugh too.

Then a redheaded girl they call Maureen says, "What do you call where you keep food cold in the kitchen?"

"You mean a fridge? Or refrigerator?"

"We say *ice box.*"

The first girl jumps in. "We call it a fridge too. Don't mind Maureen. She lives in the outback."

Maureen looks a bit hurt, then turns to me. "I'm a boarder," she explains. "My family owns a sheep station."

Still struggling with their heavy accent, it takes a minute to figure out Maureen lives here in the school dorm like Chuck at college. I didn't even know the school had a dorm.

"I go home over summer break to help shear sheep." I had to work out, with us being below the equator, she means over the Christmas holiday.

"That sounds cool."

"Do you know what a water closet is?" another girl cuts in. She has copper highlights in her dark hair with a single braid all the way to her waist.

I shake my head. I was afraid to guess wrong.

"The toilet," she answers.

"You put toilets in closets? Where do you keep your clothes?"

"In wardrobes."

"What's that?" All I heard were giggles and chuckles.

"A piece of furniture that's like a closet, but it moves around," she mimics the moving motion.

"A mobile closet? Really?" We all laugh so hard one girl snorts up her beverage.

When my last class lets out, I tram back to the hotel to do homework on the floor of my room. Mom watches television with Dad in their room but leaves the door open between us. While wrestling with a trig problem, I worry the girls at school won't like me when the novelty of my being American wears off.

At dinner, Mom asks, "What's wrong?"

I breathe in. "It's all too much. I'm in both Latin *and* French. I can't do it."

"You're talking yourself into failing. Just do your best."

Yeah, except Dad expects straight A's. If only I could have a peanut butter and jelly sandwich. But it's not on the menu. Mom went to buy groceries but only found Vegemite. *I hate that stuff.*

The following week, I lie on the hotel room floor doing homework for a *how-to-care-for-young-children* class. I'm drawing a baby in my workbook using colored pencils, hoping to get an A to bring up my lousy language grades.

A siren blares outside. My colored pencil slips, making a dark blue line across her face. I screech, "It's ruined. I can't do this!" I rip my drawing in half, then realize there's not enough time to start over. "I hate Australia!"

Mom's head shakes, a warning which only makes me madder.

"Why did you bring me here?" Pushing up from the floor, I scream, "I want to go *home!*" To stop my head from exploding, I grab it and yell, "I hate it here!"

"Debby, stop," Mom pleads without moving closer. "You'll disturb the other guests."

I clench my fists at my sides. "I hate it here!" I repeat even louder.

In a flash, a force strikes my face.

My cheek is on fire. *Dad slapped me!*

I cover my cheek with my hand while shooting darts of hatred from my eyes.

He recoils.

I run past him out the door, slamming it behind me, to race down the stairs, clutching the narrow rail to keep from tripping.

The curving staircase ends at the entrance of the nearly empty restaurant. I cross to the nearest table near a long glass wall, plop into a chair, my elbows on the table, my head in my hands, and gaze outside at the deserted swimming pool. I scoop the ice out of the water glass, fold it into the white cloth napkin, and hold it against my throbbing cheek.

I flag the wait-staff and order a fudge sundae. With no ice left in my water glass, they bring a second one along with a dry napkin. I nod my thanks and turn away, not willing to engage.

When the hot-and-cold black-and-white dessert arrives, I release the tablecloth edge. I savor the sweet fudge and creamy vanilla ice cream and recall how Dad hit my brothers to stop them from fighting. Once Chuck was so mad at Mike, he threw a knife. It missed him and stuck in the bedroom door. When Dad came home, Mom dragged me outside. Still, I heard his rage. But Dad quickly forgave my brothers and took them camping, leaving me at home, no matter how much I begged to go.

Another time, Mike was fighting with Chuck, and Mom stepped in to stop the brawl, but she got hurt instead. Dad bellowed, "Now you've hurt your mother," and struck Mike. With no place to hide, I backed up to the wall, my arms rigid at my sides, my lips quivering. When Mom saw me, she yelled at Dad. "Charlie!" Her tone broke his rage. She flicked her head toward me.

Everyone froze.

Dad deflated when he saw me cower. He crouched to look me in the face. "Sweetheart, you don't have to be afraid. I will never lay a hand on you. That's a promise."

Through the expanse of glass, the smooth water of the undisturbed pool shimmers like gold in the late day sun. Yesterday, I dove in and propelled myself across its length with wide arm swings and fast kicks, feeling the cool water flow over my skin. Today, I replay in my head the scene with Dad. If I go up to change into my swimsuit, I may see him, and I'm not ready to face him.

CHAPTER THREE

HORSES UNDER THE EUCALYPTUS 1965-1966

On Saturday after my first week of school, we're having breakfast in the hotel restaurant. I'm aching for something to do to banish my boredom when Dad announces, "We're going for a drive." Jumping into the back seat of Dad's Holden, his Australian company car, I'm comforted by the familiarity of a road trip.

Dad drives through town and comes to a six-road intersection with only stop signs, freaking Mom out, but intriguing me. He quickly learns the gutsiest driver goes first and maneuvers across like a stock car driver in a race.

Once outside the city, he keeps to the left side of the road with ease, even as the traffic diminishes. Mom, with nerves pricked, braces for a mishap at every intersection. After more than an hour, he turns onto a quiet dirt road, lined with towering eucalyptus on either side. I'm glued to the backseat window, looking for koala bears in the trees.

Mom yells, "Charlie, look out!"

From the crown on the graded gravel road, Dad swerves to the wrong side, narrowly missing an oncoming car, then touches Mom's thigh to reassure her. "We're okay."

Minutes later, he turns down a lane. I stick my head out the window, excited to see horses in a paddock sharing a pile of hay. I bite my tongue, afraid to hope.

When I was four, Dad took the family on a trip to Kentucky. On a two-lane road, we passed white-railed paddocks, one after another, with horses—mares and foals—grazing on bluegrass. I stretched my hand out the window on the hot day to touch them, but they were out of reach. Dad kept driving, ignoring my pleas to stop. That's the day I fell in love with horses.

Dad pulls in alongside two other cars parked along the fence line. We join a group of people gathered next to a small shed, where three students groom their horses. Just beyond is an arena filled with colorful jumps. Dad introduces Mom and me to his boss, a slender man with a kind face who suggests I join the group riding lesson with his son.

My stomach flips, and my arms lock at my sides. I remember all the times I'd gravitated to horses, but only rode them in my imagination. "I don't know how."

A woman, as tall as Dad, reaches out to shake my hand. "Hi. I'm Molly. I teach all the lessons." She has cropped hair tucked under a straw hat, and a sunbaked trustworthy face. "It's a basic class. You'll do fine," she says.

Dad flips his head, his form of encouragement. We're here to impress his boss. *No pressure…but this is my chance.*

I follow Molly, who unties a horse and drapes the rein over her arm. "This is Tchaikovsky. We call him Teddy. He's a sweet gelding; he'll take good care of you." She directs him alongside a block of stairs. The helmet she straps onto my head is loose, but I don't complain. I climb three steps and mount the saddled horse. Molly adjusts my stirrups and places the reins into my hands, flipping the extra leather over the top of my closed fists.

"You ready?" Molly asks. Nodding, I follow five other riders into the arena and mimic what they do with their horses, mostly walking in circles and across the ring diagonally.

After the lesson, Molly leads the class down a dirt road for an easy version of a trail ride, leaving parents behind to chat.

My hands grip the reins, one in each hand. She'd shown me how to post a few steps in the lesson. I'm insecure in the saddle with no horn to grab if I feel unsafe. When they pick up the pace along a gravel road, I can't seem to catch the rhythm of the horse's movement and pull back to a walk. Afraid of being left behind, I lengthen the reins like Molly had shown me and lightly squeeze my legs against the horse's sides. I didn't expect a fast trot and lose my balance. Unable to grab any part of the saddle, I fall to the left side and hit the ground hard with my shoulder and head, knocking the ill-fitting helmet off. The horses stop on the trail in front of me.

I'm mortified, drop my head, and pull myself up. The stirrup is at my chin. I can't even get my foot in it, let alone get back on the horse.

Three years ago, my friend and I crossed a frozen river, intending to steal a ride on the two horses loose in a snow-covered field, smaller ones, nothing like this long-legged beauty. I couldn't get on those either.

Molly dismounts and brushes me off.

"You okay?" she asks.

"Mostly embarrassed," I say and move into position to try again. I'm not helping Dad show off to his boss. I've never been athletic, no matter how much I tried to keep up with my brothers. Another rider holds my horse as Molly gives me a leg up, helps me find the other stirrup, and hands me the reins. The riders silently wait, but I feel their eyes on me. After this mishap, Dad won't let me have a second lesson. *Now, I'll never learn how to ride.*

When we prepare to leave, Dad says, "Molly seems to think you have promise, so you'll be returning for weekly lessons…if that's okay with you."

"Yes. Definitely." I nod like a bobble-head doll as fireworks go off in my head. *I've found where I belong.*

Every weekend, Dad drives ninety minutes to my riding lessons. He and Mom watch as Molly teaches me to balance in the saddle. I become more confident at the trot and feel ready to conquer the canter. I learn cavaletti jumps, starting with low bars and moving to three-foot-high walls. When I fall, I brush myself off and, with Molly's urging, I get back on and try again.

After four months in the hotel, we move into a two-story duplex with an enclosed stone patio and a fountain on the stone wall. Water trickles from a stone face into a small pond edged with perennial beds and high walls. The surrounding streets, lined with shops, rumble from heavy traffic. There's no grass, no place to keep a horse.

By August the basic dressage movements become more difficult, and the jumps advance from cavaletti to rails between fixed standards, then advancing to four-foot jumps. I fall off more than anyone when approaching or going over jumps, once breaking a wooden crossrail.

Molly marches into the arena and takes hold of my horse. "You're souring the horses. They won't jump for anyone if this keeps up."

My face flushes. I want to hide or shrink into a tiny ball.

"I'm putting you on Chopin, my champion horse, to help you get over your fear of falling. I call him Freddy. He'll jump even when you fall off. He loves to jump!"

After switching from the school horse to Molly's champion competition horse, I'm led into the arena full of jumps. Still nervous, I go flying over his shoulder on the first one. But I get back on and tell myself, *you can do this.* His poise gives me the confidence to clear all the jumps the second time around. I ride up to Molly, who's sitting on the fence. "Can I ride Freddy all the time?" Smiling, she shakes her head.

Molly teaches me to polish saddles and to mix grain unique to each horse, and yet, even when I ride, life down under doesn't feel like home.

In January, on my sixteenth birthday, Molly invites us for dinner with her family in their home, where they are surrounded by horses. Mom makes me wear a dress, which means I won't be riding. She says, "You look very nice when you clean up." She never leaves the house without putting makeup on. "Since it's your birthday, put a bit of my lipstick on. It's a pale peach."

I apply it to my lips and press them together, thankful for Mom's attention. I admire her grace, her beauty, and though I prefer to play in the dirt, I appreciate her efforts to teach me how to be more like her. But even wearing a dress, I plan to sneak away after dinner and visit the horses.

Mrs. Moore, in their small informal home, dishes up each plate and brings them to where we are sitting on the sofa and armchairs in the living room. I balance mine on my lap—a rich stew with beef, potatoes, and carrots, unlike anything Mom ever cooked.

After I help carry dirty dishes to the kitchen, Mom says, "Molly needs you outside."

I follow her out to where Dad is leaning on our car when Molly walks up with a horse, all tacked up, his mane and tail braided (she calls it *plaited*). I recognize him.

When I rode him last week for my lesson. I asked Molly, "What should I call him?"

"He doesn't have a name yet."

His animated rocking horse canter had made it difficult to keep my butt in the saddle. After class, I asked Molly, "Do I have to ride him again? I can't sit his canter."

"You'll get used to his rhythm with practice. He's a good horse for you."

Now, I see a bow on the left side of the gelding's bridle. Bubbles of excitement rise from my nervous gut like newly poured champagne.

Dad beams. "He's yours."

I glance at Mom for a reality check. She nods, with a glimpse of worry behind her smile.

Dad pats the horse's neck. "He needs a name. What would you like to call him?"

No wonder Molly looked at me strangely when I said I didn't want to ride him. He was already mine. *I'll find a way to ride his canter because he's my dream come true.*

After I kiss Dad on the cheek and say in his ear, "Thank you," I wrap my arms around the bay Thoroughbred's neck, breathing in the aroma of shampoo used to make his coat shine. Dad's mouth lifts into a half-smile. "How about Kentucky?"

"I like that." *Where I first fell in love with horses but couldn't even touch one.*

I run my hand down the crest of his neck to his shoulder, feeling his lean muscles, and down his leg to his hoof. After looking from Molly to Dad, then Mom, I hug *my* horse.

Dad boards Kentucky at Molly's. Summer transitions into a mild, snowless winter. I ride Kentucky every other weekend until Dad suddenly becomes unavailable to drive me.

"Mom, will you take me?"

She shakes her head. "Honey, I can't. I still don't trust myself to drive without getting us in a wreck. I might kill us both."

Driving age is eighteen in New South Wales, and I'm only sixteen.

When I complain at school, one girl I hardly know says, "Take a train."

The next morning, after studying a bunch of transportation schedules, I catch a tram, then a bus, and finally an electric train to get to a little town near Molly's facility. Not yet there, I walk a half-mile down the long eucalyptus-lined dirt road to see Kentucky—a five-hour trip in all. I arrive hot and sweaty, my legs weak. But I'm excited to ride my horse.

I'm in the tack room looking for his saddle when Molly stops me. "You can't ride him."

"Why not?"

She looks down, scuffs her feet. "He doesn't belong to you anymore." She turns away. "I have a class to teach. If you want to help, you can brush him and prepare his grain."

I don't understand what she means, but she gives me no chance to ask for an explanation. I came all this way and now I can't ride him. It's not fair. *Damn you, Dad! Now what have you done?* I prepare for the second shoe to drop.

Before I leave, I throw my arms around Kentucky's neck. "Sorry, boy. I guess this wasn't meant to be." Even though the trip was long, it was worth it to see him, to feel his soft coat, and to smell his sweet horsey sweat. Two hours later, Molly's mom gives me a ride to the train station, saving me a long walk as dusk settles in. A starless night shrouds me on the path to the kitchen door.

"Where have you been?" Mom screeches. "I've been worried out of my mind."

"I went to see Kentucky," I say unapologetically. Her eyes widen. Good thing Dad's not here to see my defiance.

"Never do that again."

I'm home in one piece. Why is she mad? "He's my horse, and I wanted to see him. You couldn't help. I figured it out."

"Promise me. Never again." She drills her demand into my head with her eyes.

I'm dumbstruck by her response. Since we arrived, she's let me roam wherever I want without restrictions. I nod reluctantly.

"Don't mention any of this to your father." I shake my head with wide eyes. She walks away, still talking. "Your dinner is in the fridge. Be in bed before he gets home."

Dad is probably out with his executive buddies at the Savage Club. I don't want to face him when he's been drinking. I head up to my room, but I can't sleep.

A week later, I come home to study for exams and find movers all over the house packing our things. We were scheduled to stay in Melbourne for three years—long enough for me to finish high school. It has been less than two. I'm near the end of the first term of what Aussie's call Year 11, with an exam in two weeks. It determines our only grade for the term, and I'm worried I won't pass. It's been a tough semester for me, with too many hard classes and not enough horseback riding, which helps center me.

In the kitchen, Mom is supervising two men packing dishes.

"What's going on?" I already know. It's the other shoe.

"Go pack your suitcase. We're leaving."

"But after school tomorrow, right?"

"No. They have been informed you won't return."

"I can't stay to finish the year? What about my friends? I want to say goodbye." I only have a few—Sally, and my best friend Pam, the daughter of the lady that helps Mom with the house. And my boyfriend Lloyd, who I fell for when we met a few months ago. We talked for hours. He invited me to the Australian-American ball—it's like prom. I don't care that he is fighting bone cancer. He's the love of my life.

Mom says, "Call and say goodbye. We've been ordered home without delay. The movers will finish by tomorrow; they'll ship it all back to the States."

"Why?" I brace myself.

"You know your father. He spent money we didn't have, buying rounds at the Savage Club, being the big man around town."

"Is that why Kentucky isn't mine anymore?"

"His boss found out about his financial mismanagement." Mom shakes her head, her eyes unfocused.

"Was it gambling?" Dad always bet on card games. On everything, including raindrops racing down a windowpane.

She answers with a shrug. "The company covered your dad's over-drafts but couldn't deal with the embarrassment."

"And Kentucky?"

"He's already gone. Sold to cover his board bill. I'm sorry, honey."

I lose my balance as my world spins. Mom pulls me into a hug, and I accept the comfort, but only for a moment. I push her away. She looks hurt, but I don't care. Kentucky is gone. And my friends. My life ruined again. *I hate Dad.*

"It'll be alright. Go pack your clothes." She returns to wrapping her fragile collectibles, her favorites—the glass hummingbird, two porcelain deer, and the slender lady—figurines that she won't let anyone else touch.

I run out of the house, a place that has never felt like home, and down the street, to find privacy in the shade of two towering euca-lyptus trees, their branches brushing my shoulder. With no power to change anything, I cover my face and bawl. I want to scream at Dad—to hit him until he feels my pain. After I shed, shake off, and tuck away my remaining emotion, I walk past the stone pond into the kitchen to roll a cold hotdog in a piece of bread and stuff it down as I float around the house, watching the movers box up my life.

I didn't want to come here. Now, I don't want to leave. Who knows where we'll end up next? At least when we go back to the States, I can reclaim my Scottie, Tina. She'll comfort me and help me transition to being in another new place back on the other side of the world.

The next day, the men return to finish wrapping the dishes, linens, and the minutia from our lives here. They even wrap up cigarette butts, and the glass ashtray, packing them separate but together, taping up the boxes and stacking them against the wall. Mom says they'll crate them after we leave. She moves through each room, checking that nothing is left behind.

I call a few friends and promise to write, but I know I won't. I never do. Opening up makes the loss too real for me. I don't want to think about all the people I am leaving behind or I'll crumble into a thousand pieces, not even Lloyd, who I was sure I would marry.

In Detroit, spring is in full bloom. The boisterous crowds in the airport speaking with an American accent leave me disoriented. My hybrid accent, developed over the past eighteen months, had helped me fit into the easy-going Aussie atmosphere, but it will soon fade back to my Midwestern tongue, robbing me of everything but my riding boots and memories.

Dad drops Mom and me off at Grandpa and Grandma's house, then goes in search of a job. I approach their backdoor and hear Tina barking through the screen door to the kitchen. I drop my suitcase in the drive, bolt through the open door, and reach out for my little dog. She jumps into my arms and licks my face and ear. I laugh and cry tears of joy into her wiry black coat, now sprinkled with silver. We spend every minute together.

Seven days later, Dad returns. He found consulting work with Caterpillar and is moving us to Peoria, Illinois. I reach for Tina.

Mom shakes her head.

Now what?

She wrings her hands while she talks. "We can't take her back. She's Grandma's dog now."

But she's my dog. When Mom presses her lips together, I know I can't win. My heart shrivels to an agate stone—its weight heavy in my chest. I pull cookies from the jar and a soda from the fridge, then head to the basement with Tina to curl up on the mattress in a cubbyhole across from the ping-pong table.

Dad leases a house on a busy highway with almost no backyard. When we arrive, Mom buys a coffee pot, a fry pan, a set of dishes, and rents two beds, two stools, a sofa and a little tv to get us by until our furniture returns from Melbourne. A few days later, Mom sits me down to break the news. "Grandma called. Tina ran away. They can't find her anywhere."

"She's looking for me. I know she is."

"I'm sorry, honey. In the city, there's not much chance of finding her." Mom drops her head, then leaves to start her new bookkeeping job, looking sharp in her pencil skirt and blouse.

What can I do? I can't get to Detroit to rescue my dog. I want to scream. Instead, I open the fridge for chocolate ice cream, plop a scoop into a bowl, then crawl into the unmade rental bed in my room, locking the door to prevent anyone offering hollow comfort.

CHAPTER FOUR

CONSEQUENCES 1966-1968

I'm grumpy when Mom and I enter the school office and sit across the desk from the dark-haired woman with glasses.

The counselor mulls over my transcripts. "I will transfer these credits, but you'll need to take two summer classes if you want to begin as a Junior in the fall." I slump in the orange molded chair. "I'll sign you up for the standard college prep classes." She has short, teased hair in the shape of a helmet and a drawn face from her harried schedule.

"I want to take art."

"Those classes were filled by students who have studied art since their freshman year. And Driver's Ed is filled until next summer. I'll put you on the wait list for earlier, but dropouts are rare."

I'll be almost eighteen when I get my license. I hate my life.

On a sweltering summer day, a flatbed truck unloads two huge crates on our lawn—our belongings. One crate that was dropped in the ocean grew a two-inch layer of green mold inside and out, announcing our arrival in town with its putrid smell.

When fall classes start, I'm reluctant to raise my hand. I hug the hall edges, focusing on room numbers, while three hundred students move en masse between classes. My life is in shades of gray.

I jolt back to life when Sally catches up with me after our AP Physics class. "So, I hear you like horses."

"I really miss riding."

"I ride my horse, Cinnamon, on hundreds of acres with trails all over some hilly woodland just south of town. I board her at a farmer's barn. He owns the land. You can come with me on Saturday, and I'll introduce you to the farmer. He is older and doesn't ride anymore. Maybe he'll let you ride one of his horses."

I light up. "That would be great."

After her mom drops us off on Saturday morning, a farmer wearing overalls covered in dirt and manure approaches us. He's older than my dad, worn down by life. His house and barn need paint and repairs but seem mostly functional. After Sally introduces me, he asks, "Can you ride?"

"I trained for nine months in Australia in basic dressage and arena jumping."

He leads me to a dark box stall. "This is Princess. She's a half-Saddlebred and she's only green-broke. Show me what you can do with her in the arena, and if I'm satisfied, you can take her out on the trails with Sally."

I breathe in the smell of alfalfa and horse sweat and reach out to scratch her shoulder. She moves away. I wait until she turns her head back toward me, then I reach out with my down-curved hand. She sniffs, then licks it. That's a good start.

The farmer helps me saddle her and leads us to an enclosed corral to watch me ride.

I circle her in a walk, letting out as much rein as she'll respect. Then I take up the reins and ask for a slow trot, crossing the corral to change direction from left to right. After thirty minutes, Sally invites me on a trail ride with some other kids. The farmer nods. "You can ride her whenever you want. She needs the work." *I do cartwheels in my head.*

Princess knows the trails and behaves well, happy to be out of her dark stall. As she moves, I feel her power under my seat and her sensitive mouth in my hands.

Sometimes, as much as once a week, I ride the trails with Sally, although less in winter. It's fun to ride after the snow falls, but my hands and face freeze in the biting wind.

In July, a year after we returned from Australia, my brothers showed up at our house needing a rest stop. Mike in his Karmann Ghia is driving Chuck from Michigan to stay with him in LA. When I help carry in their stuff, I ask Mike, "I have my license now. Can I drive your car? I'm supposed to meet Sally to go riding."

"Can you drive a stick shift on the floor?"

"You could teach me." I would love to show up at the barn driving his snazzy sports car.

"It's not the car to learn on." He walks away, heading for the extra bedroom.

"Then could you give me a lift to the barn? Or Chuck?"

"We drove all night and need sleep."

I call my friend Denise from math class, who also likes horses. She agrees to drop me at the barn on her way to work. I wait for her at the end of our long drive.

We pass the mall and head down a country road to where I ride the farmer's horse. "So," Denise says, "did you read about the horse trainer?" I shake my head. "She was riding on the shoulder of the road near here. Her horse pulled to a dead stop. She flipped over his shoulder, hit the pavement and broke her neck. She's dead! Just like that." Denise snaps her fingers.

I roll my eyes. "That won't happen to me. I know how to fall." I climb out. "Thanks for the ride. I'll find a way home."

"Just be careful!" She calls back to me, then drives off.

After working with Princess in the arena, we've built a partnership. I rush to her stall. But it's empty.

As I approach the owner's house, he descends his porch steps, his face stern.

"Where's Princess?" I ask.

"I sold her."

My breath catches. "Why?"

He walks away without answering. I call out, "Do you have another horse I can ride?" The farmer shakes his head, not bothering to look back at me.

Sally's horse is gone. She's out riding the trails without me. *How will I find another horse to ride?*

A kid walking nearby, who'd just finished riding, says, "The guy across the street has a horse. He gets him all tacked up but doesn't ride him. He'd let you ride...if you can handle him."

"I'll take that dare." After training in Australia, I believe I can ride anything.

I follow him to a corral with six-by-six posts and wooden rails to hold a big Appaloosa. He's saddled, giving me no chance to get a sense of him before mounting. I'll start with an easy walk around the corral.

As soon as I get on, I feel him, through the reins, take the bit between his teeth, leaving me with no control when he gallops toward a fence too high for him to jump. *I need to get off. Fast!*

I pull my leg over his rump, but before I can step off, the big spotted horse raises his head, tucks his haunches, and slides like a rodeo horse. My foot barely comes out of the stirrup when I slam into the unyielding post.

Lying face down in the mud, I try to push myself up, but I have no strength, only pain. The Appy's owner runs around in a panic outside the paddock but doesn't come to help me. *He's probably afraid I'll sue.*

When I roll over, a knife-like pain stabs my back, and I call out, "Someone, help me." But no one answers. Fear races through my core. My parents are working.

I yell to the Appy's owner, "Write this down and tell whoever answers what's happened." *I hope my brothers answer the phone.* I wait for what seems forever as the pain increases and races down my legs.

I'm still lying in the mud when Chuck walks through the gate. Muscles like straps tighten across my chest. My breathing is shallow—

probably just a spasm. My brother stands over me with his hands on his hips.

"Help me up."

Chuck puts his hands under my shoulders and tries to lift me, but I yell out from the lightning strike of pain. "I can't."

He gently lowers me and yells to the owner, "Call an ambulance."

Within the hour, I'm in the hospital. A doctor tells me, "You must lie flat on your back for a week, only turning on your side with a nurses' help. You've damaged your spine—an L-1 compression fracture." When he walks out, the nurse threatens, "If you move without our help, you'll spend the rest of your life in a wheelchair."

I'm still in denial when, a few hours later, Chuck comes in to cheer me up. "For a girl with a broken back...you don't look so bad."

I roll my eyes, knowing it will hurt if I laugh.

"Sorry I can't stick around, but Mike has to get back to LA." Chuck looks down, his shoulders rounded. "I shouldn't have tried to lift you. You went sheet white. It scared the shit out of me."

"Hey, you showed up when I needed you and rescued me. Thanks."

After he leaves, I soak my hospital gown with tears. My arms are too heavy to wipe them from my cheeks. The nurse comes in, hands me pain pills, watches me swallow them with water, and then departs with barely a word. The quiet seeps into my bones. *I'm on my own again.*

At the start of my senior year, I hide my brace under high-necked blouses. Dad loses his job at Caterpillar and moves Mom and me out of the three-bedroom house, into a two-bedroom apartment, while working as a used car salesman. After a few months, he lands an engineering job in Terra Haute, Indiana. Mom and I balk when he expects us to move with him.

Mom says, "I won't make Debby start another new school. We'll stay here so she can finish her senior year." Dad drops his head, and I return to my bowl of cereal.

Four months later, I toss my brace into the closet. Mom and I continue to grow closer—like roommates. On a hot April day after school, I walk into a shop to buy an ice cream cone and inquire about their Help Wanted sign. A woman emerges from the office and says, "We can talk back here."

I dash home. "Mom, I've got a job scooping ice cream at Baskin Robbins. I can walk to work after the bus drops me off." At last, I'll have a paycheck to put gas in her car when she lets me borrow it.

CHAPTER FIVE

FAMILY SECRETS 1968

The night before my high school commencement, I'm watching TV when Bobby Kennedy is shot. I rush in and wake Mom. "They killed him! Bobby Kennedy is dead!"

She squeezes my hand. We sit arm in arm watching the news for another hour, then Mom says, "Let's go to bed. You have a big day tomorrow."

The second Kennedy assassination renders a pall over the ceremony. Amid packed-in families seated in stands, I spot Mom. She's alone. Mike is back in Vietnam. Chuck is in LA. Dad is in LA too. He moved there after he lost his job in Terre Haute.

The following week, Mom asks, "What do you want for graduation?"

I hesitate before speaking, unsure if she can afford to give me what I really want. "Are contact lenses too expensive?"

"Let's find out how much they would cost. In the meantime, I was thinking about those blended synthetic hair extensions we saw when we were at Carson's in the mall." That is so on brand for Mom. She's always wanted me to feel more beautiful. I try, but I'll never be an actress or model like she had been. She had ambitions before she met Dad.

"It would be fun if I put it up into big loops on my head, like on the mannequin, although I'm not sure how much I'll get to use it." I rub my finger across my chin. "Can I get the contacts, too?"

"If they aren't too expensive, sure. We can splurge a bit. It's a very special occasion."

The next day, I'm sitting on a stool in the store watching the trained technician blend different colors of fibers. I'm shocked at how many are pink. When it's complete, the switch is a perfect match for my cinnamon hair. Mom also buys a fabric-covered-Styrofoam-head to style the piece on and a blue case to store and carry them in.

A month later, after finding an envelope in the mailbox from the only university I applied to, I rush upstairs, drop my book bag, and tear it open. When Mom arrives home from work, I follow her into the kitchen and sit at the table, grinning like a Cheshire cat.

I blurt out, "I've been accepted at Indiana University where my friends are going." She sets a pizza on the table. I hand her my letter and tear off a slice of the pepperoni cheese. She sits down to read it carefully, then drops the letter.

Oh, no. Now what?

Mom says, in her usual calm voice, "I'm proud of you, Debby. You're all grown up, but you'll always be my little girl."

Mom is quiet during dinner. *What isn't she telling me?* I finish the last slice and stuff the cardboard box into the trash can, then return to my chair. I start my second Coke and wait in silence for her to speak.

She talks to her nearly empty wineglass. "I'm sorry, honey. There's no money for you to go to college."

"Because of Dad gambling?" I ask, clenching my fists.

"And job changes. We emptied the account to cover the most recent bounced checks."

"Before he left for LA, I heard the cops come during the night and take him away."

Mom finishes her wine and rises to fetch the Chianti bottle on the counter. She returns to her chair and says, "You need to find a better job if you want to save for college."

"I'll apply for financial aid. I can still start classes in the fall."

"Your father will never fill out a financial statement, let alone sign it."

"Why?"

"He just won't." She refills her glass from the bottle. "I should have left him years ago. I've been unhappy for a long time…since you were born, and he was off with some floosy. He only returned because you were the daughter he wanted." She drinks from her glass and slowly sets it down, like in a tea ceremony. "Not that we haven't had some good times, but the bad outweighs the good. I can see that now."

I'm startled by her revelation. "Why did you stay with him?"

"I stayed for you kids."

Great. Now I get to carry the burden of her unhappiness, as well as my own. I never would have guessed she had been so unhappy. But since Dad left, she's seemed lighter.

The following week, Mom gets me a job stuffing and sealing envelopes for bulk mailings at the insurance agency where she works, but in a different office. I quickly settle into my new routine until one night, Dad barges through our door.

"Ready to become a *California girl?*" he asks me.

I'm not sure what that means, but it sounds better than what I have planned—a whole lot of nothing.

"We'll stop in Vegas on the way. Chuck will meet us there for his birthday and ride with us back to LA." Vegas and Chuck tip the scale for me, not that I have any choice but to live on the streets. Another road trip. *Some things never change.*

Mom says, "Debby, go downstairs into our storage space and bring up some boxes from the last two moves. I'll put the furniture in storage until we get settled." If Mom is going to California, then I am too.

We pick Chuck up in the Las Vegas Airport. He greets me with a smile and a hug and says to me, "I'm ready to hit the casinos. Wanna come? I'll teach you."

I twist out of his embrace. "I know how to play blackjack as good as you."

Dad says with a slap on Chuck's back, "Let's get checked into a motel. There's an affordable one on the main drag,"

Mom remains quiet.

After we check in, Dad tells me, "The casino is next door. You can come watch me and Mom shoot craps. Or you can hang out with your brother. We'll meet up at eight and see a show."

"You can watch me win enough to make up for what your dad loses." Mom glances sideways at Dad. He raises a brow and strides toward the casino.

Chuck nudges me. "I'll give you a twenty for your graduation present. Lose it or double it, but that's all you're getting. I'll head for the slots after a few hands of blackjack."

We gamble at Caesar's, where Chuck teaches me how to order a free drink while playing blackjack. "Just tip them a buck." He moves to the slots, playing three at a time until the show starts.

The next day on the road, Dad's driving, and Mom's going over maps to pick the best route. Chuck and I are in the back seat, keeping our voices low. "I can't believe I lost all my money." I shake out my empty wallet. "I'll have to ask Dad for some change if I want to buy a Coke."

Chuck whispers, "You need to learn to quit when you're ahead."

"I was in awe of the gorgeous show girls who balanced those enormous headdresses. I was surprised by their bare chests with only their nipples covered. They must get cold."

He stares out the window at sagebrush and sand. "I didn't notice."

I twist around in my seat to look at him and wait for an explanation.

He leans close and whispers in my ear. "I'm *gay*."

I shrug and shake my head.

"Ever heard of a homosexual?"

"My chemistry teacher mentioned it last semester, even wrote the word on the board. I don't remember what she said. I was too stressed about how I hurt my chance at college by flunking my typing test."

Chuck lifts his left brow, waiting for me to say more.

"You have sex with men?" I ask meekly.

Chuck puts his finger to his lips and stares at the back of Mom and Dad's heads. "They don't know."

"Does Mike know?" I shake my head to clear the fog after drinking last night. Chuck is trusting me with his secret.

"Mike figured out I was *with* Jack back in high school."

His best friend, Jack, taught me how to kiss when I was 14. "What about Cathy and Sue?"

"The girls gave Jack and I cover to keep us out of jail for being gay. It wasn't a total lie. I was kind of bisexual back then."

Mom would be okay knowing Chuck is gay because she often says, "If you're happy, that's all that matters." But Dad, with Chuck being his namesake, would go ballistic if he learned the truth. Before I tell anyone, I need to learn more about Chuck's secret life.

CHAPTER SIX

MOM'S BALLGOWN 1968

I burst through the front door of the LA apartment where we've lived for a week. "Mom! Where are you?"

The sofa and armchair are empty except for the hastily folded sections of the morning paper. A glass ashtray overflowing with stubbed out Lucky Strikes, and a half-filled mug of coffee amid water marks on the coffee table are evidence of Dad's early morning departure for work. Smoke, its stench masking the mildew, drifts through rays of light that stream from an open bedroom door, telling me she's home.

"I'm right here. You don't need to yell."

Mom strolls out of her bedroom carrying a dust cloth, lifting a cigarette to her orange mouth. Her lipstick, applied with precision, accents the fullness of her lips. Mom's chocolate eyes glisten. Her beauty and grace remain undiminished by her fatigue.

"Where's your ball gown? I need to borrow it."

"Breathe, Debby. You're not breathing," she says in her soft, low voice.

I've developed an unconscious habit of holding my breath, but I hate when she reminds me. It's another way of saying *calm down*. Being intense is part of being a redhead. It used to bother me when she said it—I felt dismissed—but lately, things have been better between us. So I take a breath and wait for her answer.

Mom scoops up the full ashtray and empties the butts in the nearest wastebasket, then wipes it clean with a dust cloth. The smoke from the cigarette dangling between her slender fingers records her movement as she points me toward the kitchen table. "Can I get you something to eat?"

"I-don't-want-food." I slowly enunciate each word, so she hears me. "I-need-a-formal-dress."

She swipes at a cobweb in the corner of two walls with her rag. When she's satisfied that she's captured the ghost-like strands, she turns back to me. "What have you eaten?"

"A burger." I yank off my jacket and drop it on the chair. "Would you listen? I need a gown, not food. Do you have the purple velvet with you? The gown you wore when you attended the American Consulate party with Dad in Melbourne ...the dress you said I could wear to the ball with Lloyd," I say adamantly.

"Yes, I have it. But it's *really* more of a plum or aubergine."

Mom and her vocabulary. She took elocution lessons at fifteen, planning to become a Broadway actress. Her desire for the limelight is an integral part of her identity.

With a head shake, I move past her into her bedroom. "Where is it?" I stare at the stack of suitcases along the wall.

"Hanging in the closet." She tucks the dust rag into the back pocket of her sleek jeans, tight to emphasize her small waist and full hips. "What's the hurry?"

Mom follows me into the bedroom. "You've been gone all day. Did you meet some nice boys?" Although Mom says I can do anything, she believes marriage is every girl's best path to security.

"You told Chuck to take me with him to give me something to do until I start my new job next week at the telephone company. I helped Chuck hang decorations for a ball in Hollywood."

"His friend Bobby, who was helping too, invited me to the ball. Chuck resisted but Bobby pleaded my case and offered to be my date. When I flashed my sad puppy dog look, Chuck relented."

"I was worried. I didn't know where you were. I know Chuck would never let anything happen to you, but..." She studies my face, pulling some loose hair out of my eyes. "It's such a big city. And you don't know your way around."

"I'm fine, Mother." My jaw tightens. "I'm eighteen. I can take care of myself."

She shrinks back. Her vulnerability peeks through her controlled veneer. "I know. But you'll always be my baby girl." As she turns away, she wipes her eyes. She cries at the strangest times.

Standing in her closet, I grab a handful of wire hangers. They screech when I slide them along the metal rod. A single stream of light peeking through the sliding window on the far wall isn't much help. A box on the floor tips, loses its cover, and photos of me when I was ten slip out. At school, kids made fun of my thick waist. When Mom found me hiding in my room, she scheduled a professional photo shoot to help me feel beautiful. I couldn't show the pictures at school because everyone would accuse me of bragging.

"Oh, be careful with those," Mom says. "They are precious to me."

I pick up the one where I'm wearing a poofy-sleeved blouse, a short-striped skirt with a flared red petticoat, and holding a parasol over my shoulder. "I don't remember me ever looking this cute."

"Let's put them back so they don't get damaged."

I return the photo to the box. Mom takes it and slides it to the back of the closet shelf.

I'm glad Mom kept them. Even now, they lift my mood.

I resume searching, reaching behind the stacked sliding doors. Halfway back, my fingers slide onto a wire hanger with a narrow strap looped around it. The halter neckline. *That's it.* I drag it out from between the mash of summer dresses, winter coats, and men's shirts.

"Here. Let me help you with that," Mom says, reaching for the padded hanger. She hooks the crushed velvet gown on the back of the door and smooths out a wrinkle with the flat of her hand.

Mom knows clothes. She knows how to polish her beauty and won't leave the house until she feels *put together.* I was a tomboy growing up, wearing clothes more suited to tearing through the woods to steal a ride on a stranger's pastured horse with a bridle made of twine and no saddle. After attempting to jump onto their backs, falling in the snow, my friend and I headed home to avoid frostbite on our fingers. When I turned sixteen, I stopped wanting to be one of the guys. Now, I dream of being desired by them, but tonight I just want to make my brother proud.

Mom touches my shoulder. "Focus, dear. You get cleaned up, and I'll fetch your makeup bag."

"Mom, it starts at seven—in two hours."

"You need to be more patient if you're going to live in LA, especially when you're driving. It's insane the way people dart in and out of traffic. It's not like driving in Illinois."

"Dad's been teaching me how to navigate the freeway on-off ramps, merge across six lanes of traffic, and maneuver through the interchanges. He made me recite the street name for each exit we passed: *Canoga Park, Tampa, Winnetka." He seemed proud of how fast I learned.*

I bop into the bathroom to wash my face. Mom places my cosmetics bag at my feet.

She sits on the toilet seat to light a cigarette and asks, "Where is your hair piece?"

"In my wig case." Mom leaves her cigarette in the ashtray to rummage through the closet for the blue case. I sneak a drag to calm my nerves before I put on my face.

When she returns, I clip the hairpiece onto the crown of my short-cropped hair and stack its long strands into two-inch loops, using hair spray to hold them in place. I pull out wisps to fall across my cheeks. I feel as glamorous as Mom, when Dad took her to an ambassador's dinner. Mom could put on the Ritz to lift Dad's professional or community status. As a couple, they were the talk of every party. It's the part of Mom I want to emulate, especially tonight.

CHAPTER SEVEN

MY FIRST BALL 1968

Mom drops me at the party and waves as she re-enters the heavy traffic on Sepulveda Blvd. I hope she doesn't get lost finding her way back to the apartment.

A long blue awning draws me toward the unassuming building. I join the stream of people moving through a narrow entrance that opens into a large hall of sparsely filled tables, each with a crisp white tablecloth and a vase of fresh flowers. I spot Chuck by his coiffed carrot top mop, sitting near the dance floor with his friend Bobby, and join them after checking Mom's mouton fur jacket she insisted I wear to complete my ensemble.

Gripping my beaded clutch, I cross the open space to sit next to Chuck, taking care to not wobble on Mom's four-inch heels. Bobby fetches me a stemmed glass of white wine.

"Such a gentleman. Thank you." I'm using Mom's theatric voice to sound more grown up.

Bobby flashes a big grin, then sits beside me. His slicked back hair glistens in the light.

Still nervous, I sip the wine and examine the decorations. In one afternoon, we transformed a once drab room into a glamorous space with draped streamers, stretching twisted crepe paper from the base of the central chandelier to all the edges of the room, covering the ceiling with a rainbow of color into a grand pinwheel. The only other color in the space comes from red velvet curtains framing the stage.

I smooth my skirt along my thigh. When a loose piece of synthetic hair tickles my bare shoulder, I tuck it back into place with a hairpin. I've created a mask to hide my nervousness. I edged my lids in sable eyeliner, added silver and mauve eyeshadow, and sprinkled glitter to highlight my high cheekbones and double-layered false lashes caked in black.

Bobby cocks his head to one side. "Your eyes are just like Chuck's —brown with glimmers of gold. Stunning!" He glances between us and grins, his dark eyes matching his coal black hair that is straight and just touches his shoulders. "You two could be twins."

Bobby, born in Mexico City, is cute, much shorter than me without my heels and hair, even with his three-inch platform shoes. He's gay— not a possible boyfriend, but fun to be around.

Across the room, elegant couples flow into the hall, extravagant beauties bedazzled in jewels with hair piled higher than my own. Mom's dress fits right in. With my hair loops and heels, I stand at six feet—a few inches taller than Chuck, though he'll never admit it. In our family, height is a measure of power.

I notice all the tall women are accompanied by men dressed elegantly in tuxedos but who, in comparison, are wanting in stature.

With a befuddled expression, I turn to Chuck. "Why are all the women so tall?"

He leans down and whispers in my ear. "They're *drag queens.*"

"Huh?"

"They're guys...dressed as women."

I pause, look at the beauties, then back at my brother to be sure he's serious. They are spectacular—high cheek bones, long sleek legs, and overflowing bosoms. *How'd they do that?*

Lost in a wonderland beyond my wildest imagination, I'm eager to know more. Chuck continues to hide his secret life, reluctant to reveal any more than bits and pieces. If I want to stay in his life, I need to wedge my way into his circle of friends.

Chuck wanders off to mingle in the crowd, offering compliments to his friends. Bobby stays to keep me company. People begin to gather near the stage, forming a line for what looks like a competition. I ask Bobby, "What's going on?"

"It's for the best *queen.*" He pauses, looks me up and down, and whispers, "You should have a go." He must be joking.

"They'll never know." He smiles like a Cheshire cat, eager to be the only one who knows the truth except for Chuck, who won't allow it. Bobby plots our subterfuge. "I won't tell...and no one else knows you." His eyes twinkle as he plans our scandalous intrigue. "You're sure to win...because you're real."

I like to show off as much as the next person, but I'm nervous. "Won't they get mad?"

"It's all for fun. They like to strut their stuff. No reason you can't too."

Should I? I'm wary... but I want Bobby to like me. *Can I get away with it?*

Mom had raised me to be bold. For her, life is a theater, each with a part to play, though lately she seems worn down by all of Dad's troubles. I doubt she ever imagined me in this situation.

Chuck rejoins us. When Bobby fills him in, all he does is shrug. *If he's okay with it...*

Bobby sips his champagne with eyes on me, waiting for my answer.

"I'm game, but first I need to freshen up in the ladies' room."

"Keep your guard up in there," Chuck says, leaning over to whisper in my ear.

It's the first indication that I need to be cautious. "Why?"

He pulls back. "You look amazing. The beaded velvet gown. And your hair..." He gazes around the room. "Someone might make a pass."

I look for a snicker, but instead, he looks worried.

"That's what gay guys like. To be with the most beautiful. And they won't know..." My brow knits as I struggle with his warning. Then he adds, "You'll be okay. Just keep your wits about you."

Yesterday, I had no idea gay balls and drag queens existed. Tonight,

I will step out of my nice girl persona and Catholic upbringing to take a walk on the wild side. If the nuns could see me now!

I rise from my chair, holding the table edge to gain my balance on Mom's spiked heels. Spotting the Ladies' Room sign, I weave through open spaces in the ballooning crowd, some with jealous eyes on my cleavage as I pass, my best feature since my bare back is marred by freckles. My coloring may come from Mom, but my curves, out of style since the popularity of Twiggy, come from dad's side. I had idolized the fashion model in high school, wearing pixie hair, short skirts, and lots of black eye-make-up. But I could never achieve Twiggy's svelte shape. At least my height and a low waist help me pull off Mom's velvet gown, and the A-line skirt hides my inherited fat thighs, so they don't diminish the overall illusion of glamour. The snug fit of its haltered bodice that barely contains my bosom makes me feel sexy but also vulnerable.

As I approach the entrance to the loo, both tuxedos and ball gowns are in line for the Men's and the Ladies' room. I might be the only *real girl* in the room. I choose the line for the restroom without urinals to avoid seeing men lifting the front of their dresses to pee.

I'm a bit light-headed as I find an empty stall and rush in without looking around. Pulling the door closed, I double-check that the latch is secure. At least the tile floor appears clean. I struggle with the fullness of my skirt in the cramped space, then perch above the seat like my mother taught me to avoid catching anything. After pulling my girdle back into place and checking my stockings for runs, I step through the crowded aisle to the sinks to wash my hands.

On either side of me, two broad-shouldered babes with muscled arms and admirable cleavage reapply their lipstick in the mirror. I join the ritual. They smile graciously, nodding their approval. I bow my head sheepishly, tuck up a few curls, and walk out.

Locating Chuck on the far side of the dance floor, I stride in his direction but pull up short when Bobby rushes up to me. "Here. You need this." Bobby wraps a silk-like lavender scarf around my throat.

After a second, I realize he means to hide the absence of an Adam's apple.

"C'mon. You don't want to miss out, do you?" He moves in the direction of the gathering contestants.

I shrug. "Guess not." With Chuck deep in conversation, unable to confirm his approval, I turn back to Bobby, his face eager. "So, what do I do?"

"You need to swagger your walk." He eyes me up and down as he speaks. "And make grand gestures." He throws out his arms. "Imagine you are royalty!" Being short, his movements are less than regal, but I get the gist.

As Bobby ushers me toward the line, I stroll forward with outstretched arms, stepping into the role. I try to embody Gypsy Rose Lee from the movie I'd watched with Mom. "How's this?"

"Better...but keep working it." He approaches a group of *ladies* at the end of the line, then turns back to me and says, "Marion will help you." He turns to a beauty bedazzled in red satin to verify the affirmative response he expects. "You don't mind, do you dear? It's his first time." Bobby is determined to maintain the illusion that I'm a guy in drag. When he hands me into their care, I hesitate, nervous about being found out. Then I remember. This is all about having fun.

Marion graciously nods, reaching out an oversized hand to invite me into their circle. With my hand, I give her my trust.

As the line inches near the stage, each of the *ladies* takes a turn coaching me. Giggles bubble up my throat as I listen to their instructions of how to be a woman, but I hold my composure, speaking with my deepest voice. Their fawning and insights enchant me. Being in close quarters with them, I am grateful Bobby had wrapped a scarf around my neck. I run my hands the length of the scarf and flash my fake nails, polished with a deep plum. The *ladies* smile their approval. Without knowing anything about me, they welcome me into their fold. By the time I stroll across the stage, my nerves are settled. I strut out, grateful for Mom's example when she walked the runway in charity fashion shows or was all decked out for a party, with a grand entrance on Dad's arm.

Down the steps on the far side, I rejoin my party at the table, where I receive a toast from Chuck and a kiss on my hand from Bobby. When they announce the winner, it's not me.

"Another worker who helped with decorations tipped them off," Bobby says. "Otherwise, you would have won." He sounds disappointed. I'm relieved. It is a great story, but who can I tell?

I can tell Mom. She'll get a kick out of it...after I tell her Chuck is gay. She'll be okay with it. But I can never tell Dad. He would only shame Chuck.

CHAPTER EIGHT

TELLING MOM 1968

It's late when I crawl out of bed. Mom is sitting at the kitchen table with a newspaper and a cup of black coffee. Dad's at work. I grab a donut off the counter and sit next to her. "Can we talk?"

She folds the paper and stubs out her cigarette. "If you'll help make lunch."

"Lunch?" My left brow arches, lifting the corner of my mouth.

"Yes, dear. It's almost noon. You must've had a good time last night. You slept through half the day." She points to the loaf of bread on the kitchen counter.

I take out four slices of soft white bread and lay them on the bare laminate surface.

"Last night was great. A blast. But that's not what I want to talk about." I hesitate. "Well, I mean, kind of, but not really."

She pulls mayo from the fridge, then turns and gives me a funny look. "You're rambling, Debby. Take a breath." She places the glass jar on the counter next to the ceramic mixing bowl and opens a can of tuna.

I take a breath. And then another, as she scrapes chopped onion and celery from the cutting board into the bowl, then adds the tuna.

I'm not sure how to start. "It's about Chuck..."

She folds mayo into the flakes of fish, then raises her eyes to catch mine. Her eyes probe into the depths of my psyche to read my thoughts. Sometimes I'm sure she can. She says, "What's wrong?"

"Nothing. Well, not really."

I fumble, replacing the twist on the plastic bread bag, trying out phrases in my head, worried about how she might react. *Tell her a little at a time. Don't shock her.*

After returning the bag of bread to the fridge, I move over to the table and sit down, turning in the flimsy chair to face her. "You know the party last night...the one I went to with Chuck?"

"Of course. You wore my dress." Her eyes drill into my core. "What's wrong? Did something happen to it?" She plops a heaping spoonful of tuna mixture onto the white bread, leveling it with the knife.

My head feels like it's about to explode.

She spreads a thick layer of mayo on the other two slices of bread, then glances my way. "What's going on?" Her eyes soften in that special way only a mother can do. "You know you can tell me anything. Just say it."

She knows me too well, knows how to wheedle things out of me. Anyway, I don't want to hold this secret alone. I open my fists, rest my hands in my lap, and do as she asks.

"Chuck is gay." I just blurt it out. I should have framed it better. I sit rigidly still, waiting for her to respond.

She returns the jar to the fridge, pulls out the head of lettuce with one hand and the juicy plump tomato with the other, and kicks the door closed with her foot. She doesn't speak while she tears off leaves of iceberg lettuce, folding them to fit the bread.

I sit, holding my breath, my eyes creeping wider.

She cuts two slices of tomato, one for each sandwich, then says, "I guess I always knew."

Air rushes into my lungs with a whoosh. "You *knew*?" I scrunch my shoulders and lift both hands, palms up, reaching for some unseen element that will help me understand my mom.

"Yes, honey. I am his mother." She finishes making the sandwiches and puts the ingredients back in the fridge. "When did he tell you?"

"On the drive from Vegas."

"And you weren't shocked?"

"Not really." I pause and think back. "Maybe a little surprised." *Am I actually talking with my mother about Chuck being gay? It's surreal.*

"In my day," Mom says, looking up at the ceiling, "*Homosexuality* was not something you discussed. I guess times are changing with the sexual revolution and all."

She's being too nonchalant. Like we're talking about an event on the news. Detached.

"Chuck told me they prefer the term *gay*." I gulp down my soda and return my eyes to her, to search for a hidden response. She never judges, but she never gave even a hint that she knew. What other secrets is she keeping? Or am I better off not knowing?

She says, "I suspected my intuition was true, but my suspicions were confirmed that last year we lived in Michigan,"—Mom wipes her hands on the terrycloth towel attached to her apron—"when he was with…"

"Jack," we say in unison.

"You knew about Jack?" I ask, surprised by her openness.

"I worried Jack would be a bad influence on him. They were too close. Jack was wild and careless."

So, she can be judgmental. "I didn't think Jack was wild; I hung around them a lot." I laugh to myself, remembering how Jack taught me to kiss. *I wasn't old enough to recognize he was in love with Chuck. But Mom saw it.*

She rinses the dirty knife and lays it in the sink to be washed later. "I had hoped to save him from the pain of that kind of life."

A sadness washes over her, but she quickly tucks it away. I try to understand the mother I thought I knew, getting a glimpse of the pain she hides under her elegance and charm.

She places my sandwich on the rainbow-colored placemat in front of me, grabs hers and sits across from me, positioning her plate in the exact middle of the placemat. When I lean on the table, it wobbles, splashing coffee out of her overfilled cup.

"Shit!" She clamps her hand across her mouth. "Sorry, honey. I shouldn't swear."

"You can say *shit* in front of me. I say it twenty times a day."

"It's not ladylike to swear. But if that's the worst word you ever use, I guess it's okay."

I grin like a Cheshire cat. *Right, Mom, whatever you want to believe.* I lift my sandwich and take another bite, licking the mayonnaise out of the corner of my mouth.

"The wobble is driving me crazy." The cheap dining set came with the apartment. She looks me square in the eye. "Do you have a book of matches?" and raises one brow like she's wearing a monocle. "I know you're smoking now."

I jerk back. My pack of Virginia Slims is hiding deep in my purse. *I've never smoked in front of her. How does she know? Do my clothes smell of smoke?*

I hand her the matches from my purse. She slips it under the offending table leg like I'd seen her do many times before in a cafe or a bar.

As Mom eats her sandwich, I study her face, seeing fine lines I haven't noticed before. The glimmer in her eyes has dulled but hasn't disappeared. Her auburn hair, cut short, reveals her pixie ears; the hair at the nape of her neck forms a ducktail. She could pass as my sister.

"How do you do it, Mom? All these years?"

"What?"

"Hold it all in." I cock my head to one side.

She knocks ashes off her cigarette into the ashtray. "Practice I guess." She smiles and takes another sip of coffee but leaves her sandwich untouched.

That's how she does it. How she survives it *all*. She just accepts what is.

I'm learning things I never suspected about my mom. When I asked for help with school, she'd say, "Ask your father." When my brothers and I did verbal battle with Dad, challenging his certitude about everything, Mom never said a word. I thought she didn't have any opinions. Without realizing it, I had assumed she wasn't smart. I was wrong. She is plenty smart. But her true strength comes from her empathy—how unlike Dad, she listens to her family and to her friends, a trait I hope I inherited or at least can soak up now that I better understand her.

I haven't told Mom that Bobby invited me to the club where Chuck tends bar after he finishes his nursing shift at the hospital. I don't think she's ever encountered a drag queen, either. We'll start easy with a gay bar and a game of pool.

The next Friday evening, I exit the freeway at Vineland Avenue in North Hollywood with Mom beside me. A few days ago, Chuck took me to find my first car and take out my first loan to buy a 1958 fire-engine red MGB with a black ragtop. I call her *Baby*. Mom names her cars, too, but she calls hers *Betsy*.

At the bottom of the exit ramp, I rip around the corner gas station and pull into a rear parking lot. The *Back Door* sits at the end of a small strip mall crammed against the freeway interchange towering above. I park at the end of the narrow lot next to an older black Buick sedan.

Mom climbs easily out of my low-riding English sports car and stands with her hand on the open door. "Are you sure about this?"

I place one hand on the corner of the windshield and the other on the rear panel behind the seat to leverage my weight onto my feet. "Bobby said Chuck works here."

"Is this what I think it is?"

"He's a bartender." I lift my purse strap onto my shoulder and pop the car door closed.

Two guys walk past with their arms wrapped around each other's waist. Mom whispers. "At a *gay* bar?"

"Yeah." Above our heads, cars zoom by on the elevated Highway 101 that traverses the San Fernando Valley.

I take three strides toward the back entrance, then turn to see if she's following. Mom remains planted between the two rows of cars. "Just think of it as an adventure," I say, throwing back in her face the phrase she's used all my life whenever I was reluctant to go along with whatever Dad had in store for us.

She squints at me with one side of her lips curled slightly.

I glance at her sideways. "Bobby invited us for a drink and a game of pool." She pulls back, unlike the Mom I know—the woman at the center of every party, especially when I was in elementary school, gliding down a runway wearing a swimsuit, a gown, then a wedding dress for a charity fashion event; or playing the female lead at the local theater to applause and acclaim. She's been different since we left Australia. Still, I can't let her chicken out on me.

"Mothers aren't supposed to visit their sons in gay bars."

I shake off her reluctance with a twist of my head. "Why not, Mom? You raised us in bars."

"I did not!" Her jaw clenches.

She's defensive. My flippant attitude is too near the boundary of her tolerance. "We stopped at every Elks Club, Moose Lodge, and VFW in every Podunk town along Route 66."

She looks at the ground, then raises her head and stares at me. "They were places to eat. Or they had entertainment—someone playing the piano or a pool table. My uncle has a pool table at home and taught me to shoot."

"I didn't know about your uncle, but I remember sipping Shirley Temples from Michigan to the Pacific Ocean." I walk back to where she's standing. "So?" I pause for effect. "Are you up for this?" We stand there for what seems like minutes. Another group of men glance at us when they walk past, then enter the bar.

"Are you sure?" she says under her breath.

"I told you about Chuck being gay because he wouldn't. He's ashamed of who he is. You don't want *that*, do you?"

She softens. "Oh, honey. He knows I love him. I will always love him, no matter what."

"I don't know, Mom. I think we need to show him it's *no big deal*." Again, I'm stealing phrases from her, pleased with myself, giving her a piece of her own medicine.

"Okay." She nods, takes one step toward me, and says, "One drink."

"That's not enough. I promised Bobby I'd shoot some pool."

I wait. She's looking at me like she's never seen me before.

"One drink, and we'll see…we'll play it by ear."

I hope this night doesn't turn into a complete fiasco. She's trusting me. But I don't know what we're walking into. I've never been in a gay bar either.

When I open the rear door of the club and step in, Mom pushes up against my back as the heavy door closes behind her. I stop to let my eyes adjust.

"Can you see *anything?*" she asks.

The hall is narrow, painted soft black, with three doors on the left. The first is marked *Private*. Probably the office. The next, *Ladies*. "I bet one doesn't get much use." Mom giggles.

We inch forward, passing the *Men*'s room. The space opens to a narrow storefront interior filled with round tables, each with four chairs. In the center sits a fireplace encircled by more chairs. Above the pit, a round vent hood suspended by a narrow exhaust pipe, painted flat black like the ceiling, disappears into the darkness. No flames flicker in the pit, but the smell of smoke lingers.

Beyond the fire pit, a long bar hugs the wall on the left. Behind the bar, bottles of booze on lit glass shelves shimmer in a mirror. On the right, a row of tables scallops the length of a continuous bench, each with two chairs. The place is packed with guys who look up as we pass.

I reach for Mom's hand. "Come with me." *I pray my brother is working tonight.*

CHAPTER NINE

A BAR IN NORTH HOLLYWOOD 1968

I push forward with Mom in tow through men who part like water behind a speedboat.

At the far end of the narrow space, where the bar curves into the wall, a small, raised dance floor glistens with shifting colors from a spotlight above. A jukebox and cigarette machine illuminate the entrance to the street with their glow. Behind the bar, Chuck is wiping down the bar top.

"I see two open stools." I squeeze Mom's hand.

Chuck flips his head around at the sound of my voice, his fox-red hair flying as he turns. His eyes widen, his brows shoot up, and his mouth drops open. Feeling Mom pull back, I let go of her hand.

I sit on a barstool, stifling my glee at pulling off the surprise. "Hi!"

Chuck crunches his face into a steely stare. "What are *you* doing here?"

"Bobby invited me to shoot some pool. Is he here?" I'm blocking Chuck's view of Mom until she slips onto the next stool.

"Hi, honey. Got a cold beer for your tired old Mom?"

Chuck's eyes get big again, but his mouth remains closed. He focuses his dismay on me.

"I'll take one too. Do you have Bud?" I smile, hoping he'll ignore the fact that I'm underage. I've been drinking in clubs since I met my first boyfriend, who attended a Terre Haute college, while drinking with my parents. I was seventeen. He was twenty-three.

"I thought you didn't like beer?" Chuck's words seep through his clenched teeth.

"It's growing on me."

He scowls.

Being flip isn't working. I drop the attitude. "I'm hot and thirsty. Beer is cold."

He reaches down for two long necks and pops the caps. "You want a glass?"

"For Mom. I'll drink out of the bottle."

He's mad at me, but he'll get over it. He pours Mom's beer into the glass, keeping the head to a minimum, just like Dad taught us when we were kids, and places it on a paper coaster stamped with the bar's name. As he sets the bottle in front of me, he leans over to my other side from Mom and whispers, "She knows?"

Mom answers. "Yes, dear." Even in the dim light, I can see her reach out with her eyes. The eyes say it all. When Chuck doesn't avoid her gaze, she smiles. "I've known for a while. It's okay."

I take a swig of beer. "We'll talk later, Chuck, when you're not working."

"And Dad?" Chuck asks, looking back at me.

"No. Do you think I'm a complete idiot?" I stare back, arching my brow. "We'll work on him...won't we, Mom?" I turn to her, looking for support.

"Yes, dear." She turns back to Chuck. "You know how hard-headed he can be. But he'll come around. You'll see."

Mom. Always the optimist. That's where I get it from.

I feel someone walk up behind me. It's Bobby, my partner in crime from the previous weekend. "Hi." His grin is genuine and welcoming. "I'm glad you made it. Ready to rack 'em up?" He rises on his toes to be eye level with Mom. "Who's your friend?"

"Mom, this is Bobby. Bobby, Mom."

"She looks like your sister," he says, looking back and forth between us.

I'm tickled but not surprised—I've heard it before. I wag my finger between us. "Can't you tell? Red hair? Brown eyes? She hasn't aged a day since she had us."

"That's not true," she injects. "I have plenty of gray hair thanks to the two of you. I'm just smart enough to use a bottle to cover it up." She lets out a giggle. Chuck and I smile and clink our beers together. She reaches out to Bobby. "Nice to meet you. You can call me Carleen."

We shoot doubles and win a few games, then I step back to watch Mom perform. She became the life of the party wherever we lived, whether it's a weekly bridge game in Flushing, a charity fashion show for the Australian-American Ladies Auxiliary Club in Melbourne, or a pool game at a gay bar in LA.

Three solids in a row drop into pockets like she moves them with her mind, the cue ball lining up with the eight as if she'd placed it. The guys migrate toward her hearty laugh and bright guileless eyes. She accepts them as they are. No questions asked.

After I switch from beer to scotch, Chuck digs up some cold sandwiches for us from a fridge behind the bar. More guys gather to cheer her on, and I wander back to the fire pit where Bobby is deep in conversation with Roger and Jimmy. Mom and I crushed them in a pool game earlier.

"Come join us," Bobby says. I sit in the chair he pulls up for me. "Roger has given us a logic puzzle. Tell her the story. Maybe she can help us solve this one."

Roger is older, with salt and pepper hair, closer to my dad's age. Though he doesn't have the flashy good looks of some of the other pretty boys, his face radiates kindness. He's holding court like a senior statesman.

Roger nods to me. "Ready?" I nod back. "Okay. A man comes out of an apartment and gets in an elevator. He pushes the button for the first floor. When the door opens, he gets out and leaves the building.

"That evening, he returns, gets on the elevator, pushes the

seventh-floor button. When the doors open, he walks out, goes to the end of the hall, takes the stairs up one floor, finds apartment 805, opens the door, and goes in. Explain the logic of this."

I shake my head and shrug. "You mean why did he take the stairs in the evening and not in the morning?"

"That's it. You can ask me anything, but I can only give yes or no answers." Roger takes a sip of his beer.

"So," I ask, "did he do it because he needed the exercise to lose weight?"

"Good question. No."

"Did he stop to see a friend?"

"No."

"Was he afraid he was being followed?" I'm having a blast, but my pride demands I win, after years of family game nights when my brothers and I conspired to beat Dad.

"That's a good one. No. Keep going."

I ask more questions, getting the same response for almost an hour. Between my attempts, others who gradually join in the game throw out their best guesses. The camaraderie makes me feel at home, like when my family used to spend time together at the lake while we had our boat.

"I give up." I say with a shrug.

"You sure? You're so close."

"I hate giving up, but my brain is mush. Just tell me."

Roger pauses for emphasis. With a satisfied grin, he whispers the answer in case someone in earshot hasn't yet fallen victim to his game. "He was a midget."

I hold my wrist to my forehead. "Oh my god. Why didn't I think of that? He couldn't reach the button."

My laugh triggers a satisfied smile from Roger. He leans back in his chair and sips his cognac. "You asked a lot of good questions. You're smart. Like my Denny."

I cautiously ask, "Is that your lover?"

Roger smiles and flips out his lighter when I pull out a cigarette. "Thanks." I take a long pull of smoke.

"Denny? No. He's my youngest son. I have two boys."

"You're not gay?"

"I was married for fifteen years before I came out."

"Is that when you decided you were gay?"

"Decided? No." He glances up into the infinity of the blackness above. "I'm gay because God made me this way." Then he looks me in the eye. "No one would ever *choose* to be gay if we had a choice."

I sit back, worried I have offended him.

Roger downs the rest of his drink and raises his glass to signal Chuck he wants another. "I married because that's what was expected. I was in the closet hiding from myself and my family, and it wasn't fair to any of us."

He reaches for my pack of Virginia Slims, tilting it up to get my okay. I nod. He pulls out a cigarette and ignites it using his Zippo, then slowly inhales the smoke.

"My whole life was a lie until I met Carson who gave me the courage to come out. We've been together ever since." Roger reaches behind him for his partner's hand, his eyes softening when they touch.

Chuck dated girls in high school and college to keep up appearances. Mike brought him to LA to get him away from Jack, not knowing he was dropping him into a mecca for gays. I didn't understand any of that until now.

Most of the guys gathered around the fire pit drift off into smaller groups of two or three, some returning to watch the ongoing game of pool up front. Others migrate to the raised dance floor to dance, dropping coins into the jukebox. I watch from a distance the unfamiliar image of two men intertwined, groping each other as they sway to the rhythm of a romantic song, like couples do in a straight bar, then turn back to Roger. "Keeping it secret must be hard."

Roger, Carson, and Jimmy's eyes grow big, staring at me. Coming up behind me, Bobby muffles his laughter. *Now what have I put my foot in?*

"We take *everything* dirty," Bobby says, barely containing his giggles.

Funny. My brothers had educated me well about sexual innuendos. I get it. Anything *hard* relates to a guy's hard-on. I note the rule and push on to learn more. Chuck doesn't openly share like this, and I don't want to miss my chance to better understand him.

"We live lives full of ridicule and judgment, making us ashamed of who we are," Roger says. "And afraid."

"Why afraid?" Roger seems confident, self-assured.

"Of being discovered. Of losing our job. Our family. That's the worst. Isn't it?" He looks at Bobby. "The family."

Bobby's face drops. "Yeah. Telling my parents was bad. Homosexuals are not accepted in Hispanic families."

Jimmy chimes in, "It's even worse if you're Black. We get beat up. Put in the hospital. Or killed."

Even in the dim light, I can see the flames dancing in the darkness of their eyes, a kind of hell they've been forced into through no fault of their own. What would Dad do if he knew?

Chuck appears with a scotch for Roger, a raised brow for me, then returns to his post behind the bar. Roger takes a sip, then a long drag off his cigarette. Tipping his head back, he lets the smoke escape from his lips in tiny white ringlets that stretch as they rise toward the ceiling.

"I wish I could do that."

Roger's eyes sparkle as he releases even more smoke rings.

A handsome young blonde sitting next to Jimmy says, "The worst for me was telling my dad. He disowned me. Now when I call and my mom answers, she hangs up." He blows out a long sigh. Jimmy squeezes his hand.

I ask Roger. "When you told your wife, how did she react?"

"It's a lot like dealing with death—once I broke through her denial, she became furious. Blamed herself. Then the bargaining. And when that didn't work, she went into months of depression. I tried to help, but it made it worse. It took a while, but we've become friends again. The hardest thing was telling my two boys."

"Did you ever love her?" I ask.

"Still do."

Bobby says, "Some guys don't make it." He's just returned with two bottles of Mexican beer, each with a lime sticking out, and a pair of empty glasses. He pours beer into the glasses, squeezed the lime, then places one in front of me. "Try this."

With a sip, my lips pucker from the pleasant bite, and I respond with a nod. I've had deception in my life, like pretending I wasn't lonely when we moved every year. But I can't fathom Roger's anguish.

"Bobby, what do you mean some *don't make it?*"

"Suicide is high in the gay community. Especially for those who stay in the closet. Or if their family rejects them when they come out."

I can't believe a parent would push their own kid to the point of suicide. I look to the front, seeing Mom poised for her next ace in the hole, half the bar standing in a circle around the pool table like her fan club. "*My mom* is cool with all of you."

"Your mom is different. She's great." When the guys watching her cheer, his eyes light up. "And she shoots a mean game of pool."

"She wasn't cool when I wanted to burn my bra." I chuckle, remembering my last year of high school when it was just Mom and me. "She said I'd regret it when my boobs sagged."

The guys give me a double take and laugh. Roger says, "You're a hoot. Like your mom. And optimistic. It's refreshing."

"Maybe things will change," I respond.

Roger shakes his head. "Not in my lifetime."

As I look up, my brother walks from behind the bar over to our table. "Looks like a serious discussion. What kind of bull are you two feeding my little sister?" he asks.

"They're educating me."

"That sounds dangerous." Chuck's lips curl into an endearing lopsided smile. He flips his hair off his forehead. "Last call." Chuck points at me. "Not you, Debby. You're driving. I'll bring you coffee."

"How about a Coke? That'll perk me up. Is Mom about ready?"

"I hope so," Chuck says. "The guys have lost everything but their shirts to her."

"I wish she'd beaten the pants off 'em," Bobby chimed in. "That would've been a sight to see." They all flash cheesy grins, even Chuck.

"Mom's playing for money?" I ask.

"They twisted her arm," Bobby reports.

Chuck nods. "It escalated from the usual quarter game to a couple of bucks. The guys are eating it up. They all want her to be their *mom*." Chuck grins. "They asked to see her driver's license to be sure she was old enough. She loved that."

My plan is working. He's accepting Mom and me into his gay community.

He turns back to the bar. "I'll get those drinks."

"Chuck, tell Mom she can finish her game." I turn back to Roger and Bobby. "One more question?" They nod, so I ask, "What's dressing *in drag* all about?"

"Besides the fact that it's tons of fun?" Roger reaches for his nearly empty glass. "Being in drag is like stepping onto a stage and letting it all hang out. It's living without fear, even if only for a few hours."

Chuck delivers our drinks. His ears perk when he overhears our discussion but doesn't say anything. When the time is right, I'll ask him if he's ever dressed in drag.

"What about you, Bobby?" I ask. "Ever try it?"

"Me? Yeah. Once. A couple years ago. Way too much work. Besides, I'm too short. Drag queens need to be statuesque."

I shrug off his self-deprecation. "I think you'd look elegant."

His half-smile is timid, but his eyes glisten from the praise.

As I finish my soda, Mom walks up. The sparkle from winning at pool remains, but her lids droop, revealing her fatigue.

"You about ready, Debby? I'm all pooped out."

"I should think so. You've hardly sat down all night."

"I couldn't stop a winning streak. And the boys were all being so nice."

Chuck comes up behind her. "Moths to a flame." He's there in case she loses her balance. He puts his arm around Mom's shoulders. "I need to close the bar."

Mom and I give him a hug and walk arm in arm out the back door to the nearly barren parking lot. When we reach my car, I open the door for her.

"Do you think Dad is worried? He doesn't know where we are."

"I told him we were going out. He's probably working late, like every night this week." She sticks out her chin a fraction of an inch. "I'm tired of sitting around the house. If he doesn't like that I went out for an evening with my daughter, then that's just too bad."

"Wow. I like this new rebellious spirit, Mom."

She says, "When he left us on our own for six months, I changed."

I'm thrilled with Mom's response to Chuck's true self. But Dad isn't ready. A year ago, I told him to not use the *n* word in front of me. He looked shocked but backed off.

After tonight, I understand why Chuck has protected his secret for so long.

CHAPTER TEN

WE ALL COME UNDONE 1968

The sun peeks over the mountain tops at the start of my hour-long commute as I cross the valley to where I work. From the metered ramp, I merge into the first lane, accelerating into the moving mass of steel, twist the radio to a favorite station playing Bobby Darin's "Dream Lover," then jump on the brake, leaving only inches between my bumper and the stopped car in front.

Learning to drive on two-lane roads in Peoria did little to prepare me for six lanes of cars in either direction, traveling too close to stop safely, especially if someone like me is changing the radio channel.

At work, I enjoy typing the installers' time sheet codes into a machine that produces a long tape of punched holes. I'm earning the money for my car payment, gas, and a few fast-food meals. If I earn a promotion, I'll make enough to afford an apartment. Scruffy, my best friend, coworker, and softball pitcher, and I compete at achieving the fastest time for keying in perfect coding. "Bingo!" Scruffy calls out. Today she beat me. I'll win tomorrow.

While scanning the Sunday paper for cheap apartments, I spot an ad with a horse for sale a few miles north of our apartment. I yearn to feel a horse's soft lips nuzzling my hand and to hear a welcoming nicker. Mom won't understand, so I don't dare tell her. *I'll just look.*

After calling for an appointment, I pull on jeans and the riding boots I wore in Australia and jump into Baby. The address leads me to a ten-stall barn with arenas for flat work, some filled with jumps, and turn out paddocks surround the structure. When I approach the barn, a woman greets me. She's leading a sweet thoroughbred gelding all tacked up and ready to ride.

"This is Thunder. If you'd like to ride him, I'm giving a lesson in ten minutes. You can put him through his paces and see what you think."

"That sounds great."

I'm rusty—haven't ridden since I fractured my spine—but I soon fall into the rhythm of his trot. The four-year-old chestnut has a smooth canter, only once giving a little buck when I ask him to change directions and pick up the other lead. I want to buy him. But there is no way I can afford the purchase price or pay for his keep. *This is crazy. I can't afford an apartment for myself.*

After the lesson, I untack, brush, and pick out Thunder's hooves. I even comb out his mane and tail, though they are already free of tangles. I'm stalling for time, soaking in the smell of his sweat from the workout and the sound of his whinny, greeting other horses as they pass by. I pull a carrot from my pocket to feel his soft lips and the warm breath on my palm. He sniffs my hair and snorts at the smell of my shampoo.

I tell the owner, "I can't afford him right now," ashamed I haven't been honest, but grateful to be with a horse and for the time away from my dysfunctional home. "I would like to take some lessons." I schedule one the following week. After returning Thunder to his stall, I watch him chew the hay he pulls from the net, his jaw moving in rhythmic circles.

"Where have you been?" Mom asks when I walk in. She's furious when I answer. "Save your money. You'll need every penny to survive in this city."

I don't like her telling me what to do, but she's right. Mom has had to be practical. I better listen. After canceling my lesson, I never return to that barn but promise myself, one day I'll have a horse right outside my door on my land. I don't know how, but I'll cling to my vision of a happy life to get through the hard times.

Mom can no longer hide her unhappiness. Dad's been treating her worse than ever. I wouldn't blame her if she left him. If she files for divorce, she'll be breaking from the Catholic faith she adopted to marry Dad.

I avoid my problems by partying. I dance until the clubs close, joining new friends at Denny's for breakfast until the early hours.

My favorite escape is playing women's softball with the girls after work. I'm a great catcher. The telephone installers coach our team. After a practice and every game, we occupy a corner of the local pizza place. The guys teach me how to guzzle beer, how to pour it down my open throat. Tonight, I beat them at their own game, forcing them to upend their mugs once again. No one's bothered by me being only 18.

On another night, I stay out late drinking with some friends I've only just met. We go for breakfast after the bars close. After two hours of sleep, I drag myself to work, using my anxiety about being late to drive through the exhaustion, using all I learned from watching Mom to hide the telltale signs.

The next morning, Dad corners me. "I know you're on the pill."

"What? No! Where did you get that idea?" I ask, tamping down my rising rage. *Geez, I'm not even having sex.* I'm still clinging to my Catholic beliefs by waiting for my wedding night. I drive off without further discussion.

The muscles in my gut contort, turning it inside out, making me want to puke, my stomach retching from last night's combination of too much beer and Peppermint Schnapps from some guy's flask. He'd said, "The mint will settle your stomach." We'd nestled in the backseat of his VW bug, drinking, and making out into the wee hours, until I threw it all up in his car. Instead of helping me, he yelled, "You should never mix drinks."

"I'm sorry, but no one ever told me. I just started drinking."

I've already forgotten his name, which is okay with me. I crawl out of his car, return to the dance club and sneak into the ladies' room. I clean myself up, vowing to eat something whenever I drink…and to never again drink Peppermint Schnapps.

In the morning, I wake up in a daze and stumble into the bathroom to get ready for work. I put down the ragtop of my MGB and collapse into the bucket seat, tasting the salt in the air from the beach fifteen miles away. The wind blows my short mop on end as I zip along Topanga Canyon, waking me for the gauntlet ahead.

The traffic on the 101 mirrors my life—stuck, with nothing but questions ahead, powerless to alter what's before me. As the mass of cars inch along, I talk to the majestic pile of rock and rubble that encircled the valley. "Good morning, mountains," I say out loud. "I know I can count on you to not abandon me." The absurdity makes me giggle. They existed long before man and will remain after we've turned to dust. They're constant, dependable. Not much in my life has been, except Chuck. Maybe he doesn't tell me everything, but if I need him, I know he'll be there for me. I position my head to block the piercing rays of the rising sun with the rearview mirror and wipe a tear from my cheek. I take in their steady strength to give me the mettle to survive the upheaval I sense coming. "You give me the strength to get through another day."

With only four hours of sleep last night, I doze off at work until a coworker shows me where I can nap. "Pac Bell provides a room with a bed for anyone who becomes sick at work." My illness is emotional. If I'm not careful, I'll be out of a job.

On the way home, I hit a traffic jam caused by a wreck on the freeway. Turning onto Roscoe Blvd. at last, I search for a parking place in front of our Canoga Park apartment and a spot opens up near the building's entrance.

Chuck, who lives with friends, is standing outside our apartment smoking a cigarette. I reach for the door handle to enter, but he puts his arm across it, blocking my path. I catch his eyes. This is no joke, no boyish prank. He flips out his pack and knocks it against the edge of his left hand, breaking free a single cigarette.

"Want one?" he asks, looking up. His usual grin is absent. "You're going to need it."

As I reach for the cigarette, easing it free, I crunch up my face. "What's going on?"

He tucks the pack into his shirt pocket, then reaches into his jeans for the lighter Dad gave him when he graduated from high school. Mike got a lighter too. Dad never gave one to me. Even though all my family smoke, they tell me I shouldn't. Why am I the exception? Mom told me, "It's a dirty habit for any young lady."

Leaning against the frame of the door, I loop my purse over my left shoulder, bring the filter tip to my lips, and wait for a light.

"Did you know nicotine provides a calming effect?" Chuck asks, flicking his Zippo into action.

"No, I didn't. I'll use that when I tell Dad I'm smoking."

"How many?" he asks.

"Cigarettes? About a pack a day, though most of them burn up in the ashtray at work because I'm busy. Everybody there smokes as much as I do, if not more."

"Goes good with a beer. I could use one about now." Chuck tips his head back to practice blowing rings.

I watch the precisely formed loops leave his lips, stretching larger as they rise, dissolving into nothingness. "I'd love a beer too. Horrible traffic on the way home."

A few nights ago, Mom and I sat at the kitchen table having a beer and talking about when I was young. Mom only reminisces when she's drinking, which seems to happen more lately. Remembering the beers left in the fridge, I move toward the door.

"Stop!" Chuck shouts. "You can't go in there." Panic edges his stern gaze.

"Why?"

His eyes soften with pity. "It's finally happening. They're splitting up."

I'm without words to respond, so I take another drag off my menthol-flavored Virginia Slim.

"Mike's in there trying to stop it. He's home on leave and threatening, if they break up, he'll re-up for another tour to stay in Nam."

"That'll be his third. It's suicide." A quiet panic floods through me when I realize I have no impact on Mike's choices.

"I think that's the point." He looks around to see if anyone's lurking nearby. "There's a lot that you don't know," he whispers. Chuck takes a long drag from what's left of his cigarette, the ash burning close to its filter. "I hate to be the one to tell you this, Sis, but Mike's not the only one who's tried it. Actually, I think you're the only one in our family who hasn't."

My eyes shoot open, and I cough out the smoke I've just inhaled. "What are you talking about? Suicide?"

Chuck nods.

I suck back my breath.

"Well, it's not obvious unless you know what's going on," Chuck explains. "Dad with his fast cars and alcohol...and Mom." The door flies open and Mike storms past, yelling back at the door.

"When I don't come back, it's on your heads."

"Mike. Wait." I reach for his arm, but he yanks it away without even a glance. I see moisture streaming down his face and rage in his eyes. Before I can say more, he's gone.

I enter the apartment before Chuck to search for Mom. Maybe I can pry out of her what Chuck didn't finish. Surely, she hasn't tried to kill herself. I can't believe any of this, but I know he wouldn't lie.

Dad is standing in the living room, his eyes filled with a fiery pain I've never seen. I try to pass without engaging him, but he sees the smoke in my hand.

"Get rid of that cigarette!" He grabs my arm and flips me around to face him.

I pull away, silently defiant.

"You know why they call them nails, right?" He holds me in his steely gaze, waiting. When I don't answer, he does. "They nail you in your coffin."

"Just following your example." He releases his hold on me. My retort wounds him. I'd not seen him this fragile since Grandpa died a few years ago.

The beet red in his face has faded to gray, like the salt in his peppered hair. Then I hear a door click open behind me. It's Mom coming out of the bathroom. Without a glance, she rushes into my room.

I look at Dad. Not knowing what else to say, I shake my head, then turn my back on him to follow Mom. When I reach for the bedroom doorknob, I hear a sharp crack. Dad slammed the door as he left. Good riddance.

On this day, he and I became strangers. I had been his doting little girl, but no more.

In my room, I sit next to Mom on the bed, straining to hear her tear wrapped words.

"I'm sorry," she says without looking up. With my arm around her shoulders, I support her slumped form, listening, as she has for me.

"I can't take it anymore." Her hands cover her face, trapping her tears. She shakes from the weight of her sorrow. "I just can't," she mumbles, weeping like I've seen only once before. Her shoulders rise and fall in my embrace. I'm afraid she'll crash and break open, never to be whole again.

"It'll be alright," I say, hoping to comfort her. "One day, we'll look back at this and laugh."

She stops sobbing, raises her head to search my face for what seems like minutes.

"What?" I ask.

"When did you become the mother and I the child?"

I shrug, not knowing how to answer. "I guess we learn from each other." A tiny smile grows on her face. In my belly, a tickle rises through my throat and emerges as a giggle—a little girl's giggle. Her smile grows and we laugh together, not robustly, but enough to break the cycle of pain—if only for a little while.

The next day, Mom confirms she is leaving, returning to Peoria to get her old job back. Dad hasn't returned since charging out last night, hasn't even called. None of us know where he spent the night.

I stand in the bedroom door while Mom packs her bags to leave. "Are you sure this is what you want?"

"Oh, honey, I still love your father. But I can't stand his lies anymore. Nor the gambling. I never know if there will be money for rent. Or if the lights will stay on. I paid it all with my salary. We had barely enough for food. For twenty-five years, I've put up with it." She closes the last suitcase and secures the clasp. "I'm done. I deserve some happiness."

But what is she going back to? Another family rented our Peoria apartment the day we left. The furniture's in storage if she can find the money to pay the bill. She'll need a smaller place—one she can afford on a bookkeeper's salary. It's more than I'll be starting with. We might do better together, but I won't return to Peoria. I want to move forward, to build a life with beaches to walk and mountains to draw strength from them I know I'll need. I don't want to live with her fears. She's too fearful to stay in LA, and she needs to get away from Dad.

The next morning, I help carry out her bags. After a long desperate hug, I watch her slide into the driver's seat.

"You could come with me," Mom says, her eyes pleading.

I shake my head. "There's nothing back there for me anymore. I'm already addicted to this sunshine." I lean into the open window. "But I'm worried about you driving that far on your own."

"You need to focus on your own life." She waves her hand to dismiss my concern. "I'll be fine." When she pulls out into the traffic, I stand on the sidewalk with my arms wrapped around, hugging myself, wondering how I'll manage without her.

CHAPTER ELEVEN

THE PARTY 1968

"Mike's returning to Vietnam," Chuck says while lighting my cigarette outside the apartment. Mom left yesterday. "His threat to stop our parents' divorce failed; it's struck him deep. He overreacted and signed up for another extended tour."

I shake my head, unable to find words of any consequence.

Mike shows up after a night with friends. "Dad paid the rent for next month and has now disappeared. He bragged about widows, eager to pick up the check, swarming him, wanting to take him home. Mom crushed his ego by leaving. He's looking for someone to rebuild his pride and restore his manhood."

Wasn't it Dad who's crushed Mom's happiness by cheating and gambling all those years?

Mike says, "But I don't know which wealthy woman he picked to move in with."

I hear the resentment in Mike's voice, but I don't share anything I've learned. Mom didn't spill her heart out to him. Only to me. I change the subject to a club I heard of with a live blues band. An hour later, Mike disappears like Dad did.

The next morning, Mike comes strolling into the apartment carrying a large canvas with blue and orange oil paints applied in sweeping strokes using a palette knife. When he leans it against the wall, I reach out to pick it up.

"Careful. It's still wet."

"She's naked." I look up at his grinning face. "And pregnant."

"Yeah. Isn't it great? She modeled for me. Do you like it?"

Despite my attempt at being nonchalant, my jaw drops open. "Is she your girlfriend? Is the baby *yours*?"

"Nah. It's Bruce's. They're both friends. Cool, huh?"

"Why'd you bring it here?"

"To hang for the party tonight. My buddies are coming and bringing their girls."

"Here? When?"

"Tonight. The place is ours. Might as well enjoy it. You should come too."

"Thanks. I do live here, you know." I try to look snarky. "Is Chuck coming?"

"Yeah. He's bringing Michelle."

Michelle works with Chuck at the hospital. I met her the night Chuck invited me to see where he worked. We ate Twinkies from the machines because the cafeteria had already closed. I loved seeing him in his element as a nurse's aide. I wonder if Mike knows about Chuck's *other* job at the bar, but I don't bring it up.

Mike pulls out his wallet and shaves off a twenty. "Can you pick up some snacks and sodas? And maybe some pretzels? I'll get the beer."

Though I get away with drinking beer in a club, I don't want to push my luck in a liquor store. I pocketed the twenty, grabbed my purse, and paused for one more look at the painting.

Mike rarely shared his art with me. Once, when I was in fourth grade, Mom asked him to show me how to draw a face. He showed me with pad and pencil. "Start halfway down, then cut the lower half into thirds." I use it even now, though I don't practice drawing very often.

Mom once took my brothers and me to a series of art classes at the museum, my first. My drawing was ugly, and I didn't want to share it.

The teacher encouraged me to keep working on it and, on our last day, he included my pastel in the class show.

That night, Mike's friends fill the apartment. A few hours into the party, after drinking too much beer, I climb on top of the fridge for a place to sit. The ceiling's barely high enough for me to squeeze in, stooped over. My legs hang over the door, but I lift them to let anyone reach inside for a drink.

When Michelle grabs a beer, she says, "What are you doing up there?"

"No place to sit." I'm impressed with my own cleverness. By sitting on my makeshift perch, maybe Mike's friends will see me as cool instead of as his troublesome little sister.

She says, "With the inside fridge light encircling your face, you look like an angel."

Hungover the next morning, I clean up the mess from the party, thinking about Mom as I vacuum. I miss her already, like I did when I was young, left alone for too many hours while she worked. I feel abandoned, even though it was my choice to stay.

On Monday, two days after the party, I pull into a parking spot in front of our apartment complex. Chuck is leaning against the brick wall next to the gated arch entrance. I lock my car and stroll over.

"What are you doing here? I thought you had to work tonight."

"Not until eleven." He takes out a cigarette and lights it. "Mike called. We've got a problem."

"Now what?" I sling my purse over my arm, tuck my keys into my pocket, and hold out two fingers to bum a smoke.

He lights another one off the end of his and hands it to me. "The manager put a lock on the door. We can't get in. Mike went to learn why. The manager checked our apartment because the neighbors complained about noise from our party. He says we owe money to cover the damage and won't give us our stuff until we pay."

"What damage?" Then it hit me. "Wait. He went inside when no one was home?"

"Damaged carpet and walls are what he claims. Landlords keep master keys; the laws let them do anything. Plus, Dad didn't pay another month's rent—it was due today."

"That's blackmail. And a lie. That place was a mess when we moved in." My cigarette's going out; I puff on it until it glows again. "Dad lied to Mike about paying the rent?"

"The manager called him, and he refuses to pay any more." If I had his number, I'd phone Dad and give him a piece of my mind.

"What did Mike say?"

"He tried to set him straight, but the asshole wouldn't budge. Mike got mad. The manager threatened to call the cops if he didn't back off."

My hand slaps across my mouth to suppress my scream, terrified at the thought of Mike getting arrested. I imagine the cops trying to restrain Mike's two hundred pounds of military muscle. Someone would get hurt, or worse, he'd be arrested. If Mike gets in trouble with the cops, it will screw up his deployment with the Army. That part is okay with me, but I don't want Mike to go to jail.

"I cleaned that apartment, and the party didn't cause any damage." I clamp my jaw to manage my rage. "So, what do we do?" I throw up my hands, sending cigarette ashes flying. "Where am I supposed to sleep? And I need my clothes. I work tomorrow."

Chuck puts his hand on my shoulder. "Calm down, Debby. Mike has a plan." He stubs out his cigarette under his shoe and lights another. "Mike needs his gear. He ships out in two days. If he doesn't have it when he reports, he'll be in big trouble." Chuck searches the street. "Here he comes now."

Mike walks up with a crowbar in his hand. "You guys ready? Let's do this." He wedges the pry bar between the door and the jamb and yanks. The plywood splinters around the lock.

"It's just a cheap-ass hollow door." His face flushes with rage. "What kind of security is that? Especially for a girl staying alone." He looks at me, shaking his head, and tosses the bar aside. Putting his shoulder to the door, it gives way. Mike walks into the living room like he's taking possession of land after a battle. He picks up his duffle bag, then turns back to Chuck and me. Standing in the doorway, I'm amazed Mike's plan is working.

"We better get a move on before someone comes. Debby, do you need help?"

"I'll help her." Chuck leads the way into my room, grabs my suitcase and opens it on my bed. I muscle an armful of clothes out of the closet and stuff it all in. In minutes, I'm packed and out of there, carrying my round suitcase in one hand, my red makeup bag over my shoulder, and my wig case in the other hand. I place them all in my trunk. Chuck lugs my big suitcase down the sidewalk and leverages it into my back seat—the only place it'll fit. Mike, after stuffing the pry bar into his duffle bag, joins us.

"I'm out of here."

I turn, startled by his declaration. "You're leaving today?"

"I'm shipping out day after tomorrow."

"Why are you going back? Can't you get out of it...for me?" Mike joined the Army out of high school because of the draft, but from his letters I know he hates the war. I don't want him to go back to Vietnam. He might die.

"Nothing here for me anymore. Anyway, I always wanted to be in the Special Forces. I'm going to try out for the *Seals*." I don't know what a Seal is, but knowing Mike, it'll be dangerous. Last enlistment, he was a machine gunner on a *chopper*.

He's not hearing me. He's looking at the sky, staring into the future.

"Bye, kid." He ruffles my hair. "See ya later, Chuck. Don't do anything I wouldn't do."

Mike strides off carrying the painting of a naked pregnant girl in his right hand and the military duffle bag in his left. *He's a painter. Not a soldier.* But maybe I'm wrong. Maybe he's *both* an artist and a warrior, two halves in conflict with one another, each fighting to dominate his life.

Chuck lays his hand on my shoulder. "Follow me. Michelle, Tony, and I rented a house. There's room for one more." I met Tony once at the bar. I search Chuck's face for answers, seeing in his eyes the same sadness that's crushing me, grieving the loss of our family, but our family never talked about emotions. I didn't dare now for fear of being teased as a crybaby. When I look back, Mike is striding down the street, out of my life. I'm left clinging to the hope that one day I will see my oldest brother again.

CHAPTER TWELVE

FALLING FOR THE CON 1969-1973

The house I share with Chuck and two of his friends in Mission Hills has mattresses on the floor in the bedrooms, bean bags in the living room, and beer and joints in the kitchen where everyone seems to gather with our friends from work. Even Uncle Tom drops by to party. Everything is great until, one night after work, I come home to chaos. Chuck is furious with me.

"You flushed a tampon, didn't you? Don't lie. I know it was you."

"But the package said it could be flushed," I explain.

"Not with a septic system." He closes the door to the foul-smelling bathroom where two inches of sewage ferments in the tub and walks away. When the owner shows up unannounced to fix it and sees how we're living, he kicks us out after only one month.

Chuck says, "We're losing our five-hundred-dollar deposit!" I beg Chuck to take me with him to his friends' house because I have no place to go. With a taut face and a shake of his head, he says. "It's for your own good. Here's Dad's number. Call and see if he'll take you in."

I leave in tears. *I'll show him. I don't need his help.*

After staying with Dad only one night, I find an apartment in

North Hollywood within walking distance from my job at Pac Bell, great for when my MGB is in the repair shop, which is often.

Grandma's in town to see some cousins and stopped by to see Chuck. After their visit, he takes Grandma to the airport and picks me up on the way. There's no room in the front, so I jump in the backseat. When he stops at a light, I lean forward to listen to Grandma, who's telling a story about Mom back in the day. Suddenly, a car rear-ends us. I scream—only half aware of how loud I am. It hurts to turn my head, so I twist my body to look back at the offending vehicle.

Recovering from the impact and whip lashing, Chuck asks, "Are you okay, Grandma?"

"I'm fine," she says. "I'm strapped tight in my seat."

"What about you, Debby?" Chuck strains to turn halfway around and check on me.

"My neck hurts," I respond.

"Let's drop off Grandma at the airport." He turns to her. "You sure you're okay?"

When she nods, he exits to exchange info with the driver who hit us, then returns to complete our delivery. I rub my neck as they discuss which airline she's taking.

Fifteen minutes later, Chuck pulls in at the curb drop-off. After waving goodbye, Chuck says, "I'm taking us to the ER."

I'm unprepared for the impact of my head whipping, tearing my neck muscles, and putting me in the hospital for a week. They send me home with powerful pain meds that render me useless for work or even self-care. Luckily, I've worked for Pac Bell long enough to earn generous sick leave, plus they let me take off for doctor visits to get traction therapy that seems to make me hurt more.

Chuck tells me about the relief he's getting dancing at the gay bar when he's not working, so I give it a try. As he predicted, a few beers loosen my muscle spasms and rocking out relieves my back pain better than any of the meds the doctors gave me and brings Chuck and me close again.

Leaving the doctor's office, I turn left from a side street onto Magnolia, when a woman smashes her sedan into my MGB. Baby's front end is crunched, and I re-injure my neck, putting me back on painkillers and muscle relaxants after I'd worked so hard to rid myself of them, and making me less effective at work. I've missed too much work already, and my boss is watching me.

Three months later, I fall for a guy I meet at a bar who drives a Porsche. He wines and dines me, then proposes and convinces me to quit my job to travel with him. He tells me to deposit his $2,000 out-of-state check into my account. The merchants willingly accept my local checks to pay for new clothes and a nice dinner.

The next day, the girls at work throw us a farewell luncheon. "I'm happy for you, Debby," Scruffy whispers in my ear amid the active chatter around the table in the Mexican restaurant. "He seems great. Very charismatic!"

I twinkle but whisper back, "I just wish I had a ring."

Before my hopes are realized, he disappears—right before his deposit bounces in my bank account, along with the $1,500 in checks I wrote for him. I call Chuck, blubbering over the phone. I'm so over-wrought, he can hardly understand me.

"I'm too humiliated to ask for my job back. Now I can't afford to keep my apartment."

Chuck says, "It'll be alright." He covers the bounced checks and fees to keep me out of jail. "Like father, like daughter," he teases. "You know Dad often bounced checks when he was between jobs."

"I know."

Unable or unwilling to take me in again, Chuck puts me on a plane to Mom in Peoria, two years after she left me in LA, making my escape the reverse of Dad's.

He says, "I'll take care of your car until you decide you want it back."

Mom, a month after her divorce from Dad, married Dick, an abusive, alcoholic, know-it-all worse than Dad ever was. I land a job as a carhop at Steak & Shake, but I can't stand the way Dick treats Mom when I come home. He won't let us talk without baiting me into arguing with him, threatening to kick me out if I don't fall in line.

Mom looks terrified when I complain about Dick's abuse. "I'm sorry, honey. You can't stay here if you are going to argue with him." In my childhood, I took a backseat to Dad's needs, too. *I guess I'm going back to LA.*

Chuck picks me up at the airport driving a Chevy instead of my MGB. "Where's Baby?"

"In the shop. Your car almost killed me."

"How?"

"I was tooling down the freeway when the hood popped open. The wind caught it and bent it over the windshield, smashing the metal, the glass, and my head. I barely pulled over with all the blood in my eyes."

After my last crash, I hadn't noticed the mechanic's error: he forgot to replace the safety hook for the hood latch. How could I be responsible? *I was a thousand miles away.* I take the blame because I need a place to stay.

The shop owner says insurance won't cover it, "If you can't pay, I'll take the car to cover your bill." That's how I lose the MGB, my first car.

Chuck lets me stay with him and some new gay friends, one of them a florist who loves putting my hair up into a pompadour, the other a chef. But soon I feel the subtle pressure to move. I'm cramping their gay lifestyle. Chuck suggests I stay with Dad.

For two days, I float in the pool at Dad's apartment complex, looking up at the clouds passing overhead, wondering what to do with my life. From the edge of the pool, Dad hands me the newspaper with an ad circled.

"You need to get a job." He wants me out. I'm in the way of his new girlfriend moving in. So I call for an interview.

The ad for a marketing position turns out to be selling encyclope-dias door-to-door. I'm good at it. After a few months of proving myself, they take me with a crew of four to Las Vegas, giving us a company paid apartment to share along with a car.

Before the supervisor leaves, she tells me, "Open a new office and hire people. You train them, then run the crews."

We're doing well until suddenly everyone's paycheck bounces. With a call to LA, I learn Melvin, my boss and the company's owner, is a con man. Some of the original crew stay in Vegas. I drive to see Chuck in LA with barely enough money for gas. "I don't know what to do. Can you help?"

He hands me a tissue to wipe my tears and follows me to Melvin's home to return the company-owned car. He'd already shuttered the office. I can't stop crying. Chuck goes to the front door to return the keys and get the money I'm due. While I wait in his car, I bawl and beat on the dashboard, furious I was such a fool. I'd become suspicious and attempted to quit, but Melvin reeled me back in with compliments and offers for a promising future.

After a few minutes, Chuck returns down the cobblestone path, with my boss's mansion looming behind him.

"I see why you fell for it. That guy is slippery." He slides into the driver's seat of his car. "While I waited, I overheard a couple trying to recover their life savings that they had invested with him. Like you, they don't have a chance in hell to recover any of it. He's got this scheme down pat. He's already working with a new patsy to re-establish the business in another city. Unbelievable!"

I sit, listening, my face soaked in tears. "I know the couple who lost everything. They are the ones who convinced me to believe Melvin."

Chuck gives me forty bucks and drops me off at Dad's house, where he lives with his new wife. I hadn't seen or heard from him for six months while I lived in Vegas.

I catch a ride to Vegas and locate a friend from my encyclopedia crew. We rent an apartment together and barely get by working a series of dead-end jobs until my doctor informs me of a Class Four Pap smear result—probably cancer. With no insurance and no money, I call Mom, now living in St. Louis with her heavy-drinking husband who had once tried to grope me when she was away. I never told her and cringe at the thought of being under the same roof as him. But I'm desperate for a place to figure it out.

"Come to St. Louis, Debby. I'll explain it to Dick. We'll make it work."

I'm twenty-two and ashamed that I need her help, but thankful she's willing to take me in. I start out on the sixteen-hundred-mile journey driving a baby blue Chevy convertible I bought for a few hundred dollars. It breaks down halfway there, but a kind stranger—a recently furloughed marine—stops to help me. He follows me to fill the radiator each time Baby overheats, feeds me, and camps with me overnight, getting me safely to Mom's curb, where my car quits. He stays only long enough for me to thank him and Mom to pay him what I owe, then disappears as if he'd been an imagined guardian angel.

The next day, I watch from the window as the scrap man tows Baby away, making me totally dependent on Mom. She gives me a room until I find out if I have cancer…if Dick doesn't kick me out first.

CHAPTER THIRTEEN

MARRIAGE AND DIVORCE 1973-1980

Every evening, Dick says, with a glass of whiskey in his hand, "When are you moving out?"

It has been a harried four weeks since I moved in with Mom and her asshole husband. I'm tired of battling with him, but I can't move out until I find a job and maybe a roommate. Plus, I've enjoyed having time with Mom. I only saw her twice in the four years before moving here. When I've been in trouble, she's always tried to help me, at least until Dick blocks her efforts. Despite his protests, she took time off work to drive me to my surgery.

Mom hands me an envelope, my first mail at this address, and I tear it open. "It's the settlement money from my whiplash injury in LA. Can you take me to look at a car?"

She waits while I take it for a spin. It's old, but I love it—a smaller version of the red sports car I had when I was 18. *Now to find a job.*

The interns at the teaching hospital call me in for the results of my surgery. I don't have cancer. But they also tell me I will never conceive a child, because my uterus never fully developed, and the surgery decimated my cervix. *Who knew the cervix was so essential to getting pregnant.*

I am relieved I'm not dying but heart-sick for the children I will never have. Mom wipes a tear from my cheek and pulls me into her embrace.

After a few moments, I step back. "Thanks, Mom, but I need to pull it together. I have a second interview for a secretarial position at that metal reprocessing company."

Later, I burst into the apartment. "I got the job!"

While celebrating over a glass of wine, Mom tells me about her neighbor, Mark, a thirty-year-old Texan. "He's a nice young man and he asked about you."

"Mom, thirty isn't young."

I bite my tongue when we hear a scraping sound from a chair being moved on the patio upstairs. *Did he hear me?*

Mom calls out, "Hey, Mark. Come and join us for a glass of wine."

He works in human resources at a big aerospace company and looks like a ruffled professor—tall and thin, with a mostly bald head. He stays for two glasses of wine and dinner.

After Mark leaves, I tell Mom, "He doesn't sound like he was born and raised in Texas. To be honest, I'm not impressed. He's too stodgy for me."

Mom says, "Give him a chance."

When I show interest in Mark's photography, he teaches me to use his Canon camera, how to frame a subject or scene. At interesting spots around the city, he shows me how to compose light and dark shapes through the lens. "This is cool," I tell him. "It's creative and technical."

A month later, while having a glass of merlot with Mom on the patio, she asks, "Did you see the picture of Mark in front of his family's oil well in Texas? He'd make a good husband." Mark had only moved twice in his entire life. Stability is something I need. He isn't all I had hoped for, but he's all I deserve.

In April, Chuck flies to St. Louis to give me away at a small service held at our community's rec center. To decorate the sunken seating area where we exchange modest rings, I strung into garlands the carnations I made using tissues. Mark's friend from work, who officiates, pronounces us man and wife. When we kiss, I inwardly cringe. *Have I made the right decision?*

Mom made sandwiches and Dick mixed some high-octane Long Island Iced Tea for my family and mostly Mark's friends to enjoy. His family couldn't come.

When we return from our New Orleans honeymoon, Mark and I move closer to work, but further from Mom. When I drive across town to see her, she confesses Dick forced her to push me into Mark's arms. *Too late now. At least I have security.*

Later that year, Mom's sister Dee calls me from Michigan and says, "Carleen and Mom were in a head-on collision two days ago."

"I didn't know Mom was visiting Grandma."

"The police had trouble finding anyone to call because she was driving my car with Florida plates while I was in Wisconsin trying to sell a boat. I thought Dick told you."

Mom and Grandma! "How bad is it?"

"Mom died on the highway and Carleen is in critical condition. The drunk who plowed into them is fine."

"I'm on my way." I leave for Ann Arbor immediately, but I don't arrive in time to attend Grandma's funeral, and I missed Mom's three surgeries. I blame Dick. He didn't call me when Aunt Dee contacted him two days earlier.

When I see Mom in her hospital bed, she says, "I'm fine. Go home. There's nothing for you to do here. Dee knows the doctors and is managing my care."

Mom has a hole in her skull, a shattered wrist, and three broken ribs, but she won't let me stay. All the beds and floor space are claimed by others. I'm the odd man out, expelled from the family. Without any sleep, I drive back to St. Louis.

A few weeks later, Mark tells me his dad, in Mission, Texas, is terminally ill. Wanting to move closer, he finds a high paying corporate job in Houston. Since Mom's accident, I'd fallen into a deep depression, so it is a relief to move, especially since Dick will hardly let me see her and she's not strong enough to fight him. The accident traumatized her body and mind. She has a long recovery ahead of her. Saying goodbye is hard.

Mark and I move into an apartment in Houston, where I rotate through various secretarial jobs. I'd like to go to school, but he insists I work even though my paycheck contributes relatively little to our household.

After Mark's father dies, we spend a week in the town where Mark grew up, near the border with Mexico, helping his mom Juanita. Back in Houston, Mark pushes me to take depression meds which I hate because they dumb me down. I continue to burn out and change jobs until I land a position in Publicity at the Museum of Fine Arts, where I spend hours in their galleries staring at Matisse, Monet, Gauguin and van Gogh, dreaming of becoming an artist. That's when Mark's mother dies, and he inherits a large fortune. We buy a house, only because Mark hates our apartment and believes real estate is a good investment.

When we move into our custom-built home, Mark lets me spend money on furniture, trees, and roses but only to a point, until one day, I summon the courage to ask Mark for my deepest desire.

"I want to go to college in the fall to pursue an art degree."

"No," he says, flatly. "I'm not paying for a useless art degree. You'll make less than you do now as a secretary." He walks into another room, but I follow him, begging.

"Please? I'll do anything."

He stares at me for a long while. "Try architecture. Work for a firm as their secretary. See if you can handle the workload." Mark crosses his arms.

I accept a position with an architect and his staff of four in a small office. After the first week, I decide—I love it. A year later, my new boss helps me convince Mark to let me study architecture in the fall. *It's not art, which is what I really want. But at least I'll be working toward a degree…and learning design.*

In the fall, I drive to the far side of the city to attend the University of Houston where I meet new people and make a few friends.

One night, I come home when Mark, sitting crossed-armed on the sofa, says, "You need to quit school. You're gone to class too much and stay up too late working on projects."

"So instead of becoming an architect, you want me to cook, clean, serve you dinner, and keep you company watching TV?"

Mark shrugs.

I'm ready to leave him, but he delays my decision when he buys me a brand-new red Mazda RX7, my new *Baby*.

In the spring of 1980, Chuck and his partner Don, along with Mike and his wife, Judy, all come to visit Mark and me in Houston. Everyone's eating on the patio, and floating in the pool, when Don, who is a clinical therapist, pulls me aside. "You do know that Mark's control over you rises to the level of abuse, right?" I adore Don, but don't know how to respond.

A month later, after another argument with Mark about how I spend my time, I muster the courage to tell him, "I want a divorce." When I call Mom, who's moved to LA with Dick, she says, "How can you walk away from the security of his fortune?" I call Chuck, and he says, "His money will never make you happy. You deserve better than him."

We both hire lawyers, his, a pit bull. Mark threatens to leave me penniless, then his attorney attacks me viciously in a deposition, calling me *crazy* because I take anxiety meds. I break into sobs. I need to get away—far away.

Mark had convinced me to study architecture, erasing my dream of becoming an artist. I'd completed two years of the five-year program. Starting over in art would cost more than I might receive in our divorce settlement. I acquiesce to my reality and apply to a small architecture school in Santa Monica. When I'm accepted, I tell Mark I'm leaving, even though the divorce is not yet final.

To start my new life, I pack only what I need and prepare for the long drive to LA. As a sign of my independence, I leave behind my childhood nickname, *Debby*. I am *Deborah*, a woman steering my own course.

Chuck lets me stay for a few months with him and his partner, Don, a clinical therapist. Everything is peachy until one day after class. I'm about to change clothes when Chuck comes through the sliding glass doors into a corner of the garage converted into a bedroom and confronts me. "You need to find your own place."

"It's hard to find something I can afford. I don't know when my divorce settlement will show up, and I'm not sure how it much will be."

"Look, sis. It's nice having you around, but you've stayed long enough."

"Why now? It's been fun living here."

"Fun for you." He shakes his head while looking down. "But you're cramping my style with Don."

He looks at me like I know what he's talking about. I kind of do, but not really. All I know is I feel rejected when I'm most vulnerable—and betrayed by the only person I trust.

Don helps me find a place to live—an apartment in a Craftsman building two blocks off Venice Beach, a few miles from school. With its trundle bed, I only need to buy a futon. My drafting board fits in the bedroom, too.

As I'm walking out the door with my last box, Chuck says, "We'll see you at the cabin. Maybe in a week or two." He'd recently bought a cabin in the mountains near Frasier Park, two hours north of Van Nuys.

"Yeah. Sure." I give my brother a quick hug. "Thanks for letting me stay."

Don gives me a bear hug, because he understands my devastation with Chuck keeping me at arm's length. "I'll come down to Venice soon and we'll have lunch, okay?"

I nod, fighting back a tear.

Older by a decade than most students studying architecture, I struggle to make friends. My saving grace is Melanie, a woman with twin daughters, who, like me, works to make a life for herself after a divorce.

Melanie and I are under an awning on Venice Beach Saturday morning, drinking mimosas with our cheese omelets. We talk about everything from exes to clothes to classwork.

The waiter brings us fresh water and smiles.

"He'd make a nice boy-toy," Melanie says, watching him walk away. "Interested?" We both laugh at our outrageousness. Melanie helps me cut the binds that have restricted my creativity and robbed me of joy.

That evening, I lose myself in the beauty of a fiery sky over the crashing waves, my skin tingling from the salt in the air. I vow to walk on the beach every day to find my bearings and my self-esteem.

I stay in touch with Chuck through Don over lunches until Chuck invites me to his cabin two months after he made me move out. He drives with Don and their dog in their van, and I follow. We head north for nearly two hours into the mountains, then pull in below a darling cabin nestled into the steep incline, with two levels of stairs to the wrap around deck. For dinner, we enjoy a bowl of Don's chili in the kitchenette. After cleaning up, Chuck takes me for a walk in the tall leggy pines along the paths he's created on his land. After dusk, we drink hot buttered rums in front of the fireplace, telling stories. Hearing Chuck laugh makes me feel like I belong again. I let go of the hurt and soak in the joy he radiates when he's in his element, whether dancing in a bar or walking in the woods.

A few weeks later, Don introduces me to a therapist who helps me get off the antidepressant my ex-husband insisted I take. It clouded my mind. During the six weeks that I can afford to work with her, she teaches me coping skills, which give me a newfound confidence.

Now that I've burned through my divorce settlement, I'm working in the school library re-shelving books until I find a full-time job related to architecture, something that uses the sales skills I learned from watching Dad and from when I sold encyclopedias, a job close to school so I don't have to quit going to class.

CHAPTER FOURTEEN

MEETING GREG 1983

On Friday halfway through the semester, I storm back into class after retrieving my architectural drawings from Baby.

"What's wrong?" Melanie asks.

"You know how much I love my car, right?" She nods. "A vandal bent her retractable antenna. When I turn the key to off, she makes a whining, crying sound as it repeatedly tries to retract. I don't know what to do."

A guy friend in class says, "There's a car stereo shop over on Pico and National who can fix it."

The next day, I drop Baby off at the shop and find a restaurant down the block to study and eat while I wait. I call from the bar phone to check on her every few hours, but they say, "We need more time." *What are they doing to her?* After two hours more, I pick up my books and stomp down to the shop to investigate, sneaking around to the backdoor to find my sports car ransacked. They yanked out the stereo and rear speakers, cutting wires—leaving a tangled mess inside my car and no way to play music.

"What have you done?" I screech.

They exchange a flurry of Spanish. One guy who speaks English tries to assure me. "Everything will be okay. We just need another hour."

"I'll give you one hour to put her back together and it had all better work!" Then he hustles me out the door.

Still fuming, I stomp back to the restaurant and find it packed with the happy hour crowd overflowing from the bar, occupying all the tables. I scan for an empty seat and find the only one at the bar. With my butt on the stool, I plop my book bag on the floor and order a scotch on the rocks with a water-back. A guy sitting on the next stool is also drinking scotch. He stops chatting with his friends and swivels toward me with sparkling blue eyes and a big smile.

"I like scotch too. My name's Greg. What's got you upset?" When I tell him about my car, he says, "I used to work at a stereo shop. Maybe I can help."

Hmmm. I wonder if he can. Who is this guy? He seems too good to be true. "What's your sign?" I ask. For those of us who read Linda Goodman's *Sun Signs* to understand ourselves and the world around us, it's a standard question.

"I'm a Sagittarius…born in the year of *the Horse*." His brow arches —not unlike Chuck's. "In other words, I'm three-fourths horse." His smile widens and his eyes glisten in delight. Or maybe it's the scotch. I'm not sure because I'm on my second drink, but I am intrigued.

I turn up the corners of my mouth. "I'm an Aquarian…with a Gemini moon and a Sag rising." I'm air sign, well matched to the fire of Sagittarius. Our conversation continues.

With the bar chatter getting louder, I lean closer as Greg talks about *mojo*. My eyes light up. He believes in magic. Then he says, "There's a club not far from here. Do you like to dance?"

"I need to check on my car." *Can he help me?* He's cute. And if he can dance, why not spend more time with him.

He drives me down the street to find Baby in worse shape than on my last check, with more speaker cable cut and strewn throughout the interior and the entire sound system yanked out of my dash. I want to cry…and hit someone.

"It's okay." Greg puts his arm around my shoulders. "We'll take it to a dealer and bring the bill back for these guys to pay. They can't afford not to."

That sounds like a good plan. I climb into my red sports car, cringing at the mess, and wait for him to follow. We'll drop Baby at my apartment, then go dancing. On the way, he pulls in for gas, then shows up at my car window holding a single long stem rose. "I thought this might cheer you up."

I accept the rose. *Is this guy for real?* Scotch plus magic plus dancing plus a rose equals perfection. He may be the one, but I'm not ready for this. *One day at a time.* I park Baby at home, then slide into his passenger seat. He pops in a cassette—*What a Fool Believes* by Michael McDonald, the one I wanted to hear but couldn't with Baby's destroyed stereo system. *Synchronicity strikes again!*

When I wake up in Redondo Beach, Greg's making breakfast. Maybe he's my perfect match. He's thoughtful and attentive—really wonderful—but I don't want to rush into the wrong relationship. I don't have my car, so I go for a walk by myself to think. With my divorce just final, am I ready for another serious relationship?

In the window of an open shop, a taupe-colored cat stares up at me. Our spirits connect. I go inside and come out with the cat over my shoulder, naming him Beau after the French poet Baudelaire. Whether or not it works out with Greg, this cat belongs with me. I bring him back to meet Greg at the apartment, and he loves him. It feels like another sign.

The next day, we take my car to a dealer who fixes Baby. Greg goes with me to drop off the bill stamped *paid* at the repair shop that destroyed my stereo. The owner pulls the cash from the register and pays me back...then apologizes.

Greg and I see each other every day. We meet each other's friends; he even takes me to San Francisco for the weekend to meet his close friend from high school back in Indiana. Lyda is divorced with a daughter. She and I talk about women's issues and creativity while Greg spends time with her daughter. We talk until 3 am and find her daughter in Lyda's room and Greg on the sofa, both fast asleep, which endears me to him even more. Lyda and I return to our discussion and laugh until our sides hurt. We hug like long-lost sisters.

On our way home, we stop in the valley to see Chuck and Don. Greg likes them both and enjoys hanging out with them. And they adore him. Chuck gives us a key for his cabin in Frasier Park, which is two hours closer to Lyda in San Francisco, so we invite her and Melanie in LA to join us the following weekend. June is pleasant in the mountains, and we have a blast—drinking, cooking, and walking with lots of talking.

Two weeks later, Chuck and Don invite us to go camping in Yosemite. "Tawna loves camping." Chuck reaches down and strokes the head of their beloved lab-mix they found wandering in the desert. She was dehydrated and half starved, but they've nursed her back to health. "Everyone comes. Mike and Judy set up a tent with their kids in an adjacent campsite. Don's sisters bring their families and help with meals. Don's mom, Edith comes too." He doesn't sound too happy about Edith, but I don't say anything in front of Don.

Greg says, "It sounds great! Count me in."

We pack my car with Greg's pup tent and sleeping bags. Before leaving the valley, we buy groceries for the communal meals from a list Don gave me.

After driving four hours north, the scenery changes from desert to mountains and forests. It's like being at Chuck's cabin, but with rivers, waterfalls, Half Dome, and tons of tourists. We find the campsite, set up our tent, and join Don's family at the picnic table to play cards before dinner. Don's brother-in-law wins with such good humor, I don't mind losing. We clear the table and devour Don's chili, then sit by a campfire until the black sky lights up with stars.

The next day, Greg and I strike out on our own for a hike. We smoke a joint while staring at Half Dome, where I see the face of an Indian chief in the flat face of the rocks. In my head, I hear his words saying Greg and I are destined to be together—a truly magical moment.

Eight weeks after we met, Greg and I are sitting on my sofa when he tells me his company has eliminated his position in LA. "I'm moving home to Fort Wayne." His face droops like a hound dog's.

"Indiana?" *Shit.* "When?" And here I thought I'd found the right guy.

"Next week." He kisses me. "I want to stay…but I need my job."

He doesn't invite me to go with him. "Why aren't you asking me…?"

"You told me to never ask you to choose between me and your architecture. You said I'd lose."

The last time, I walked away from my marriage. This is different. I face him, steeling my courage, and say, "Ask me anyway."

He draws back. "Will you"—he hesitates—"go with me?"

I'm not about to let go of him. He's everything my first husband wasn't. Greg supports my vision for the future, and I don't see it happening without him. "Yes, I will." I sigh. "But I need to finish this semester at school."

"I'll come back for you in six weeks." We embrace to make it official.

After Greg leaves for Indiana, I won't have enough money to pay next month's rent. I'm working for an architect making cold calls to find him new business, but the pay is not enough to keep my apartment. Melanie offers me one of her twin daughter's rooms while they're staying with their dad for the summer.

"Thanks, Melanie. I don't know what I would have done without you." I move in and store my furnishings in her garage.

Starting my job eases my money issue—my apartment rent and school tuition has burned through my divorce money. I need to get credit for the semester I've left incomplete. My teacher gives me until the end of summer to finish and hand in the drawings for my final project: a four-tower open amphitheater design I had envisioned in downtown Santa Monica. With my new job and Greg being gone, I'm too scattered to get back to my drawings. I love my design, but I've lost my confidence since a male teacher criticized it.

Am I leaving with Greg to avoid failing? What if I'm falling into my parents' pattern—moving to avoid a problem? I'll be with Greg, so it feels different. But am I sure?

I catch Melanie cleaning up in the kitchen. "Am I giving up too much to be with Greg? Now I don't have time to complete my drawings. What if I hate Indiana?"

Melanie says, "He's a great guy. Is he worth the risk? Only you can answer that question." She gives me a quick hug and hands me a bowl of ice cream. "Let's watch a movie."

Greg calls me every day while he's in Indiana which helps me push my fear back into its invisible box at the base of my gut. By the time he returns, my panic has escalated. I'm moving a thousand miles away from my school, my family, the mountains, and the beach without a commitment from Greg. And I never complete my drawings. Why bother? I can't finish my last two years. After researching for architecture schools, there are none close to where I will be living in Fort Wayne.

When I pick Greg up at the airport, we kiss and hug as if he'd been gone a year instead of two months. We climb into my Mazda RX-7 with me driving to see Chuck in the valley. Once I enter the freeway, Greg says, "What's wrong?" He knows me well enough now to read me.

"What if I move to Indiana and you break up with me?" He may propose eventually without me pressing the subject, but I need to know now if he is serious.

I take the Van Nuys exit and linger at the stop sign, searching his sky-blue eyes.

"Okay, let's get married." He rifles through the glove box and finds a cigarillo Melanie left behind. Greg slides off the label and slips it on my finger as a makeshift ring. I giggle. He leans over and kisses me and the car behind us honks.

We support each other's goals, mine in art and architecture, and his in sales engineering for hydraulic seals. I'm fascinated when he talks about his work. It reminds me of Dad's engineering brilliance—but without all the drama.

After two weeks of living with Greg in Fort Wayne, he shows me an ad for a German shepherd puppy. With a twinkle in his eye, he says, "I had one when I was young. She'll keep you company when I'm on the road."

"No chance of getting a Scotty?" I had told Greg about Tina, my last dog.

The twinkle in his eyes dims. His head droops. "I've always had shepherds." He lifts his head to grab my eyes. "They're smart. And very protective."

I'm grateful for his need to keep me safe. The next time trouble comes calling, I will have someone other than Chuck to lean on.

"How about if we just go look at her?"

I nod, knowing I'll fall in love with any puppy I hold.

That night, we bring home a black and silver German shepherd puppy. "She's a silver sable," Greg explains. He's happy, and that makes me happy.

I haven't had a dog since I lost Tina because we moved to Australia. During my first marriage, I brought a stray Irish Setter home, but Mark wasn't a dog person and wouldn't let me keep him. I missed his happy face after I found him a better home. When this eight-week-old shepherd comes into our lives, my anxiety vanishes. Greg and I name her Tania.

We take turns doing steps from our second-floor apartment to take her outside to play and potty in the newly fallen six inches of snow. Longing for a house with a yard, I search for work.

Six months later, Greg and I plan our wedding for after an aerospace engineers' conference he's attending in Long Beach, CA. It's close to our friends and my family. The conference starts in three weeks, not much time to plan a wedding, but we'll keep it simple. When I tell Chuck, he suggests we have our ceremony in the national forest near his cabin and reserve a park lodge for the reception. The location is a perfect fit for our nature-based ceremony we plan, inspired by a do-it-yourself wedding book.

Before leaving for LA, Greg helps me design our custom rings—our biggest wedding expense. We also pay to fly his brother from Denver and his parents from Fort Wayne to LA.

While Greg flies out to attend the conference, I wait for our rings to be cast and set with tiny diamonds. Together, they form a heart—a symbol of our union.

After I drop Tania off at a kennel, I stand in line at the airport holding up my wedding dress draped on two hangers. While strangers offer good wishes, I wonder where I'll hang my dress on the plane. When I board, the captain offers to hang my dress in the front cabin.

When I arrive, I stay at Greg's hotel for two nights and arrange for a cake, food, and flowers before we drive to Chuck's cabin. All our wedding preparations have magically come together, just like the night I met Greg. *Our destiny unfolds.*

CHAPTER FIFTEEN

SYNCHRONICITY AND CREATIVITY 1983-1984

Chuck knocks and enters the bedroom carrying two cups of coffee. "You better get up. It snowed in the mountains last night."

I jump up and shake myself awake after too little sleep. The pounding rain kept me awake most of the night. I should have known there'd be snow. *Getting married outside was my idea. Now what?*

Yesterday, after Greg finished his meeting, we drove up to a pine-covered mountain in Los Padres National Forest, two hours north of LA, to pick the perfect spot for our ceremony—a clearing on a cliff overlooking the valley. In the homemade invitations, we asked our guests to meet us at the fork in the road where we'll have balloons tied to our cars. After everyone arrives, we'll lead them up the mountain where a local minister will marry us with the words we wrote, inspired by an outdoor wedding book. Once satisfied with our plans, we drove a few miles to Chuck's cabin, nestled in towering pines, to spend the night before our big day with him and Don.

But today, eight inches of fresh snow blankets the top of the mountain, including the location we selected to be wed. Now there's a roadblock.

Pulling on my jeans, my ribs tighten to hold back my panic. "People will arrive in a few hours, and we have no place to get married."

Chuck says, "First, eat breakfast. Then go pick a spot at a lower elevation—one with no snow. Don made bacon and eggs and corn bread. Food is on the table!"

On a cliff with a vast view of the valley below, we're encircled by friends and family. A loud "kee-aah" echoes from the sky. Don points up, "Red-tailed hawks! They're circling overhead."

Greg squeezes my hand. "That's a good omen."

We hold each other's eyes as we recite our vows, exchange rings with a kiss, then step out of the circle to plant our baby pine tree that represents our connection to the earth. Greg's best men, his brother Bob and his ex-roommate Dave, dig a hole. My bridesmaids, Melanie and Lyda, lift my skirt so I can crouch down with Greg. Together, we lower the tree in and cover it with soil. Chuck pours a bucket of water over the loose dirt to seat the pine tree into its new home as the hawks screech their approval from above. Returning to the circle, we exchange hugs with family and friends, then follow Chuck and Don's dog, Tawna, with a balloon tied to her collar, back down the path to our cars. On our way to the reception a few miles away, we pass families headed up to play in the snow.

At the lodge, our minister arrives on his Harley. I ask him, "Can I sit on it? I rode a Honda for a while in West LA." He agrees, and Greg joins me for a photo.

Inside the lodge, family and friends help lay out the ten-foot po' boy sandwich cut diagonally in serving-size pieces, along with chips, pitchers of lemonade, and a coffee pot. My maids of honor are assembling our three-tiered wedding cake when Chuck rushes up to me.

"Don forgot to pick up the keg of beer." He was busy preparing for the wedding party breakfast this morning.

"We'll have some folks run to the store down the road."

He shakes his head. "Frazier Park is dry on Sundays. Someone will have to drive to Lebec on Interstate 5 to buy any beer."

Dad, who loves playing the hero, rushes off and returns with a case of beer. Don's nephew offers to drive down the mountain to pick up the keg, an hour away. By the time he returns, the people needing to work the next day begin leaving. The reception wasn't perfect, but the ceremony was. I'm just happy Dad and Mom, who haven't spoken since they split fifteen years ago, showed up with their spouses and everyone is getting along. Dad's wife had a nice chat with Mom, and Dick actually chatted with Dad.

After one night in the hotel for our honeymoon, Greg and I fly home in time for Greg to go on the road for two weeks with his boss to start his dream job, a promotion to outside sales. I take care of Tania, running up and down stairs to take her out, grateful for her company. I'm a stranger, far from friends, hunting for a job to help pay for our wedding and save for a house with a backyard for Tania.

A month later, with an earful from neighbors complaining about Tania barking, I tell

Greg, "We need a house—now. Any ideas?"

"I'll talk to my parents. Maybe they can help with the down payment."

After touring a few houses with a realtor, it is clear we'll need to choose one in town on a tiny lot with no room for a horse. With the closest architectural program two hours away, completing my degree is out of reach, too. After living in LA, I'm burned out on commuting.

On my job hunt, I'm directed to a Women Business Owners' networking breakfast, where I make a new friend, Dian. She's a massage therapist and asks me to create a logo for her letterhead and business cards, which starts my graphic design business, working from home. But I soon give it up when I find a job with a regular paycheck.

Tania grows strong and fast. Greg says proudly, "She will be a hundred pounds soon."

House hunting, like walking Tania at night, becomes miserable in the snow, ice, and bitter cold of the Midwest winter. A violent storm leaves a thick coat of ice on everything the night before we visit a craftsman house up for sale.

Greg pulls up and gives me a hand to help me out. "Be careful."

Excited to see inside, I walk halfway up the concrete stairs, hit black ice, and fly into the air, hitting my tailbone on the bottom step.

My coccyx has ached since the fall, but I refuse to let it stop me. My friend Dian, with her magical fingers, lessens my pain. With some ibuprofen and a few night's rest, we resume our hunt, checking out a house every evening and two on weekends.

Two days before Christmas, we discover a Victorian home on a narrow one-way street, a seventy-year-old house in a neighborhood just south of downtown Fort Wayne. The homes in the neighborhood fall short of Painted Lady status, but this one is charming, with a rust-colored exterior trimmed in gold and cream gingerbread around windows and doors. A covered porch with leaded-glass windows lights a pinewood-paneled entry and narrow slat pine floors. Ten-foot ceilings on the entire first floor help the smaller rooms feel spacious. She's a beauty, loaded with character. The master bedroom is large, but the third bedroom is closet-sized. The previous owner renovated the kitchen with new built-in appliances and a large central island.

Greg says, "I can make us omelets for breakfast." He wants this house.

"I like the bigger Victorian around the corner."

Greg says, "But it needs work to be livable, especially the kitchen."

He's right, I know he is, so I give in.

I accept a position selling advertising for a business magazine to help us qualify for the loan. The bank agrees to lend us money over the sale price to paint the exterior, repair windows, and replace the old gravity-fed octopus furnace with a new forced-air system. They even include adding two skylights for the walk-up attic. "Greg, this will be a beautiful art studio. Look!" I stand with my arms out the open skylight and touch a leaf. "It's like living in trees. I can almost see the studio at school." I'm taking an evening painting class at the university's downtown campus a mile away.

We may not have a horse in the backyard, but the old oak trees line the street and drape branches above our roof in front and back, creating a natural country feeling.

Once we move in, playing with Tania gives me a break from the stress of my new job. I like working from home, but when my sales aren't high enough to cover my weekly draw, the owner, Victor, yells at me over the phone. During the monthly sales meeting at the Indianapolis office, he approaches. Towering over me, he barks his threat, "I should fire you. You've got one last chance."

I hold back my tears until the meeting ends then rush to the ladies' room to let it all out. After splashing my face with water, I escape to my car avoiding the other sales reps.

On the two-hour drive home, I flash back to another abusive boss who tricked me and my coworkers into selling encyclopedias door-to-door, then thrashed me with insults when I failed to make his weekly quota. I blubber in front of my boss, saying I'll do anything to keep my job. Each time I am dressed down by an authority figure, I feel eight again with Dad and my brothers making fun of me because I am afraid to dive into the lake, then threaten to leave me behind when they take the boat out.

At home, I stand at the window watching Tania bark at squirrels in our fenced backyard, replaying all my failings, while Greg cooks his famous Mexican lasagna for dinner. *It's happening again. I want to quit... but we have a mortgage now.*

"What's wrong?" Greg asks.

I spit it out. "I hate working for Victor."

He shakes his head. "If you're that miserable, quit and find another job."

"Really? Can I?"

Greg shrugs.

I try working for a pleasant couple selling business office furniture, but I can't learn about their product choices fast enough. *I need to give up sales.* My next job is at an electric sign company as secretary to the president. After weeks of covering for my boss because he won't take calls, I tell him I won't lie to customers anymore. He's tall and assertive, practiced at throwing his weight around. He thinks I will cower to his demands, but I refuse to put up with any more abuse. I need another job—my third this year. *What's wrong with me?*

I'm terrified of being out of work and determined to find some way to help pay for our mortgage. On the way home after quitting the sign manufacturer, I pick up a newspaper and zero in on a job at the Fine Arts Foundation. I don't know what it is, but it's connected to the arts, and that intrigues me.

I stop at a phone booth to look up the address in the phonebook and find it on my map from the glove box. It's nearby. I drop in a few coins and dial the number. The director answers. "Can you stop by now?"

I fall again on the ice in the parking lot before entering the quaint limestone building, reinjuring my coccyx, but I still go inside and hand a slender young man my resume. He's the director, a gracious man who raises money for local arts groups. After I articulate my sales and secretarial experience, he asks, "When can you start?"

I'm hired on the spot. I rush home to tell Greg. "As his Administrative Assistant, I'll type, file, and keep anything on his agenda from slipping through the cracks." There's only one part of my assigned tasks I dislike—catching up on years of back filing.

After six months of success with all my duties, I begin to cull and organize decades of old documents neglected for years—two file cabinets worth. But soon, I catch myself dozing over piles of paper bulging from boxes. When my boss checks on my progress, I confess, "I can't do it. It's too much." He looks disappointed and I'm afraid I'll lose my job.

"Don't worry about it. You're still the best Administrative Assistant I've ever had."

My face flushes. Maybe, at last, I've found a job I can keep.

On a late summer evening, we're dining out with Danny, Greg's coworker, and his wife Melissa, who I've just met. While we wait for our food, our husbands discuss seals and O-rings; she and I share our passion for quilts and creativity like we're old friends. While we savor our meals, she asks me, "How do you like working for the Foundation?"

"I love it, especially sitting in on Board meetings, and working with the different arts groups."

"But are you making any of your own art?" She'd seen two prints hanging in our living room I created at the Museum School in Houston.

Surprised by her forthrightness, I pause before answering. "I am in a painting class after work, which is great. I signed up for a three-session clay class at the Y and used Greg as my model for a bust sculpture. Working the clay between my fingers feels visceral and familiar, like I've been doing it all my life."

Greg lights up when he hears his name and adds, "You should have seen my mom when we showed her the sculpture. We put my glasses on it, and she screamed, 'It looks just like you. I don't want to look at it! Busts are only made for dead people.' We all laughed, but she still made me move it out of her sight. I bring it out every time she visits just to bug her."

Melissa turns to me and asks, "Why aren't you taking clay classes at the college?" She stares through me like I'm transparent. *She's nailed my deepest desire.*

"Greg's been asking me the same question." I glance at him, and he's watching, waiting to hear what I tell Melissa.

"The evening class fills up with students from the previous semester before I can enroll, leaving only the day class when I'm working. I asked the teacher Nancy for help, but she can't do anything for me. I just can't win for losing." I hear my dad's voice echo in my words.

"What does that mean?" Melissa asks.

"I've tried before and failed. Years ago, I took an aptitude test at a community college that said I'd be either an architect or an art teacher." I can't help but grin. "I'd like to teach college art and maybe get my work into a gallery one day." Greg returns to talking with Danny about work. We've already had this discussion.

The server removes my nearly empty plate of lasagna, giving me time to sort a flurry of reasons mixed with my fears. "But taking one class a semester will take me forever to get a degree."

"Is that what you want?" Melissa persists.

"I've dreamed of being an artist since I was twelve when Mom took my brothers and me to an art class...but I never thought I could be good enough." *My fear is holding me back.* I look at Greg, who's still absorbed in his conversation with Danny. *He believes in me.* I turn back to Melissa, lowering my voice. "I would need to take classes full time. With just buying a house, we can't afford me to quit working altogether. It's impossible to save up when I barely make minimum wage."

Melissa says, "That's what you really want? To be a studio artist?"

I nod.

"So do it."

"How can I?"

"Just do it!"

"What do you mean?" She must be crazy. It's impossible.

"Sometimes you need to take a leap and trust it will work out. Like when you followed Greg here after knowing him for only two months."

"I did do that, didn't I."

"You're extremely creative, Deborah, with amazing enthusiasm. Just go for it."

"And trust that somehow it will work out? I need more magic to pull off this trick."

"That's it." Melissa reaches out with her wine to clink glasses. I reciprocate even as my doubts flood back in.

"I need to think about this. And talk to Greg."

"Don't wait too long. And remember what I said."

I stare at her with wide eyes, shocked I'm considering taking such a big chance. "I hear you. Just do it."

The following week, my boss at the Foundation overhears me telling a coworker about my conversation with Melissa and my dream to be an artist. He calls me to his office. "Would you be interested in a part-time job at Artlink? They need a director. You would need to interview with their Artists Council. But you know many of them. Some are your teachers at IPFW. The rest teach at St. Francis."

It's synchronicity, like when I met Greg. "Yes. I'm interested. But would I have to quit this job?"

"I think we could muddle along without you."

When he smiles, my misgivings vanish, and my mind starts working out all the issues we would need to consider. Maybe I can take daytime classes and get more involved with the local art community in the evening, not as a student artist, but as a gallery director. *I want this job.*

To get the inside dope, I meet with Nancy, who teaches my evening composition class in addition to the clay classes I can't get into.

"Artlink has been without a paid director for years. We're desperate for someone to whip the gallery back into shape or we'll lose our funding. They've given us fair warning."

When the day of my interview arrives, I'm feeling relaxed and confident. To me, an interview is like a test which I enjoy taking—one of my quirks. In the meeting, I present to the committee my experience with the Foundation and my art education, closing with my sales experience, and they hire me on the spot.

Nancy says, "So does this mean you'll be signing up for my day clay class next semester?" All I can do is grin from ear to ear.

The pay is less than what I've been making, paid for twenty hours to do work that takes forty to complete, but the hours are flexible enough to let me take Nancy's daytime class. I'm giddy.

Melissa was right. I needed to throw myself off the cliff and pray that my wings will appear. I can feel my feathers growing already. Greg is worried about the money, but he tells me to go for it. He loves me and believes in me, like no one has ever before. I worry too about the cost of more art supplies. But this is my chance.

Together, Greg and I build my art studio in the walk-up attic, giving me a place to pursue my dream of being an artist. I climb the stairs to stand with my head through the opened skylight and reach out to touch the maple tree leaves that tickle the roof in the breeze. Greg and his friends from back in high school hang the drywall. When the mud on the seams dries, I paint the walls white. The light is glorious.

Greg's brother Bob visits from Denver to help build the rolling storage bins I designed to fit snugly along the bottom edge of the slanted ceiling, creating the appearance of a short wall while giving me the storage space I need. Greg says, "Bob crawled into a bin and told me to push him around. He loves your design." *That's Greg's brother Bob!*

All that's left is to paint the bins to match the walls and fill them with art supplies. *And Shazam!* I have an art studio. *Now to find the confidence to create my own art.*

PART 2

FINDING ART AND HOME

Creativity is a wild mind and a disciplined eye.

— DOROTHY PARKER

It's not what you look at that matters,
it's what you see.

— HENRY DAVID THOREAU

CHAPTER SIXTEEN

MENTORS 1985

In the clay lab, I'm on a stool in front of a kick wheel, staring at a vessel I'd created with coils of clay. After a month in Nancy's class, I've chosen Ceramics as my major.

Nancy wanders around two rows of students at wheels, lecturing on form and function. "I sat on these same stools before heading to Indianapolis for grad school. Three years later, I was asked to return to head up this department. My predecessor died of cancer from firing fumes and glaze over spray." She bows her head for a moment. "I don't want to see any of you in the kiln room when we are firing, nor in the spray booth without wearing a full respirator. Got it?" We all nod, struck by the fierceness of her caution. "You will be graded on your intentions for the design of your thrown vessels and hand-built sculptures, the progress in your craft, and critiques. During critiques, any suggestion you may have for another student's work must be changed into a question. So let's keep it positive."

Though younger than me, Nancy becomes my mentor. She sells her art at galleries in big cities like NYC but also writes grants to create public projects. With her guidance and support, just maybe, I can become an artist too.

I've signed on for a full load of studio art classes while working at

Artlink. In between my classes, I write grants, develop promotional materials, and plan exhibitions. With no funds to pay a janitor, I clean the toilets before each art opening, which is easier than writing the NEA grant renewal application. I'm not getting paid for all the extra hours I put in, but I am compelled to excel. I'm investing my time to learn all I can in my studio classes, plus maintaining top grades. I strive to make the Artlink gallery a success, so my old boss looks good after recommending me. Even though I haven't talked to Dad since our wedding, I feel his presence pushing me to make all A's.

At the next Artists' Committee meeting, we discuss next year's schedule of events, which include ten exhibits. Nancy tells me, "Each year, we try to give a solo exhibition to a big-name artist in the spring." She casts her eyes around the group. "Since this is the first year of the UN's *Decade for Women*, let's pick a woman."

The committee members throw out names, starting with lowered expectations of regional and local artists, many who have already had a solo show at Artlink. But they can't agree on one. Unfamiliar with most of the names, I'm out of my depth. *I have lots to learn about women in the arts.*

When they seem stuck, I ask, "If you could have anyone, who would it be?" They glance around the circle until Stephanie, a teacher at St. Francis, speaks up. "Miriam Schapiro." Others agree, but chant, *"We'll never get her."*

"Who is she?" I ask, despite my embarrassment for not knowing.

"She's a New York City artist. You know Jackson Pollack?" Russell, a painting instructor, asks.

"Of course."

Nancy says, "She's part of his generation." My mouth drops. "Her feminist art raises women's crafts like crochet and sewing to the level of high art. I'm surprised you don't know her work. She's known for using the heart symbol in her early work. You'd like her."

I had been creating large heart vessels all semester. Intrigued and determined to accomplish the impossible, I say, "I can try."

The meeting quickly disperses.

I research her, then call her New York gallery looking for information on how to proceed. Bernice Steinbaum, the owner, answers the phone. Out of sheer naiveté, I ask what she would need to bring Schapiro's artwork to Fort Wayne, unaware that Miriam will soon grace the covers of both *ART News* and *Arts Magazine* with her recent work—cutouts like Matisse created late in his career. Bernice gives me a list: catalog, shipping, and insurance. I make notes. When she's done, she says, "Can you do that?"

"I'll get back to you."

When I glance at my notes, it hits me—Miriam's work is large. I'll need a trucker with experience handling valuable art. And I need to raise *big* money to pay for it all. I call Mack, my old boss at the Foundation. After all, he got me into this job. I run down the details when he answers the phone.

Mack says, "We can help you with part of this, but you need a sponsor. Lincoln Life Insurance Company is a major supporter of the arts donating to the museum and the foundation for years. I can introduce you. Then it will be up to you to sell your idea." He writes a number on a slip of paper and passes it to me. "This is the direct line to the president."

A lot is riding on this call. If I can't raise the money, I'll fall back on the art of regional women artists to fill the gallery. But I want Miriam Schapiro. I need to prove to myself and the committee that I can pull this off.

A few hours after we talk, he calls back to tell me they will sponsor the show. Before I call Nancy, I need to confirm with Bernice at the New York City gallery. I make the call.

"I've got the funding. What's next?"

Bernice talks about the specific pieces she wants to include in the show. "I'll send you photos and written content to include in the catalog. I'll want to see a proof before you print. We should talk in person. When will you next be in New York City?"

I gulp. "I've never been there." She doesn't respond. I scramble for a solution. "A group of art students are going next month. I could probably join them."

She laughs. "No one has ever admitted to me they've never been to New York City. I like your honesty. Come see me and we'll talk about details for the show. And you must come to see Miriam's new art."

When I call Nancy, she says, "Artlink will pay for your plane ticket. I'm one of the faculty supervising the student trip, so I listed you in the group. We're leaving in two weeks." My head is spinning. *This is happening.*

On Thursday, we check into the hotel. I'm sharing one room with three girls I barely know from St. Francis. Nancy, who has her own room, finds me in the hall. "Look what just hit the newsstands." She hands me copies of Art News and ARTS magazine. "Shapiro's work is on both covers!" My stomach drops. *Miriam is at the top of her game. I'm in over my head.*

Friday morning, after a taxi ride to SoHo, I enter the storefront gallery and see six-foot tall cut-out dancing figures painted in bright colors. Two art magazines chose them for their covers this month. A staff member leads me into an office area in the center of the gallery, where Bernice sits barking orders to her staff, who rush in and out. Behind her hangs one of Shapiro's fabric hearts adorned with lace, buttons, and ribbons.

"We're having bagels with cream cheese and lox. I'll fix you one."

I know she'll think I'm a country bumpkin, but I have to ask. "What is lox?"

She does a double take, then laughs. "It's smoked salmon. Just try it."

I've eaten sushi. Not for breakfast. But...I can do this. I bite into the onion bagel smothered with cream cheese plus a slice of raw fish on top, swallow, then smile. "I like it."

After Bernice answers some staff questions, she goes through all I will need to do to bring Miriam's work to Artlink. "Miriam will come for the opening. I expect it to be big. I'll send you a bill for her airline ticket. The catalog needs to be in full color. And you need a promotional poster, also printed in full color to distribute around the city, promoting the exhibition."

"I can do that." I gulp. We may only be a small Midwest gallery, but I'll make it happen. Somehow.

"You must come this evening for Miriam's opening." I nod, not knowing how I will cope with being shoulder to shoulder with a New York crowd. Everyone here is either affluent or an artist.

That night, the opening is packed with media critics and art collectors dressed to the hilt. I'm glad I brought a nice dress, but my feet are sore from all the walking and standing in heels. I bump into a man who says, "How do you like the art?" He gives me his card. It says he's an art reviewer for the *New York Times*. I tuck it safely in my clutch. After the crowd thins, Bernice invites me to go for drinks and a late snack with Miriam and a few friends, including the guy from the *Times*. It's nearly midnight. I slide into the backseat of someone's car that smells of rich leather, with no idea where we are going. The lights along the storefronts twinkle in the gentle mist. At the restaurant, I mostly just listen as I float in a wonderland filled with New York City's arts' elite.

A week later, I'm back in Fort Wayne, sitting in my office, wondering if it was real. I fantasize about one day having my own show in a New York City gallery. As I finish up the grant application, I wander into the main gallery, seeing the blank walls like I'd never seen them before. Panic runs through me to my toes. The dim, uneven lighting against the walls reflects hundreds of cracks and old nail holes in the plaster surface—too much to cover with spackle.

I can't hang Miriam Shapiro's art on this mess. The entire gallery needs resurfacing as well as better lighting. I call Mack at the Foundation, nearly in tears. "We need more money."

He says, "Just hang on. I have some ideas. I'll get back to you sometime tomorrow."

Once back in my office, I call for estimates to have new drywall installed and painted on a tight schedule, plus the electrical and track light installation, then finish running the numbers. Setting that aside, I start working on the design of the poster and brochure, using the images Bernice sent me. That night, with lists of details and deadlines running through my head, I can't sleep. I jump up an hour early to make coffee before Greg can, giving me extra time before my clay class to consider where to hold the reception.

When I get to the office, Bernice calls. "I've decided to come with Miriam to talk with your art collectors at the dinner about adding one of Miriam's new works to their collection."

We iron out details of their arrival two weeks later, and she gives me an update on when to receive the moving truck with the art. She repeats the importance of me getting lots of publicity: coverage in the papers and on all the network news shows. "An interview with Miriam on public radio is a must." *I don't know the staff at our local NPR. Maybe Nancy does.*

As opening day draws near, I'm more on edge than ever, worrying about what will happen if I let something fall through the cracks. When the committee comes to help me hang Miriam's art, Nancy quells my fears. "Look at this! The gallery looks spectacular. This will be our best ever show."

Once our New York guests arrive, the event becomes a blur, most of which I can't remember.

Our opening night is the talk of the town. Bernice praises me for the event coverage I had arranged on all the local channels, plus a full color spread in the newspaper. After a preview of the gallery, I walk them out to the white horse-pulled carriage to take them to the dinner. Greg picks me up and we race to greet her at the restaurant.

The next day, Bernice infers my one failure is that I was unable to persuade our primary sponsor or another collector to purchase one of Miriam's works. Actually, Bernice didn't tell me she expects us to sell a piece of art out of the show until she arrived, and I wasn't sure how to go about it. I tried a few inquiries, but didn't have the confidence or connections to push a sale through.

Miriam and Bernice ask me to drive them around to different secondhand stores before they leave for New York to collect buttons and odd bits for Miriam's art. As she looks through the containers of loose buttons and such, Bernice talks to me about my plans for the future. I tell her about my clay hearts. Miriam says, "To become a professional artist—if that is what you want—you need to commit to working in your studio and let go of the arts administration. You can't do both well."

On a cold January evening, I meet Nancy at a nearby pub after class. She's become more than my mentor. She's a good friend. I sip on my white wine spritzer listening to her ideas about artists she knows who may give a lecture to our class. The entire class will be eager to learn all the new techniques they will teach us, but all I can think of is how far behind I am with meeting my class requirements because of my responsibilities at Artlink.

I clasp my glass with both hands, staring at the melting ice disappearing like my time is to achieve my goals. Like Bernice said, I need to choose.

Nancy comes back with another round of drinks and says, "What's on your mind?"

"I'm running on empty but behind in many of my classes." I rub my brow. "How will I complete enough clay work to graduate next year?" I sip the fresh drink for courage. "Something has to give. I think I need to quit working at Artlink."

"I'm not surprised," she says without pause. "It's a full-time job, no matter what they tell you. Too much with a full load of studio classes."

I expected more resistance; she helped me get the job.

Can I walk away from my paycheck? What will Greg say? I look to Nancy, a decade younger than me, for her sage advice.

"Your art has progressed in the last year, especially your heart forms. You should submit to the clay show in Indie. Maybe the one with the horse and girl figures?"

I saw my heart sculpture design in a dream—the symbol of a heart cut through the top with an infinity symbol. Nancy brought in a teacher from Alfred University to teach our entire class the technique, which helps me scale my work up to over thirty inches tall. After hand-building smaller versions, I create a mold from a plaster and Styrofoam heart that I sculpt, one hump open to the front, the other to the back. Then I lay slabs of clay in the finished mold. When they stiffen, I join the front to the back along the sides with a coil of clay, then attach a slab of clay for a base. One takes up most of the space in the electric kiln. Nancy has encouraged me to create multiples of the form with different grazes and surface design.

She circles her drink on the coaster. "Do you want a career in arts administration or as a studio artist? It's impossible to do both well."

"Do you think I can make it as an artist?"

"You'll need an MFA, especially if you want to show in New York. I'll help you put together a portfolio if you want to apply, but you would need to go out of town. You can't get an advanced degree here. I'll ask my friend, who documents all my work, to teach the class how to photograph 3-D art for your portfolio. It's all about the light."

I brighten with her encouragement, but my lingering doubts persist. Me in graduate school? I'd be reaching for a higher level of education than anyone in my family. My grandfathers were blue-collar workers. My grandmothers were homemakers.

"You should go down to Bloomington to visit Indiana University's main campus. Most of the teachers have left since I graduated, but I still know a few. I'll make a call. If that's what you want."

"Art is hard for me. Especially drawing." I unclench my hands and reach for my water glass; the cool surface relaxes my fingers. "I love Ceramics—the feel of the clay between my hands, and when my work comes out of the kiln transformed. Every fiber in my body tells me I'm meant to work with clay."

"That's the way it is with clay. You either hate it or you love it.

"All my life, I've wanted to be an artist, ever since Mom took my brothers and me to an art class at the museum. Mike, who took art in high school, taught me the right way to draw a face but never encouraged me after that. I've been afraid...of not being good enough." Dad's disappointment when I didn't get straight A's still rings in my ears.

"Confidence is the most important part of being a successful artist. We all have bad days when doubt creeps in. But it's got to be there in the bottom of your gut—a deep-seated belief in yourself. Or you'll never survive the business."

I look up at Nancy. "Will you help me?" My voice is timid like a kitten instead of the bad-ass director of Artlink.

She smiles. "In the fall, you start your senior year. We can talk about your portfolio after class tomorrow. And if you leave Artlink, I can hire you as a studio assistant, to fire kilns and mix clay. Interested?"

"That would be great. I'll just move into the studio."

Nancy laughs. "You'd have to sleep in a respirator."

So, it's decided. I'm going to be a studio artist. Now I need to tell Greg. He worries when I spend money on art supplies.

"Let's toast to your future as a big-name New York artist." We raise our glasses and clink them. "Isn't today your birthday?"

"I almost forgot. I'm thirty-six. Kinda old to be figuring out what I want to do with my life."

"Some people never do."

After a hug, Nancy exits through the back door. I walk to the front, feeling like my feet don't touch the floor. As I pass the bar, a crowd huddles in silence, watching the small screen above the bar.

The Space Shuttle Challenger has blown up on take-off. Everyone on board is dead...including the schoolteacher.

I shout, "No! How?"

A guy standing next to me says, "It happened this morning. It's been on all the channels since."

My mouth drops open as a tidal wave of horror washes over me. While I had been discovering my future, they've been losing theirs. What a senseless waste. One I will never forget. None of us know how much time we have. While I can, I must grab onto the life I'm meant to live. To honor the shuttle crew in my own small way, I will mirror their courage by pursuing my passion, get into graduate school, and complete my masters.

When Greg comes home, I run to the door. "Have you heard?"

"A seal caused it," he says, his face flushed. "We told them this would happen." His company hadn't made the shuttle seal, but they were among the many companies trying to find a viable solution.

"That's all we talked about at the last SAE—how an accident was imminent. If they'd only waited…"

When he finishes ranting about the shuttle accident, I tell him about Nancy suggesting I go to Grad school. "I want to quit Artlink to focus on my art."

A part of me still expects him to get mad like Dad, but he doesn't. Instead, we talk—about our financial fears, and about what grad school would mean to me, how I want to find a gallery to sell my art and teach, like Nancy. In the end, we both commit to my dream.

If I'd stayed in LA, I might have become an architect, but here in Fort Wayne, I have Greg's support, mentors, and a community of friends. I may finally achieve my dream of becoming an artist.

CHAPTER SEVENTEEN

PUSHING THROUGH THE UGLIES 1987

In early May more than a year later, I bring home *Blue Horses* by Franz Marc, a library book Nancy recommended to inspire horse imagery in my watercolors. With a Diet Coke, I head to my attic studio to sketch from horse calendars and equine magazines to replace a live horse model. Smaller canvases stacked against the short wall wait their turn on my easel. A variety of paintings will hang in the school gallery. Greg is building four-foot-tall plywood pedestals in the basement to support my thirty-inch-tall vessels at eye level.

I'm working late, squeezing a tube of cerulean-blue watercolor onto my palette. Large square sheets of 140-pound cold press water-color paper, torn from a sixty-inch-long roll of 100% rag, stretch across the floor. With my long-handled brush, I mush and swirl the blue into the red and yellows, mixing colors, especially gray, to add depth like George, my favorite teacher, taught me in his evening painting class.

I've been painting for two years, learning the basics, only a fraction of what I need to master the techniques, materials, and color theory. As always, with each stroke, the imposter in me slashes my thin veil of confidence, as if it were an enemy's effigy. My next choices destroy the integrity of the running girl and horse forms as they disintegrate into mud. Traditional watercolorists build up delicate transparent layers of color—but not me. *What am I doing?*

For a better perspective, I step back and lean on the crooked brick chimney that juts through the center of the attic to find something good in this disaster. I sketched with water, then added pigments to watch the layers of intense colors magically mix in wet shapes framed with dry areas. But the stylized imagery looks overworked. *Is this my style?* It's a mess. I want to melt into the narrow wood slats on the floor and disappear.

Deep down, I've always known I'm not good enough to become an artist. When drawing, I struggle with proportions; even my line quality often reverts to sketchy lines—a telltale sign of an amateur. Am I crazy to keep going?

Why did I choose watercolor—the most difficult medium, unable to paint over mistakes like with acrylic on a canvas? I first studied watercolor at a community college in Santa Monica, during the summer between semesters of architecture.

I can work fast in watercolor to cover the walls behind my clay hearts before graduation. Our senior show is only a week away. Not enough time to start over. The frames wait to be assembled—metal edge strips, plexiglass to protect the paper, wire to hang—parts all piled under the skylight.

What a nightmare. With these atrocious watercolors, they will laugh me out of the program. I want to rip the ugliness into pieces. But if I stop, the section of wall assigned to me behind my hearts will be empty. At least, with Nancy's help, I have thirteen heart vessels.

Tears streak down my cheeks. I can't let Greg see me like this. He's supported me through changing jobs, then quitting for art school. I can't let him down. The money I've spent on art supplies can't go to waste.

As a child, I wandered in the woods and in the desert—whatever landscape surrounded our latest temporary home. Nature inspires and comforts me, and I want to show that sense of sanctuary in my work. If I can't create the balance I found in nature, my art will fail—like I always have. Throughout my life, I've been told I'm too much—too loud, too energetic, too talkative, too inquisitive—I've heard it from family, teachers, and friends. I try to do better, but like my dad, I mess up and quit. This time, I refuse to run away.

I dial the phone. It rings three times before Nancy answers. She must've been working in her garage clay studio. "Nancy? It's Deborah."

"What's wrong?"

My quivering lip must be altering my speech, revealing my distress. "I've ruined my watercolors. They're muddy. And horribly overworked. I want to start over with blank sheets of watercolor paper. But there's no time."

"Muddy is part of the process. Art needs to go through the uglies to gain the depth and complexity to make them rich."

I huff out the air I've been holding.

"Keep working. Add more layers. Deepen the color. Add some texture. The image will emerge again."

"I don't know." I'm almost blubbering, embarrassing myself.

"Use some gouache to pull back some white. I'm sure it's not as bad as you think. When you get stuck, pull up a chair and stare at it for as long as it takes—until it tells you what it needs. Don't give up."

"You really think I can save them?"

"Trust me. Push through your fear and they will improve. Take advantage of watercolor's transparency. Imagine you're illustrating a person's life, their experiences layered year after year, combining into who they become. Don't worry if they're a little muddy. That just means the colors are *luscious*."

I can't imagine that word ever being used to describe my work, but I say, "Okay. I'll try." Still, my doubts linger.

She adds, "Don't try. Do."

I laugh at her Star Wars movie reference; she reminds me of Master Yoda. "I'll keep at it."

After hanging up, I wipe my eyes and go back to work, praying Nancy is right—that somehow I can pull this off.

Nancy teaches that what we are looking for can only come out of the process of making art. But will I recognize it? If I can find the powerful woman buried deep within me and allow her to emerge through the image, maybe I will find my voice in the color.

Keep working, Deborah.

I suck down two six-packs of diet soda, working throughout the night to allow my naked girls running with the horses to emerge from the paper. All three compositions stare up at me from the floor, questioning me. And from smaller watercolor pads on easels. *Are you done yet?* I stare back while waiting for the paint to dry before adding more layers. *Talk to me. Tell me what you want. What color? What brush? How can I best share your story?*

A flash of being laughed out of the gallery by teachers and students returns.

Remember Nancy's words. *Trust the process.*

Since I was a kid, I have had a recurring dream about flying and teaching others to fly...but we only stay airborne if I believe. Ever since that first dream, I've gravitated toward people and stories involving magic and the power of self-belief. Yet still, I struggle to find my path to manifest that belief.

While watching *The Oprah Show* for some added comfort and inspiration, I imagine appearing on her show, sharing my journey to success, then return to my attic studio and see myself stepping out of my fear like a garment, ragged with wear. It falls to the floor to transform into drops of paint. Then I pull out a fresh piece of paper and pick up my brush to create a new cerulean-blue horse using broad strokes.

CHAPTER EIGHTEEN

THE EXHIBITIONS 1987

After many late nights of matting and framing, I select my favorite watercolors to hang in the outer halls of the Performing Arts Center behind four of my thirteen heart vessels on pedestals. All the graduating seniors in the art program have only one day to hang work in the group student show. As I make a last swipe with a cloth across the Plexiglas protecting my watercolors, a friend approaches—the local gallery owner who deals in art from established and emerging artists. I've spent hours in awe as he pulls back the protective tissue between signed and numbered prints in his flat files. After a hug, he examines my work. His visit is unexpected. I appreciate the courtesy, but my work is nowhere near ready to appear in his gallery.

Robert tilts his head, raises his brow, then says, "I'm putting together a show of about a dozen works to hang in my gallery to introduce the hottest local emerging artists to my collectors." He moves a few steps closer to one of my large watercolors. "I'd like to include this one." His lips curl into a smile.

Flushed with humility, I nod. "Okay. If you really want it."

"I'm not in business to flatter my friends.

I pull back.

He gives me a reassuring, lopsided smile. "Is it for sale?"

"Yes." I look down at the cloth in my hand, needing time to decide on its value...and mine. "I can bring it to you on Sunday after we take down this show."

"That will be fine." He nods, then moves down the hall to consider my classmates' work. I'm thrilled to have my work hang in his gallery, but I don't expect it to sell.

Robert sends out printed invitations to the opening reception for his *Emerging Artists* exhibit. When the night arrives, I enter on Greg's arm wearing a white dress and full makeup with my head held high. Robert waves me into his private office.

"I sold your watercolor," he says and pauses, making me hang on his words. "To Lincoln Life."

My eyelids disappear inside my head. He smiles wide and lifts one brow.

"For their Corporate Collection."

I can't breathe. "Really?" It's a dumb thing to say, but I am dumbstruck.

He turns to the work, pointing to a streak of blue green in the horse's mane that curls around the running girl's leg. "They came in this afternoon, before the opening, and chose yours because of its layers of vibrant color, along with two others from the show." He turns back to me. "I'll have a check for you next week." He studies my face as if he hasn't seen it before. "One of their executives wants to talk to you about a commissioned piece. If you're interested."

I force the air out of my lungs and measure my next intake to sound professional. "Yes. Of course."

As he wanders back into the crowd. I signal Greg, standing across the room, to join me in front of my watercolor. I steady myself on his arm and point to the red dot on the label. "Know what that means?"

As I fill him in, my confidence rises, and his smile grows bigger and bigger.

Mack, my old boss, comes over to talk with Greg while I search for Nancy. She spots me and breaks free from her conversation.

"I see congratulations are in order though I can't say I'm surprised."

"I still need to hang my solo show. I'm worried." When I realized most of my work wouldn't fit in the group show, Nancy suggested I reserve the main gallery at school to show it all together after graduation. My family can't make it to my commencement, but maybe they will attend my solo opening.

Nancy asks, "You almost ready?"

"Greg still needs to put a final coat of paint on the pedestals. I have some finishing touches to a watercolor plus framing it."

"How are things going with Purdue?" Nancy knew both Indiana University and UCLA wait-listed me. I don't want to wait another year.

A few weeks ago, she'd suggested, "If you want to start in the fall, apply to Purdue. They don't offer an MFA, just a two-year MA degree, but they have a nice clay department run by a friend. If you're interested, I can call and make an introduction." I applied the following day.

"I met with the head of the department last weekend," I tell Nancy. "After seeing my portfolio and with your recommendation, he accepted me into the clay program and offered me a lab assistant stipend which will help cover the cost of an apartment. I found a place starting in the fall—just need to mail him the deposit."

"How's Greg dealing with the fact that you'll be gone a lot?"

"I'll come home on weekends—most of the time. He understands how important this is to me. Anyway, it's my turn. I left my life in California when his job moved him here."

"Following your dream isn't always easy, but it's only for a year, giving you time to develop a new series of work. I'm sure you'll get into Bloomington next year."

"I've started some sketches for the new series," I swallow hard, "but I'm going to miss Greg something awful."

The following week, I send out invitations to my solo opening for "Heart of Woman." I'd reserved the auditorium, where we'd set up in a circle around a nude model for the Life Drawing class, a space large enough to show all of my work. With big wooden easels removed, Greg and I place my thirteen hearts on pedestals he'd built in the same circle, surrounded by watercolors and oils distributed on three walls. Seeing it all together takes my breath away.

On the night of the reception, Greg picks up a cheese and a veggie tray at the deli and a tropical flower arrangement for the table from a neighborhood florist. His folks drive up from Indianapolis and, to my delight, Mom flies out from LA. I've been wanting to introduce her to my women teachers who've also become my friends.

After greeting people at the gallery, we take a smaller group to our house for more wine and conversation. When my favorite art teachers, all women, arrive, they gather around Mom, who lights up with their attention. *What are they telling her?*

I expected Chuck, but he hasn't shown up. I'm worry something bad has happened. *I'll call him in the morning.*

At the hors d'oeuvres table, I talk with my friend Dian, who introduced me to aroma therapy and spirit cards. We've discussed the symbolism in my work. While she chats with my teachers, I walk across the dining room to Mom who is examining my diploma for my BFA, propped against the crystal vase of exotic flowers.

She holds my face. "I'm so proud of you, Debby."

"Thanks, Mom. But you know how much I hate that name. It reminds me of when I felt powerless. You chose it for me. Why can't you remember it?"

"I'm sorry, dear. It's hard at my age."

"Nancy said we look like sisters. It's true—you've hardly changed." I thought back to when we played pool at the gay bar where Chuck worked. It seems like another lifetime.

She blushed. "Not anymore."

I blame Dick for that. Thankfully, her husband stayed home.

The party had been perfect. Finally, my life is coming together. Greg and I head up to bed after midnight, leaving the clean-up for tomorrow.

At ten o'clock the next morning, I drag myself down the stairs to clean up the mess from the party. Greg cooks a fabulous egg dish, and we eat before we start. Then, he tackles stuffing soiled paper plates and plastic cups into a trash bag. I carry empty serving dishes to the counter next to the sink. When the phone rings, Greg gets to it first. He stretches the wall phone receiver on its long cord to me. "It's Chuck."

CHAPTER NINETEEN

A DEBT TO REPAY 1987

I wipe my hands on a towel and plop on a stool.

"You didn't come for my opening." I lean my elbow on the counter.

"Sorry. How was it?" Chuck sounds tired, but it's three hours earlier on the west coast.

"It was great! We had a good crowd. My teachers loved meeting Mom."

"She called me this morning and told me all about it. Congratulations."

"Thanks." There's a long pause on the other end that makes me tighten my core. His unusual reticence jerks me awake enough to read between the lines, like I do with Mom. "What's going on?"

"There's something I need to tell you…" Again, a long pause. My brow crunches.

"What is it?" I set aside my exhilaration to focus my radar on my brother. Red flags wave in my peripheral vision. As I wait, possibilities scramble in my head. Is it Don? Dad? Mike? Not Mom. I just saw her last night.

He speaks in a muffled tone. "I'm sick."

"The flu?"

"Debby...rah," he corrects himself. "I'm dying."

I gag on my coffee, unable to speak.

"I have a..." He trails off at the end.

"I can't hear you with all the static."

"AIDS. A-I-D-S." Hearing him spelling it scares me. "Do you know what it is?" he asks.

"No." I'm holding my breath, terrified, intuitively fearing his answer. "Tell me." He sounds nervous. Like when he told me he was gay.

"It's been on the news." So, I should know. This is my fault...for not staying in touch. I stare at the floor. Greg braces his hands on the counter, watching.

"We haven't had time for tv. I've been in the studio. Greg was building and painting pedestals for my hearts. What is it? This AIDS?"

Being far away from Chuck for four years has left me clueless, unaware of the AIDS epidemic ravaging my brother's community. People don't talk about the virus in Fort Wayne, at least not in the crowd we run with.

"It's a virus. Mostly gay men are getting it. It's really bad."

"How bad?"

"It's terminal and there's no cure. Don has it too."

My heart pulses in my throat. "Mom didn't say anything." *Why didn't she tell me?*

Chuck interrupts. "I told her not to. I didn't want to ruin your graduation. That's why I waited until today. You needed to hear it from me."

That's what Mom was holding back last night. I had hoped it was about her leaving Dick, but I didn't have a chance to corner her. How long has she known? Since she's on a plane, I can't ask her.

"How long do you have, Chuck?" *He's only 40.*

"A year, maybe two if we're lucky. We've already survived longer than most."

I'm grateful he's still alive, and furious he withheld this from me. "How long has this been going on?"

"We don't know. The disease can sit dormant for years. They don't know much. There's nothing you can do."

He doesn't want my help. I anchor my elbows on the counter and cradle my brow in one hand to hold the weight of my head. Suddenly, it comes to me—what I must do. I catch Greg's eye. He's across the island, his hands twisting a dishtowel.

When I hang up from Chuck, Greg's arms fold securely around me. It's like he knows. I need to be there. For Chuck. I step back, out of Greg's arms.

"Chuck and Don are both sick. He's dying."

Greg reaches for me, but I step away. I *don't want comfort. I want action.*

Since we moved here, we've talked about one day moving back to LA. But going back would mean diving into the tar pit of my family's conflicts. After I've fought to build my confidence.

"What do you want to do? Go visit him?" I don't think he's ready for my answer.

"Let's move back."

His eyes widen a bit. "I don't see how that's possible." He tightens his jaw.

I haven't considered the repercussions. I just know it's the right thing to do.

"He's saved my butt so many times. I need to be there." Those rescues were all before Greg, but I've told him about them. Does he remember?

When I was living in Houston, I tried helping Mom by getting her alcoholic husband into rehab, but she thwarted our one chance at an intervention. She accused me of meddling. Is that how Chuck will see me when I show up?

Each winter, we grow weary of the snow and ice. Whenever Greg is on a business trip to LA, I'm jealous. I miss the beaches and the sunshine. That's why I had applied to UCLA. A flight of fantasy perhaps. I planned to attend Indiana University at Bloomington. Instead, I'm going to Purdue.

Greg asks, "What about Purdue?" With a furrowed brow, he waits for my answer. I'd signed a lease on an apartment but haven't sent my deposit yet.

I touch my thumbs to each of my fingers at my side, a habit that helps me manage my anxiety. "Maybe I can get out of it."

He shrugs. Not the response I was hoping for. He says, "Let's talk about it later. We still have a lot to clean up from the party. And an exhibit to take down." He releases one end of the dish towel he'd been twisting in his hands and shakes it. "I'll dry."

CHAPTER TWENTY

UNEXPECTED OPPORTUNITIES 1987

A few hours later, I'm upstairs at my drafting board, trying to add order to the chaos of matting and framing materials left over from my art show. Greg is cleaning up the basement where he'd built the pedestals for my hearts. Staring out the window at the base of the stairs to my attic studio, I trace with my eyes the intersecting angles of my neighbor's rooflines, backlit by the overcast sky. I'm lost in my thoughts, ruminating over Chuck, his illness, and how to get to LA when I hear the phone. I'll let Greg get it. I don't feel like talking to anyone.

He yells up the open staircase leading from the entry hall. "It's for you."

I grumble, then lean back to spot him on the landing. "Who is it?"

"They didn't say." He gives me that look with his scrunched brow.

I knock over a cup of colored pencils when I twist to go. "Damn it!" I leave the scattered pencils for later, stepping over to avoid breaking any, then walk down the hall to the closet-size third bedroom that serves as my office. Sitting, I reach for the receiver on the green princess phone. "Hello?"

"I'm calling for Deborah Lucas," a man announces on the other end.

I don't recognize the voice. "That's me." Maybe it's Chuck's doctor to tell me he'd exaggerated his condition. I'm desperate for some good news.

I suck in a breath to steady myself and wait for the stranger to explain why he's disturbed me.

"This is Adrian Saxe."

I can't place the name. I don't know what to say. The silence stretches on.

"At UCLA?"

The head of the clay department. He wasn't there when I visited the campus. Nancy had shown slides of his work in class from Saxe's exhibit at the Contemporary Museum of Art in LA. He's one reason I'd applied to the program, and they have a *car kiln* on order. I could build even bigger pieces on its cart and just roll it in to be fired. Adrian is on the phone. Quivers run up my arms, across my shoulders, to the base of my skull. *Pull yourself together.*

Adrian says, "I'm calling because we have an opening in our graduate program. We'd like to offer you the spot. If you're still interested."

I nearly drop the phone. But I stop myself from jumping on his offer. *Think, Deborah. What do you need to make this work?*

"I am." I use the phone voice Mom taught me when I was little. Soft. Alluring. *Take your time. Work the system. Use all the skills Dad taught you.*

"However," I speak as slow as I can manage, "I have already accepted a position at Purdue." *Breathe. Go slow.* "UCLA is my first choice. But I'm not sure I can afford to pay your out-of-state tuition. Purdue's offered me money through a graduate assistant program."

No matter how Adrian responds, I know damn well I'm not going to Purdue. But I must be careful. I don't want to blow my chance to go to UCLA. Am I being stupid asking for money? Nancy taught us, *if you don't ask, you won't get it.*

There's silence on the other end. Despite my doubts, I wait, biting my tongue. I'd learned how to close selling Arizona desert plots in a casino while living in Vegas. *The next person who speaks loses.*

"I might be able to offer more," Adrian says. "Can I get back to you in a few hours?"

I sigh, then pray he didn't hear it. I use my phone voice to say, "I look forward to your call."

I hear Mom's voice in my own. I used it at my first job in the Plant Service Center at the telephone company in LA. Because of it, they chose me to record phone messages for customers, and for our installers calling for new orders when the lines were busy. From Mom's theatrical training, she taught me to project my voice to the balconies. Sometimes, it irritates people—friends and strangers alike. But I can't help it. Mom's training is ingrained.

When I hang up the phone, I replay the conversation in my head, worried he won't call back. But maybe he will. Maybe it's synchronicity. Just like when I met Greg.

I trip rushing downstairs to tell Greg but grab the rail to save myself from falling. Greg is in the kitchen fixing a snack of leftovers. I cross the room, working on how to spring the news. He looks up. My eyes give me away, smiling even before my lips curl. I want to jump into his arms, but I hold back. *Don't jinx it, Deborah. You're not in yet.*

"What are the chances you could arrange a transfer back to LA?"

A few hours later, Adrian calls offering a waiver to cover out-of-state tuition and a generous stipend to help with school expenses. I'm stunned.

On Monday morning, Greg calls his old boss in LA. It takes a few days, but he gets a job offer from two different departments in the Santa Monica office. Now we need to sell the house.

To make more money on the sale of our home, I find a service that allows us to list without paying the six percent agent fee. Within hours, someone appears at our door asking if she can show our home to *one* couple. She says she'd only ask for the commission if they buy our home today.

I need to be in my first class in LA in six weeks. I talk with Greg privately. We return to her waiting in our entry and agreed to her terms.

Later that day, we show the couple our house. They are barely outside when their agent returns to offer our asking price. It seems too good to be true. Later, we learn they'd lost out on a bid for a house two blocks away. It ends up they like our house better.

As soon as they leave, I call my brother with the news. "We're moving back to LA."

Chuck sounds pleased, although he doesn't totally believe me.

"It's true." I hand the phone to Greg for him to confirm it.

That same day, Greg and I paint the storm window trim, required to close the sale on the house. The detailed brush work takes longer than we think, but we push through, climbing up and down ladders until it is done.

What we need to make the move has all come together. School, job, house. Now all we need is to find a new place to live close to my school and Greg's office. We both remember well the tangled LA traffic and hope to minimize its claim on our time and energy.

The events unfold as if orchestrated by another worldly power. My life is looping again back to California. Our home goes to a couple who will cherish it, and we are returning to LA to the beach where Greg and I had walked on our first day together. I regret it took Chuck being sick to bring us home to the mountains and the ocean. However, I fear I'm losing Nancy's guidance too soon, but she said we'd stay in touch. And I'm leaving behind my good friend Dian.

I don't understand Chuck's disease. AIDS. A strange name. Can it really be killing him? I pray for a cure. But will they find one in time? Wringing my hands, I realize I am my mother's daughter. A caretaker and a worrier.

CHAPTER TWENTY-ONE

RETURN TO VENICE BEACH 1987

In September, I'm surrounded by boxes, unpacking dishes in the small kitchen. The movers stacked them three-high in every room and piled them up to the rafters in the detached garage, all waiting their turn to be unpacked.

The rental house located a mile from Venice Beach down the road from my old apartment is small but is an easy commute to Greg's office in Santa Monica and close to UCLA main campus.

We're renting an odd little house, a cube stacked two-high with a flat roof, designed long and narrow to fit the cut-in-half lot between larger homes. We're a block from the Venice canals, copycats of Italy. This close to the beach, the rent is high, but it's worth it to avoid a longer commute to school.

After putting contact paper in the cabinet, I unwrap the plates and glasses, emptying another box while waiting for a repairman to fix the refrigerator that came with the house. As I dry and put up the last of the dishes, Greg calls.

"Anybody show up yet?"

I look at my watch. "Not yet."

"What's wrong?" He picked up the tension, though I'm attempting to sound calm.

I close my eyes, not wanting to remember, unable to forget. "It's the critique class last night." About a dozen students from painting, sculpture, and design each offer a piece of their art for comment. "I presented my slides from *Heart of Woman*." My chin drops to my chest. "It didn't go well." *Why am I telling him now instead of tonight?*

"What did they say?"

I swallow hard. "My work is too pretty. If I want to be a serious artist, it must be tougher." I collapse into a nearby chair. "They don't get my symbolism—the magic in hearts, horses, and angels." I've been drawing angels from my dreams ever since my printmaking at the Houston Museum of Art School. "They know nothing about the history of clay vessels and claim I won't be successful if I don't make it ugly, or at least tough."

"What about the professor?" Greg asks.

"He's a *conceptual* artist—so nothing."

"What's that?"

My tone is sassy, resentful. "The instructor crawled through broken glass, even stabbed his hand with a surgical skewer. He researched how to do it without causing permanent damage." I shiver, imagining the self-mutilation.

"Did he use pain killers?"

"Not until after.

"He gets paid for this crap?"

"Big time. It's the new art."

Greg reminds me, "There's a lot more to the art world than that craziness, like Miriam Schapiro."

"I mentioned Schapiro in class. They aren't impressed. They said, 'That won't hack it in LA.'" I shake my head. "What am I going to do? My committee are all men."

"That doesn't make sense. The core of your work is women's spirituality."

"I'm scared I'll never fit in here." Coming to LA may be the biggest mistake of my life.

Greg asks, "So can't you change committees?"

"No. I asked. They stay with me for all three years. I want women, but none in Fine Art are on tenure, only instructors who stay two years. I can't find women interested who are outside our department either." I'm overwhelmed—by the campus size and intensity, unlike Fort Wayne, adding to my anxiety about Chuck and Don.

By November, I'm exhausted from fighting traffic to visit with Chuck and Don. We brought pizza for dinner. There's nothing more for us to do. Only Chuck takes care of Don. We're only in his way. *Chuck may not need my help, but I need to be here.*

I stand in the hall and peer through the open door. In their bedroom, oxygen tanks line up like soldiers against the wall to supplement Don's breathing. I push at my brow, trying to rub my worry away. I love living near the beach, but our rent is eating up our house sale profits.

At home one evening, I ask Greg, "With the high rent here, should we move to the valley?"

"We signed a lease; we're stuck for now. Can you spend less on art supplies?"

All the blood drains out of my face. "I need them."

"It'll be okay," he says.

I don't believe him. "LA is even more expensive than when we lived her four years ago. And Chuck doesn't seem to want my help. Did we screw up moving to LA?"

"We're together. That's what matters." He wraps me up in his arms. "Chuck will call when he needs you. You'll see."

Feeling his warmth, I snuggle against his chest. "Don seems weaker every time we visit. Chuck will be lost without him."

"Maybe he'll pull through. Chuck's giving him the best around-the-clock care."

"They can't afford a full-time nurse, and he's doing it because he loves Don. I just pray Chuck doesn't end up in the hospital from working too hard."

CHAPTER TWENTY-TWO

A CHANCE TO HELP 1988

A few months later, I'm outside with Tania when I hear the phone.

"I've been trying to reach you"—Chuck's voice sounds strained—"but I never know when to call." After a pause, his stress eases. "School must keep you busy."

Something is wrong. "Is Don okay?" I moderate the panic in my voice. I hate when my family withholds information because they think I can't handle it.

"Don's not been in the hospital for a month." A tense moment passes. "It's about Tawna."

The big brown lab-mix has been the light of their lives ever since they found her in the desert. Chuck had often talked of coaxing her into the car and nursing her back to health. She's been family ever since.

"She collapsed this morning and couldn't get back up. Teddy helped me get her into the van and we rushed her to the vet." Teddy, Don's nephew, lives across the street and lends a hand when needed.

"How is she?"

"She broke her hip." His voice quivers. "She was in so much pain.

There's nothing the vet could do." He composes himself. "I couldn't bear it."

I gasp. "You put her down?"

"I held her as the vet administered the shot." Even with his emotions restrained, I feel the knife stabbing his heart like we're twins.

"I'm sorry." I stare out at Tania in our fenced yard, grateful she is healthy, guilty for my good fortune. Chuck is losing *all* his family. It's not fair. "What can I do?"

"I'm having her cremated. I just wanted you to know. Don is taking it pretty hard, not saying goodbye. He said, *as long as one of us was with her…*" Chuck's voice cracks.

"You gave her a wonderful life. She loved you both. I could see it in her eyes. Every time you walked into the room, her head popped up; her eyes would follow you."

"She was a funny old girl, wasn't she?"

"She was the best. Now she's in doggy heaven."

"That better be the same place people go, or Don will be pissed." When I hear his chuckle, I let my shoulders drop. They'd crept up to my ears.

The following week, Chuck calls again, this time from the hospital. Getting my brother to go to the doctor, let alone a hospital, is like uprooting a tree. He's an exceptional nurse but sometimes knows more than the doctors, making him a self-proclaimed horrible patient. He stays apprised of the latest research, working with AIDS-LA.

"I went to see my doctor to fill a prescription for some cough medicine with codeine. But he insisted on tests. When one came back positive for pneumonia, he admitted me. I agreed because I'm worried I'll give it to Don."

"That would be bad." Don on oxygen with pneumonia…I didn't want to imagine it.

"Debby-rah." He chuckles. "Sorry. You'll always be my little sis. But I'll try."

"It's okay. I like Debby-rah. What do you need?"

"They have me hooked up to IV fluids and antibiotics. I'll be in here a couple of days. So, I need a favor."

"Anything." Finally, a chance to help.

"Don's home alone. I left him food in the fridge that he can microwave, but I need someone to check on him. Can you do that? Teddy won't be off work until this afternoon."

"I'll make the time. After I see Don, I'll come give you a full report. Are you in Sherman Oaks?" He worked there and knows everyone.

"Of course. The nurses are fussing over me. The attention is nice, but I hate being told what to do. And I'm worried about Don. He might need his port flushed."

"What's that?" I don't want to screw this up. He'll never ask again.

"Don will explain it." Since Chuck doesn't sound worried, I push down my anxiety. He says, "Thanks for doing this."

"Hey, what are sisters for?"

Before leaving, I give Tania and our cats dry food and water, lock them inside, and jump into my little white truck. When Mike told him I was looking for something to get me to school, Dad called out of the blue and offered to sell me his truck, asking for the retail price without a family discount. *He must be hard up for cash.* It's perfect for hauling around my clay, and we'll need it if we move again, so we bought it.

Chuck and Don's house is silent. I plop my purse onto the sofa and knock on the master bedroom door. Finding it ajar, I peek in. Don is in their king-sized bed, propped up against the headboard of their brass rail four-poster bed, his throne made complete with a half dozen bed pillows and assorted throw pillows, many handmade. A marble finial ball swirled with green, cream, and rust tops each bedpost. He sits with a quiet dignity, draped in a mantle of crocheted Afghans tucked around his shoulders.

He smiles. "C'mon in." He's lost weight and his face is paler.

"So, you've heard? Chuck is in the hospital." Don's voice cracks from the dryness in his throat, a side-effect of the oxygen that keeps him alive.

I soften my voice. "He asked me to check on you." *Am I being too nonchalant?*

"I'll bet he's running the show on the entire floor. All the nurses come to him with questions. He could have been a doctor," he says, with pride in his voice.

"Being bossy runs in my family." I walk up to the end of the bed. "How are you doing?"

"Pretty good. I had a little bit to eat. But I need my port flushed. Can you help me?" *Here we go. Steady, Deborah. You can do this.*

"Chuck mentioned it. He said you'd show me what to do."

Don folds back the teal blue Afghan and white bed sheet to reveal his port—a plastic tube taped and sewn into his side.

"They can't find a vein in my arm anymore. This makes it easy. My meds go directly into my blood stream. But if it doesn't get flushed every day, the blood clots and plugs it up. Then they need to tear it out and find a new place on my body to sew in another port."

Stepping closer, I bend to examine the tubing coming out of his chest. "What do I need to do?" I reach to touch it.

"Stop!"

I back up, startled, scared I've done something wrong.

"It's okay," he says in a reassuring tone. "Put on surgical gloves first." He points to a cardboard box of flimsy green gloves on the nightstand. "AIDS is spread through blood—any bodily fluid." He closes his eyes, then opens them. "We need to be careful. I wouldn't want…"

"Chuck told Greg and me to take a fresh glass from the cabinet, but not much more."

"That's only a precaution. The virus dies when it's exposed to air. It needs a direct body to body transfer, like if you touched my blood with a cut on your hand. Wearing the gloves prevents that. But mostly, it's transferred through sex."

I pull the stretchy gloves onto my long fingers; they make my hands look as big as a man's. "I've tried getting information out of Chuck. He'd rather talk about antiques or his garden."

"Your brother has many secrets—some he keeps from me."

Like Mom and Dad. Even now, our family keeps secrets. Don, being a therapist, understands family dynamics better than me.

Don says, "Chuck thinks I don't know he visits the baths."

"Steam baths like at my workout gym?" I ask, feeling like the naïve little sister.

Don looks away as he explains. "It is where gay men go to have careless sex."

My tongue tightens against the roof of my mouth, but I force out the words. "Is that how he caught it?" Don pales at my question. I can't believe I asked him that. *Damn it.* I search his eyes, desperate to understand. I'd wanted to respect their privacy—had never even entered their bedroom before today. Usually, when we came to visit, Don sat on the sofa with his legs stretched out, wrapped in an Afghan with Tawna lying at his feet. Being in this inner sanctum, I feel intimately closer to them both. The reality of their situation sinks like a stone in my heart.

"We don't know for sure." He looks out the window. Fuchsia Bougainvillea climbs up their brick facade spilling over the windows, its luscious flowers suspended. "AIDS can lay dormant for decades. We both had lives before we met. But your brother is the love of my life. He tries to fill a great emptiness inside. It doesn't matter what he does, I'll always love him."

Don, falling back on his training as a therapist, nurtures their relationship, whereas my entire family is screwed up.

"Does Chuck still go to the baths?"

"No. He wouldn't risk giving it to someone else." Don closes his eyes and takes a long, labored breath from the oxygen seeping into his nostrils. "Since I tire easily, I better talk you through flushing my port."

I open a place in my brain to store the instructions, separating it from what I learn at UCLA, like how not to burn myself when welding metal sculptures.

"Chuck didn't tell you how sick he was last winter, did he?"

My eyes close as I shake my head no.

"He almost died."

My mouth drops open.

"He pulled himself back from the brink to take care of me when my heart became infected. It doesn't pump very good anymore. That's why I'm so weak." He glances at the four-foot-tall oxygen tanks against the wall, ready when needed. In the corner, a dog bed lies empty.

"You must miss Tawna."

Don looks up. "I think losing her is what put Chuck in the hospital. His white blood cell count tanked. When our emotions take a dive, the virus attacks what little immune system we have left. I don't know what I would do if something happened to him." A tear rolls down his cheek.

Reaching for the box, I offer him a tissue. I am honored Don is opening up to me, but the muscles in my gut clamp down when I hear my brother may be close to death. I don't know how to reassure Don, so I pivot to something I can do. "Okay. Let's do this." I say, looking at his bared port. "What's first?"

Don points out the little black bag containing the needle and glass vial, patiently talking me through the draw and elimination of air bubbles. He pops the cork on his port. I inject the clear fluid. As instructed, I properly dispose of all the contaminated items, breaking off the needle first to keep it from being reused. Then I tuck Don in and watch him drift off to sleep. I sit next to the bed, watching him struggle to breathe with each lift of his chest.

Chuck almost died! No one told me. I once overheard him talking about bathhouses but didn't grasp the full meaning. It doesn't matter how they got sick. They're going to need more help. *And there is no cure.* I shiver, my skin clammy and cold.

Satisfied that Don has fallen fast asleep, I leave his bedroom door open a crack and head to the fridge to find something to wash the dryness out of my throat. The shelves are stacked with supplemental drinks for Don. From the trays on the door I grab one of Chuck's cans of Coke, pop the top and chug half of it, enjoying the tingles and burn of acidic bubbles on the back of my tongue.

Knowing Teddy will arrive soon to stay with Don, I lock the front door behind me, then place the key back inside the fake stone under the fern. I need to be here more often, and Venice Beach is just too far. Living close to school is nice, but it doesn't work. We need to move to Van Nuys—closer to Chuck. I owe him. I must get out of the lease. Greg's company won't pay for another move. Good thing I kept all the empty boxes broken down flat in the garage.

With my truck started, I finish the soda and toss the can behind the bench seat, along with my ambitions...at least for a while. Time to focus on my family. I don't know if I'm strong enough to do what Don and Chuck need. They're both very sick. And how will I keep up with my schoolwork while I care for them?

My anxiety elevates from my conflicting responsibilities. But then, I remember rare spontaneous moments of joy in my childhood when my brothers and I performed the *Monster Mash* and the *Twist* in the living room. Dad joined us to teach me the swing, then Mom stepped in and wowed us. We danced through the fires of upheaval and uncertainty. The laughter feels real even now and helps me prepare to move again. *I can do this.*

A week later, Chuck is out of the hospital, cooking, cleaning, and weeding his garden when he calls again.

I set aside the clay slabs I'm pressing into a vessel mold to call Greg and let him know I'll be home late. "I'm going to see Chuck. Why don't you grab an Arby's for dinner?" That's his favorite fast food.

When I enter Chuck's house, I peek in the bedroom to say hi to Don. He isn't strong enough to make it to the sofa today. After a kiss on Don's cheek, I hug Chuck, then he leads me to their only bathroom.

"What am I looking at?"

"The carpet," Chuck says. "It's old and stinks from being wet too many times when the shower door leaks. It disintegrates when I try to clean it. We never use the tub, and we dry off before getting out of the shower. But the steam fills the room and soaks the towels, our robes, and especially the carpet. It smells like a swamp. I have a piece of carpet big enough to replace it, but it's a weird shape—harder than it looks. I can't get it right. Screwed up the last piece. Can you help?"

He'd seen me cutting detailed pieces for my architecture models when I lived with them before I met Greg. I don't need to get close to smell it. He's right. It needs to come up, carpet and padding. "Are you sure you want carpet again?"

"Definitely. It's soft on our feet—and warm—especially for Don. With his poor circulation, he's always cold. Do you think you can do it? Like soon?" He cocks his head and lifts his brow, my brother's signature look. So many memories.

"No problem." *I'm not sure I can pull it off, but I jump at the chance to help.* I take a mental picture of the carpet pattern. "Tomorrow, I have critique. Will Friday be okay?" *I can do this.*

"I can't leave Don without access to a bathroom. How long will it take?"

"Two or three hours. I'll need to replace the padding."

"If it needs it." His eyes soften. "It's great having you here, Sis, to help me. I can't tell you how much this means to us. By the way, are you still considering moving?"

"Maybe. I haven't even started looking."

"There's a cute house for rent next door to Edith three blocks from here. Emily, the owner, is nice. Maybe you can see it when you come on Friday."

"Do you know how much the rent is?"

"It's less than what you're paying near the beach. And it's only a few blocks away. We used to walk Tawna to visit Edith. She loved that dog." His pain peeks out of his eyes, but then he shuts it down.

Don's mom Edith has a syrupy sweetness that makes me sick. I don't trust her. "I'm not sure about living next door to Edith."

Chuck says, "She won't bother you. She's busy taking care of the skating rink her husband left her. The rest of the time, she's here, which I don't mind...most of the time. Don's very close to his mom."

And not in a good way, based on what I'd observed.

"I'll look at the house. Do you know how big it is?"

"You'll have to see it. It's cute. And Emily has kept it up. She lived there until her job moved her to Orange County. Since she didn't want to commute, she rents it."

The next day, we meet Emily, who is nice. She's asking less for rent than what we're paying. The Universe continues to guide me. We take the little house to be closer to Chuck. I smile through gritted teeth when I see Edith.

Our current landlord has a long list of people waiting to move in near the canals and lets us out of our lease. We spend the next month transporting a load at a time over the mountain pass to Van Nuys. Emily's house is small, but with my drafting board and art books in the living room, I make it work. On sunny days, its sliding glass door gives me ideal illumination for my work with watercolors and with a view of the irises Emily planted in the fenced backyard. The blooming garden greets us with a sweet aroma whenever we slide the door open.

On the final day of moving, Greg calls his friends from the office to help with the big stuff. Mike shows up too. I stay out of their way. Chuck doesn't have much stamina after being in the hospital, so I ask him to help me put dishes away at our new house. Chuck tends to work through his exhaustion only to collapse the next day. Mike and I do that too, but it won't put us in the hospital.

After moving all day, I fall into a half-made bed. I'm behind at school and need to put in long hours to break through before the end of my first year. I'll spend more time with Chuck this summer when I don't have school every day.

Please, God. Keep Don and Chuck healthy until then.

CHAPTER TWENTY-THREE

CHUCK'S REQUEST 1988

On a gloomy Saturday morning, I'm sitting at the drafting board we'd set up by the window in a corner of the cramped living room. To brighten our living space, Greg cuts irises for vases inside, including a bouquet in a jam jar next to me. So, despite the dim light cast inside, the rich blue-violet flowers inspire me to pull out my watercolor palette and brushes. On hand-made paper, I sketch the unique shapes I see in the spent iris blooms, looking up close, then paint them using only three hues: blue, green, and peach.

When I need a break from the intense work, I walk Tania over to see Chuck; we're both eager to meet his new dog. Don's nephew Teddy found the Australian shepherd-mix pup wandering on Ventura Boulevard.

"Teddy can't locate an owner." Chuck's eyes light up, a first since Tawna died.

As I reach down to pet him, his mouth drops open into a smile and his multicolored, long-haired tail waves like a flag. "What are you going to name him?"

"I didn't want to get attached again. But, well, who can resist?" He pats the sofa, signaling the dog to jump up. "What about Wolfie?"

I scrunch my face. "Like a wolf?"

His eyebrow lifts, then he chuckles. "Haven't you seen *Amadeus*?"

I shake my head.

"About Wolfgang Amadeus Mozart?" He points to the pup's tail. "It's just like a metronome."

A few weeks later, I walk Tania to Chuck's for our Saturday ritual of exploring the sleepy neighborhood with our dogs. A shower overnight had left the sidewalk wet. The rain clouds had dissipated, allowing the sun to warm our backs as the dogs pull us along. Chuck doesn't mind Wolfie tugging. Despite our recent training, I let Tania keep pace with her new friend. Our walk is the perfect excuse to break Chuck away from his round-the-clock care of Don.

When we pause for the dogs to sniff a tree, I turn to Chuck. "Have you seen Dad lately?" My brothers and I took turns reaching out to Dad until he pushed each of us away—lying, breaking promises, and setting us against each other. I was tired of the abuse, but they kept trying.

"Not since our barbecue by the pool last summer." Chuck looks up as if to pull down a memory. "He really shocked me that day."

"What did Dad do?" I'm hoping Chuck will reveal more about his illness, or maybe another family secret. He only tells me what he thinks I need to know.

Chuck braces his back against the tree. "He handed Don a bottle of his favorite bourbon. Until that day, Dad never looked Don in the eye. Never called him by his name." Chuck's face lights up. "That gift meant he's accepted us. And me. As I am. I never thought it would happen."

"Wow! I thought Dad was a lost cause."

"I don't know how he figured out Don's favorite drink, but him making the effort meant everything."

"Remember when I brought Mom to that bar where you were working?"

"I'll never forget it. I was flabbergasted. You're just lucky it worked out." He tucks his chin and drops his voice to a judgmental tone, mimicking Dad to tease me.

"I knew she'd be cool. When I told her, she didn't even flinch. She hesitated about coming to the bar, but she did it." I crouch down to rub on Tania's back. "I knew it'd take Dad a while to come around. But twenty years?"

Chuck pulls away from the tree and stretches one arm up and then another, releasing his back. "Some dads never do."

Wolfie looked up with his cheery face, signaling it was time to move on. Tania charges forward, ready to resume our walk, but I gently tugged her back to my side.

"Do you ever see Bobby and the guys from the bar?"

"I've lost track of them since I've been with Don. The last time I was at the bar was after the car accident when you and I took Grandma to the airport. I never understood how she didn't get hurt."

Tanya rubs against my leg, so I reach down to pet her. "I still laugh at how we danced at the bar to relieve our back and neck pain when none of the meds the doctors gave us worked. Do you think the insurance company ever assigned an investigator? We were so sure he'd never follow us into a gay bar."

"We were being paranoid. But we had fun. With beer to numb my pain, I could stand straight. And dance."

I rub the back of my neck. "I still have problems."

"Whiplash is a bitch." He stares back. "Did you ever get much from that lawsuit?"

"Nah. Enough to buy a used car when I needed it." I purchased a used Fiat X1/9 which broke down all the time. The repairs ate up my paycheck.

"We were quite a sight. Two flashy redheads hogging the dance floor. The guys loved it." Chuck stands taller than I've seen in weeks.

The memory warms me as well. Or maybe it's the sun peeking out, or the smile on Wolfie's face as he urges us down the pavement. "I bet we could still raise a ruckus on the dance floor."

We resume walking when a cloud blocks the sun, tossing a dark mood over Chuck. He stops and stares at the pavement. "You'll soon be able to dance on our graves."

"Don't talk like that. It freaks me out." A shiver runs down me like a freight train all the way through my feet.

"I need to," Chuck pleads. "I need to know that you'll take Wolfie and give him a home."

"Of course I will. But that's a long way off." This is not the closeness I was looking for.

"One of us needs to make plans. Don refuses to."

Now we're getting somewhere. "What do you mean?"

"The laws don't give me any rights...because we're not married. Do you understand what that means?" He turns to face me. Fire and fear swirl in his dark eyes. "Don hasn't done a will."

His naked revelation confuses and unnerves me. "Why not?" I always thought Don was the responsible one because he's a therapist with a more serene personality. I couldn't have been more wrong. Don is leaving the one he loves vulnerable in the depth of grief.

"He says he'll do it, but he keeps putting it off. Edith is telling him he doesn't need to. He doesn't have the strength to fight her." He bows to hide his worried face, but I see it anyway. "She's always had this power over him. Maybe he doesn't believe he's going to die." He looks up and holds my gaze. "But he's running out of time. He needs to tell her he wants me to have the house. There's nothing in writing." A chunk of hair falls onto his face as he shakes his head. "Edith cosigned for our house loan. My name's not even on the deed."

Shit. "How did that happen?" At least he's trusting me with the truth. I hardly know Edith. Now, I hate her. She's been purposefully wedging herself between Chuck and the love of his life for years.

"When we were looking for a house, my credit was bad. Don had wanted this house for years. He'd looked for a For Sale sign every time he drove by. So, when it came available, she offered to help us buy it." Chuck stops to watch a squirrel scramble up a tree, the dogs pursuing until they hit the end of their leashes, whining to be let loose.

"She wanted control over her son." I'm fuming inside, trying not to show it. My grip on the leash tightens. Tania turns to look at me as if she's picking up on my stress.

"We got the house"—Chuck shrugs—"I was happy about that. But since, I've grown suspicious of Edith's intentions. Nothing has changed...even though I make the mortgage payment every month. When he dies, the house will belong to her. I worked double shifts at the hospital to buy the cabin. The house is Don's and Edith's. The cabin is mine."

I love his cabin. Weekends there with Chuck and Don were some of the best, surpassed only by camping in Yosemite when I first met Greg.

"If this house belongs to anybody, it's you. You've paid for it and decorated it. With all your antiques. And the beautiful gardens, full of flowers and rose bushes. That's all your doing. You do all the work. Cleaning and upkeep. And now you're taking care of Don too. She's got to appreciate that." The least Edith could do was give Chuck the house.

"If she had to pay for round-the-clock care for Don, it would cost her over a hundred thousand a year if it weren't for me. I don't think she gets that."

I'm like a balloon heated up, ready to blow. "You're going to fight her to keep it, right?"

"I'll wait to see if Edith is true to her promise to Don."

Of course, she won't be. I scream my outrage inside my head without letting it show on my face. This is Chuck's life, and I can only help when he asks.

"If she isn't, I'll have the money from insurance. Don and I both have policies with each other as beneficiaries. I've been making the monthly payments on both for years—money for when I get sick."

We walk toward his house in silence. Will I be able to care for Chuck the way he's cared for Don? Will he let me?

The clouds darkened again, threatening to burst. We increase our pace but stop when the dogs sniff at another tree. Chuck turns to me.

"Edith is planning to bury Don in the plot next to his dad. She has a place there too."

The shocks keep coming. "What about you? Is there a place for you?"

"No. I don't want to be buried. I don't want people wasting their lives crying over my grave. That's what Edith has done. She visits Harold's grave every week and used to drag Don along whenever she could. I don't want that for you," he says, his eyes steeled.

My fists curl and clench. I envision tearing out Edith's heart...but this is not the time to confront her. Instead, I ask the dreaded question. "What *do* you want?" The words scorch my throat.

"I want to be cremated. You can do whatever you want with the ashes. The Catholic Church won't accept anyone who's gay. We're depraved and evil."

My blood boils. "I hate how they've turned their back on you when you've needed them most."

"The church won't hold a service for a gay guy. Especially if it's from AIDS. I don't know what I'll do for Don. He's Lutheran."

An old anger surfaces from deep inside my gut where I'd pushed it into hiding. I was nineteen when I argued with a parish priest about gays, infuriated by his unwavering and unsympathetic stance, and haven't stepped inside a church since. And I never will. Greg and I were married on a mountain.

We arrive at the stone path that leads to Chuck's front door. He reaches down to scratch Wolfie's ears.

"Maybe the Lutherans won't be so resistant. They've ordained a few women. I know one who may help us."

Is that what he wants?. I'm worried I'll say the wrong thing and ruin it all, just when we're getting closer than we've ever been.

"So you don't want to be buried?"

He looks back over his shoulder at me with his brow raised. "Sorry, kid. You'll need to dance on somebody else's grave. I don't want one. You can keep my ashes on your mantel if you like. That way you won't need to drive anywhere to talk to me." He laughs at himself.

That's Chuck. He makes light of the hard things in life. I try to laugh but can only manage a slim smile. The burden of the tasks before me weighs like a bulldozer on my spirit. I search for a one liner that's silly, or ridiculous, but every flash of an idea seems trite or silly. Instead, I walk alongside my brother without speaking, my arm looped through his as the dogs lead us to his front door.

The sight of Don sitting on the sofa brings a smile to Chuck's face and relief to mine. Our conversation gets tucked into the shadows of my memory to wait for its time to emerge. Not yet. I'm not ready. And may never be.

CHAPTER TWENTY-FOUR

RETURN TO YOSEMITE 1988

After school lets out for summer, Chuck tells me he's taking Don on a return trip to his beloved Yosemite. "I'm inviting both our families. Edith demands I get a large RV for the three of us." He bites back his resentment. "So, I've rented one." I start to object, when Chuck pulls me outside to their patio around the pool lined with big splashes of colorful annuals.

"I'm not arguing about it because it's the best way to transport Don's oxygen tanks and medical supplies. Edith used to drive a Zamboni at their ice rink before her husband died—she can handle an RV. We'll switch off between driving and sitting with Don."

Trapped with Edith in a box on wheels for six hours each way. If I had to listen to her high pitch voice and her superior, know-it-all attitude for that long...I'd throttle her.

When Greg and I arrive in Yosemite at our assigned campsite, Don's niece Cathy, her husband Ralph, and their kids greet us. He was born in India, teaches math, loves to cook, and practices yoga daily. While the kids play in the woods nearby, the adults set up camp, then gather by the fire. The sun ducks behind the treetops, bringing an early dusk before Chuck pulls up in the lumbering RV.

The long trip has taken a toll on Don. He looks paler than when I saw him earlier that week. Ralph minimizes the bickering among kids and adults with his calm, grounded energy by just being present. He pulls the pot of chili from the cooler and slides it over the red-hot charcoal fire. They'd prepared Don's recipe—the traditional first meal at all the family camp outs—to be followed by roasted marshmallows for s'mores. I've loved eating the gooey treat since my Girl Scout camping days. But then, who doesn't love s'mores?

After dinner, Edith and Don retire to the RV while Chuck stays up for a few games of poker at the picnic table. We play with chips instead of money, letting the kids play. As usual, Chuck wins it all, flashes a big grin, then disappears into the RV.

The next morning, I wake to a thunderous noise. Sticking my head out of our tent, I'm surrounded by a herd of horses running loose through our campsite. I crawl out, yelling back to Greg, "Wake up. You've got to see this."

At breakfast, Ralph says, "They probably got loose from the horse rental place."

"They rent horses here?" I wish I'd known. My excitement over the possibility of riding crashes when I hear Chuck and Edith arguing about Don's care. Still, the horses running all around us tells me horses will be in my future. Mom and Chuck believe in signs too.

Chuck says, "Edith insists Don needs to be at home. So, we're leaving." Edith disappears into the RV. Don had only joined us for one brief meal with Chuck and Edith on either side.

They depart within the hour. As they leave, we see Don through the rear window lying on the bed in the back of the motor home. I don't know how Chuck manages.

Once they've left, the campsite doesn't feel right, but we make the best of it for the kids' sake for two more nights. Daytime temps are cool for early summer, and the nights are bone chilling outside my sleeping bag. The river is raging fast and high with all the rain, making rafting out of the question. New waterfalls pouring off hundred-foot cliffs are spectacular from a distance, but the rain has flooded the lower campsites, closing them. The forest, powerless to stop the moving water and its destructive forces, mirrors my life. Instead of dancing through fire, I'm drowning, unable to pull myself up and out of the depression threatening to swallow me.

Greg and I decide to leave the following day before nightfall. Bears trashed a vehicle in the neighboring campsite the night before. Greg says, "They're starving, flooded out of their habitat." Another sadness clutches my spirit, weighing me down. On our way out of the park, Greg takes the route to revisit a magical moment from our last trip to Yosemite—a view of Half Dome in the distance. The climbers who scale it using only handholds are crazy. My tingling nerve ends seem to calm when I look up and see the face of the Indian chief in the patterns on the granite dome. He's watching over us.

CHAPTER TWENTY-FIVE

THE SOFA 1988

With access to my lab at school all summer, I establish a rhythm working in clay. At home, I put in long hours to develop a new series of watercolors. The iris blooms in the vase have died, withered into abstract shapes that curl and twist, yet maintain the essence of their former glory. As I sketch the branching slivers, I layer the abstract shapes on handmade paper with raw, deckled edges. I then add intense greens, blues and reds to bring the forms back to life. I'm lost in the work, floating in my creativity, when Chuck calls. He has an urgency in his voice I've come to expect.

"I'm going to the grocery. I hate to ask, but can you come sit with Don for a while? Edith is getting her hair done and Teddy's in school. You won't need to do much. Maybe get him a glass of juice. If he's hungry, the liquid meal replacements are chilling in the fridge."

"I'll be happy to come, Chuck. That's why I'm here."

"Thanks." I can hear the strain in his voice and his attempt to conceal it.

I dread walking away from my watercolors, but family comes first. It's why we moved here.

"I'll be right over."

We both hate asking for help. Growing up, if we had a problem, we were pretty much on our own. Mom and Dad were at work or with friends, playing duplicate bridge, golfing, or hanging out at the Elks club, drinking and dancing. My brothers and I found our own solutions to problems as they cropped up. I'll never forget how I traveled on my own in Australia to see my horse when Dad refused to take me.

Leaving my latest watercolor to dry, I clean my brushes, let the dog out to pee, then head over to stay with Don. When I walk in, I'm surprised to see him lying on the sofa. He's swaddled in two quilts and an Afghan with Wolfie snuggled against his legs, close enough for Don to pet his face. Chuck heads out the door, and I grab a cold can of Coke from the fridge and curl up on the floor to chat with Don.

We talk about how he took me on walks to hidden city parks, our search for my first Venice apartment, and about our visit to the UCLA campus and sculpture garden. Then he goes quiet, his hand on his dog, his eyes staring into nothingness. Memories of our time together will soon be all I have. He breathes in oxygen from the line split between his nostrils, supplementing his air. His sunken cheeks make his forehead more pronounced. Barely any muscle remains beneath his pallid skin. Only bone. Even the sharpness of his mind rarely emerges through the fog of his illness. How can two of the most important people in my life be slipping away?

To get me through, I remember when I was 18, being lost as my family disintegrated, calling on the mountains along the freeway for strength, until Mom finally left Dad and returned to Illinois. Their power helped me then. Breathing in the memory, I'm able to relax while a vise tightens on my heart. The pain of watching Don disappear surpasses everything I survived in my youth.

When Chuck returns, he helps Don back into bed, replaces his oxygen line. Then my brother sits on the sofa next to me, his eyelids only partway open. His cocoa-colored eyes reveal the exhaustion intertwined with his grief.

"He doesn't have long, does he?" I ask, unsure if I want to know.

"No," Chuck tells me, dropping his head on my shoulder. "It could happen any time now. He's exhausted. I think he's ready. But I'm not sure I am."

"Is there anything I can do for you?" I brace for the answer, praying it is something I can give him.

"Be ready for my call...when the time comes. I want everyone here to give him a proper send off." Chuck runs his hand across the sofa. "This fabric is dirty. I need new furniture. Want to help me pick it out? Teddy can sit with Don for a few hours."

"Go shopping? With you?" Chuck is the best shopper in the entire family. It's an honor to be invited along. And being asked to consult on the purchase is another level of compliment. "I'd love to. When?"

"How about this evening? There's a big furniture store on Sepulveda. I think they may even have a sale going. Can you pick me up after dinner? Say about 6:30?"

I nod, quivering with excitement.

Chuck and I wander through the enormous store talking about design and color, debating modern verses traditional styles. I'm having a blast...that is until Don's sister Linda shows up. I didn't know Chuck had invited her.

It was supposed to be me and my brother. She's ruined it.

The throbbing in my feet silently announces I wore the wrong shoes for extended shopping. I plop on a sofa to rest and check for blood on my heels. Seamlessly, Linda takes over, directing Chuck around the store away from me. My resentment balloons. I'm crushed when, after ten minutes, I realize he hasn't noticed I'm missing.

Ignoring my aching feet, I catch up with them to add my two cents to the discussion. "Chuck, that sectional is cumbersome. If you find a sofa you like, then add two or three upholstered chairs, the room will have better flow." But he isn't listening. After years of design training, I know I'm right. Why did he solicit my help?

"Do you really want white?" I continue, in an attempt to get his attention. "How about off white? Or something with color—it would add pizazz. Like this one." I sit down on the sofa to try it out, and Chuck sits next to me. "What do you think?"

He hesitates. "It's comfortable."

I jump up, try an adjacent chair. "Ooh. This one sits well. And it has a matching ottoman, which would look great with your antiques, without overpowering the room."

"I'm not sure about that color," Chuck says, then pauses. "I forgot my room measurements on the dining room table. So, I can't buy anything right now. We'll need to come back." He stands and moves toward the exit, leaving me with my mouth open. "I'll ride home with Linda."

I glance around for anyone witnessing my humiliation, then look up to see Chuck not meeting my eyes. "Okay. Let me know when. I'll pick you up again." I limp on my sore feet, struggling to catch up, hoping he will include me in when he chooses a sofa.

Without even turning around, Chuck walks out the door, says, "See ya later. Appreciate your help. Thanks for coming."

They walk away. I shrink into my inner turmoil, reaching for mental techniques to keep me from fracturing with old anger and new grief. *C'mon, Deborah*. He'll call when he needs you.

But why did he ask Linda to come? Aren't I enough? You'd think after all my art and design training that he'd value my opinion. Don was never interested in what Chuck did to the house. Why is his sister?

I swallow my feelings. Chuck deserves a break. He's losing the love of his life. I'm here to support him, to help in whatever way he asks. If only he would clearly tell me what that is.

CHAPTER TWENTY-SIX

A SEARCH FOR SOLACE 1988

When I get home, Greg says, "You look like a deflated balloon."

"Thanks. Just what I wanted to hear."

Greg jiggles the keys. "Let's take a drive into the mountains to get out of the city." He gets me. I'm bad at holding my emotions in, but talking helps when we take drives.

We drive north on Hwy. 5 for more than an hour. As we climb into the mountain pass the locals call the Grapevine that leads into the Central Valley, Greg pulls off for gas at the exit we've taken before to Chuck's cabin. We decide to have lunch at a cute cafe next door. Eating a big burger and fries helps me stuff my frustrations.

When Greg pays the bill, I pick up a local newspaper near the door. While he fills the tank at the gas station next door, I circle four property listings in the ad section and show them to Greg. "What do you think about buying some land and building a house?"

Greg shakes his head. "Maybe if we'd stayed in Fort Wayne. But in California? I can't see a way to make it work. Not with the commute."

"Could we look? Just for kicks." I stick out my little girl lip as leverage, which usually works with the men in my life.

"Okay," he says, "but don't latch onto any of them. We don't have money for a down payment. And we won't until you finish school and find a job."

"I know, I know. But I can dream, can't I? I just need something to help me tolerate living next door to Edith." I cover my eyes as I shake my head. "I can't stand that woman. When Chuck's making Don's medical decisions, she tries to override him. You know, he has no legal say in Don's care at the hospital, even though he's an RN."

"Greg looks puzzled. "He doesn't have any rights?"

"Gay partners aren't considered family. Often, they're not even permitted to visit a loved one who may be dying. Can you imagine my mom pushing you aside to make my health decisions?"

"I'd be fine with that." I stick my tongue out at him. "Kidding." Greg gives me a half smile with one raised brow. "You know how I hate hospitals." Greg's mom was in the hospital for a long time when he was in high school. Back then, he didn't have the skills to cope and perhaps still doesn't. He catches me looking at him and hesitates. "Despite being mother and son, they seem unusually close." Greg focuses on the road as we wind through the pass on the access road.

"That's because Don's dad was the love of Edith's life. When he died in the Korean war, her baby son became everything—even after remarrying and having three more kids." I support my forehead with my palm. "Sometimes I want to punch Edith. Chuck sees Don in the hospital only because the doctors and nurses are his friends and know he and Don have been together for years."

Greg shakes his head. "You'd think Edith would appreciate all the loving care Chuck gives Don. She's at their house all the time, goes on all their vacations. I don't know how Chuck does it."

And we're living next door to Edith. "I can't imagine Edith ever being gracious. She controls her kids with the threat of losing their inheritance, manipulates them to always get her way." My head pounds. *What if Edith takes Chuck's house away from him?*

Greg says, "Don should tell her to back off."

"Yes, but it will never happen. Not now."

Through the car window, I breathe in the mountain air and allow myself to dream of fencing an area to corral with two horses in any one of these canyons. And above the horse pasture, we'll build a home on the rocky terrain, hidden from the highway—Greg, Tania, and me in our own little world.

I ask Greg, "When did you learn to ride?"

"I never really did. In grade school, I rode with my friends at some farm with horses. It was great. I haven't had the chance since high school. So I got a motorcycle instead."

As we drive along SR 138 toward Lancaster, the mountains part to reveal a desert valley.

Just past Three Points Road, a lonely building sits surrounded by campers, trailers, and junk cars.

"Stop. Pull over. There's a real estate office."

Greg pulls up to a strip of connected stores, including a grocery-cafe where we buy some cold sodas and peanuts. On the way out, we pick up a flyer off a rack with area listings and a map. The real estate office next door is closed, leaving us to venture on our own using the map as our guide.

We cross over the California Aqueduct, a concrete waterway. "It provides water to growers of almonds and hay," Greg says. We drive on roads made of desert sand, passing barren land backed by mountain ridges. A sign leads us to the Poppy Reserve. It's closed with no poppies in sight. Despite the dry heat, blue and red wildflowers thrive amid desert scrub. Before we head home, we park on the entrance road to stretch our legs and snap photos to remember the day.

When I was ten, a chunky, lonely girl, I wandered away from summer lake parties to dream of buying land somewhere in the Michigan mitten. I imagined driving a bulldozer to fill swampy areas and shape the land into a place I could live with my dogs and horses—a place to call home. I still want that, but now, I've switched my vision from Michigan pine trees to California Joshuas, from grass to desert sand.

CHAPTER TWENTY-SEVEN

LOSING DON 1988

In late August, classes resume at UCLA. In my small studio space off the main classroom, I pull out a bag of clay to begin a new series of female figures. Pinching fat coils of clay, I sculpt fifteen-inch goddesses, my version of archetypes—women who have often felt powerless throughout history in a patriarchal system. Books by Joseph Campbell inform my choices. Elements from nature—fire, water, earth, and air—merge with the female form imbued with magic, so I sculpt them without arms to become the goddess figures I envision. As they emerge, they empower me.

When I'm next up for critique, I explain my sacred space design with an antechamber where my female figures will stand. An undergrad, barely twenty, who someone invited to join us, blurts out, "That's not what women's breasts look like. They're supposed to sag."

"She's a water goddess. Hers float." I wanted to tell him how, in my twenties, mine wouldn't hold a pencil beneath them. Since it's not true anymore, I keep the story to myself.

"What about those?" he points at wind.

"They are symbolic figures. You need only know they're feminine."

The lanky, stringy-haired undergrad insists I explain about the lack of arms again.

"They're magic, so they don't need arms," I explain.

When he can't accept my logic, his continued attacks dredge up my insecurities from a lifetime of being teased. My insides curl into a ball. Why doesn't Adrian, the head of the clay department, rein him in? Or better yet, ask him to leave? My male classmates don't defend me. The other female grad student who sits two cubicles beyond my space remains silent. I've been searching for women professors, who would understand my work and inform my committee. Without tenure track, they teach for only two years, leaving one year before I graduate.

As I wrap up my presentation, the uninvited invader resumes berating me. "Those breasts are all wrong. Why not make them realistic?" I cast my eyes down, seething without answering.

After he finishes stripping me of all self-confidence, I run to the ladies' room and break into a full-blown ugly cry. When my shoulders stop shaking, I emerge from the stall to wash my face, releasing my anger and fear, letting it flow down the drain with the water. I long to be back in Indiana where my women teachers encouraged me. I lift my eyes to the mirror. *Why are you letting them push you around? Stand up for yourself.* My body vibrates with exhaustion, pulsing in time with my heartbeat. I need to go home. Greg will wrap me in his arms until I fall asleep. Maybe spirit guides will visit my dreams to tell me how to fight back.

Oh shit. I forgot to move my art out of the main classroom.

After fetching the goddesses and lining them up, safe in my cubicle, I walk to the parking garage with my head down to hide my shame. For the following week, I keep to myself to avoid breaking down again.

I'm working on a watercolor at home one evening in October, when Chuck calls.

"Debby?" I hear him swallow hard, but he doesn't try to correct himself. "Can you and Greg come over? I'm gathering the family. I think this is it."

I release my clamped jaw. "We'll be right over."

We bring a bottle of wine and a six-pack of beer for the vigil. Mom greets us at the door. "I'm glad you're here, honey."

I glance around the living room. Edith, Don's mom, and his sister, Linda, have staked out the club chairs, cast in soft light from the side table lamps. The dining room chandelier, just beyond, illuminates the table filled with casseroles, dropped off by friends and neighbors. The fragrance of fresh flowers in crystal vases set around the room fails to cover the scent of approaching death.

After we give my brother a hug, Greg heads into the kitchen with our donation to the liquor stash. I join Mom on the cushioned piano bench facing the picture window, with drapes nearly closed. The gap allows a glimpse of the lighted flagstone walk as people approach the front door to pay their respects. I squeeze her hand as we watch Chuck usher family and friends, one at a time, into the bedroom to spend their last moments with Don.

"Oh, Debby. It's just so sad."

"Where's Dick?" Each time I want quality time with Mom, I must deal with her alcoholic, sometimes downright mean, husband.

"He's out by the pool to smoke." Chuck smokes there too. When it rains, he stands under the eaves. No one smokes in the house—not ever.

When our big brother Mike, and his wife Judy, walk in, I rise to greet them. I spot Teddy, Don's nephew, sitting across the room on the well-worn sofa and wonder if Chuck is still getting new furniture. It hurt when he didn't call again to finish shopping for a sofa, but it's not the time to ask why. When Chuck calls Edith in to visit with Don, Mom touches my arm.

"Did I ever tell you what that woman said to me a few years back at one of Chuck's dinners?" she whispers, glancing around for anyone eavesdropping.

"No. What did she say?" Mom is polite to Edith but told me before she doesn't like her.

"She cornered me just after dessert and said, 'One day, Don will give me the grandkids I've always wanted.' I cringed when she told me, 'My son isn't really gay, and he will eventually figure that out.' Do you believe the gall of that woman?"

I shake my head, shocked that Edith would approach my mom with her dream of Don having kids. Mom never bugged me about grandkids. She didn't get to choose when Dad got her pregnant with Mike before they were married. The following year, she had Chuck, then two miscarriages between his birth and mine, which I only learned about in my twenties over several bottles of wine.

"Did you tell Chuck what she said?"

"I never had the nerve. It would've broken his heart." It must be terrible for Mom to hold on to this grievance this long. "He's always thought Edith had accepted him into her family. I couldn't tell him she's a two-faced liar. When Don is gone, she may turn him out onto the street."

I shake my head. "Chuck told me he isn't on the deed. Edith is. Don trusts her to do the right thing."

"That old biddy." Mom shakes her head. "She'd better. If she hurts my son, I don't know what I'll do."

I lean away to get a better look at her standing up for him. "Mom. I've never heard you talk this way."

"I'm sorry, dear. Usually, I hold my tongue. But my son's heart is breaking and there's nothing I can do." Her fists lay clenched in her lap. "It makes me furious." Darkness shadows her eyes, but she blinks it back into hiding.

I give her a long hug. Her body shakes, but the tears don't come. She's holding them back, afraid she might fall apart. I'm doing the same thing. Chuck comes out of the room and walks over to Mom. *How is he keeping it together?*

He bends down and whispers to her, "Do you want to spend a few minutes with Don?"

"Is he lucid at all?"

"No. Not since this morning."

"Well, dear. Then I think not. If you don't mind. I've already said my goodbyes. I'm here for you...whatever you need."

"Thanks Mom. Debby, how about you?"

I let the name thing pass. I nod and follow him to their bedroom. Dick comes in and takes my seat next to Mom. Better him than Edith.

In the hall, Chuck says, "Tell Don it's okay for him to go. He's been holding on for all of us for too long." I nod my understanding.

The room is dimly lit. Don lies motionless in the center of their king-sized bed. The brass head and foot, and the marble balls atop, glisten in the lamplight, looking almost magical. Oxygen tanks remain in a row along the wall near the bed. The transparent tube connected to the first tank splits into two near his nose and is held in place with a narrow elastic band around his head. Don's skin is ashen; his only visible sign of life is his chest faintly rising. He doesn't seem in pain but struggles to take in the life-sustaining oxygen. An icy presence chases across my skin despite the warm air lingering from the sunny day. I sit in the chair on the right side of the bed to cover his frail hand with mine, and softly say, "I love you, Don. You have meant so much to me. But now it's time for you to be free from the shackles of this plague. I release you to walk with the angels, and I promise…I'll take care of Chuck."

I kiss his cheek, then walk over to Chuck standing near the door. "How are you doing?"

His face collapses, then perks up, I suspect for my benefit. "I'm okay. It's nice, isn't it? Having everyone here. This is the way it should be—family and friends remembering the good times and all the wonderful things Don has done for them."

I turn to see if Don is still breathing. "I love him like a brother." His chest rises and falls like water onto a shore on a windless day. "Just remember, Chuck, I'm here for you. Whatever you need."

"Thanks, Sis."

In the living room, I settle next to Greg on the sofa with a plate of snacks and a drink to wait for the news that will break my brother's heart…and mine.

A few hours later, Chuck comes out to tell us Don is gone. Mom kisses Chuck on the cheek. "I'm sorry, honey. What can I do?"

"Thanks for being here, Mom. I have lots of help. It's late. Why don't you and Dick head home?"

She gives Chuck a hug, then returns to her already drunk husband, looping her arm under him to steady his swaying, directing him toward the front door. Edith goes into the bedroom. A moment later, she comes out, says something to Chuck that I can't hear, then leaves. Greg tells me, "I'll walk home and leave the car for you." I kiss his cheek. The handful of people who remain start putting food away.

I approach Chuck. "So what happens now?" Like Mom, I want to wrap him in my arms and take the pain away, but I can't save him.

"I called the mortuary. They'll be here in an hour." He's keeping busy, doing what needs to be done. *Watch and learn, Deborah, for when it's your turn.*

"Why that long?"

"I want to wash and shave him before they come," he says proudly.

"Do you want help?" I ask, unsure if I can.

He shakes his head. "I want to do it myself." I choke back my useless words of comfort.

As Chuck moves toward the bedroom door, I tell him, "I'll wait here," I point to the club chair next to the fireplace. "If you need anything."

While reading last month's *House Beautiful*, alone in the quiet, I doze off, waking to a knock at the door and Chuck letting in the men in black suits. In minutes, they appear with a long black bag resting on a shiny chrome gurney and roll it out to their ebony hearse at the end of the stone walkway.

How different this was from my other experiences with death. My first husband, Mark, lost his dad, mom, and aunt while we were married. None had a family gathering at the deathbed, only the funeral. I don't know where Chuck learned this ritual, but I'm committing it to memory.

A woman minister who knew Don presides over his memorial at her Lutheran church. During the service, some of the mourners write personal notes and place them in a basket next to Don's coffin. When Chuck takes the podium, he promises, "No one will read your notes but Don."

After the service, Greg and I drive an hour to the cemetery. Twenty of us, including Mike, Judy, Mom and Dick, stand near the grave, and Dad, who arrives late, stands behind us. Edith stands next to Chuck as he places the notes, Tawna's ashes, and a ring he had given Don into the coffin. We each say our final words to Don, then walk in silence back to our cars. Chuck hangs back, resting his hand on Don's coffin.

Some friends and family had gone from the church directly to the house to set up. We enter through the kitchen; food and drink cover the dining room table with Birds of Paradise flowers as the centerpiece. The house is full of people—most I don't know. Volunteers placed flowers from the service throughout the house. Through the sliding door, guests head outside to walk around the pool bordered with blooming fall annuals, bursting with color. I pour a glass of wine, fill a plate, and walk into the living room, nearly dropping my plate onto the beige carpet. Chuck bought a new sofa—the white sectional I advised against—didn't tell me and had it delivered in time for the reception.

I find Greg outside, chatting with Don's nephew, and touch his arm. "I'm going home to change out of these shoes." *I'd better escape before I do something I'll regret.*

As I walk out the door, Mom asks to ride with me to see our house. We climb into my white truck, and I drive the short distance in silence. Once in the living room, Mom asks what's wrong.

"Chuck lied to me," I am screaming, pacing back and forth in the overcrowded living room, maneuvering within narrow pathways. "He's just like Dad."

Mom looks in my eyes and backs away.

"Why ask for my advice if he has no intention of taking it? I'm sick of people who don't appreciate my time and talent."

"Debby Ann," Mom says, her voice measured. "Stop." Mom's voice becomes soft but remains firm. "You're scaring me."

When I hear my childhood name, I shake out of my rage to recognize my father's voice inside me. *Why am I shouting?* I never wanted to be like Dad, especially not today. I touch my face and feel the radiating heat. Tania, too, is cowering behind the sofa.

Mom stares at me. She spent years managing Dad's temper. And now, manages Dick's.

"I never knew you had this much fierceness in you."

I shake out my fists. "Neither did I."

As I center myself, something changes inside me. I recognize a power. If I can control the anger and use it instead, I won't cry the next time a man scolds or dismisses me. Instead, I will speak up for myself.

CHAPTER TWENTY-EIGHT

HIGH DESERT DREAM 1989

Chuck retreats into his house after Don is laid to rest.

I can't sleep nor focus on my art. Attempting to load fragile unfired clay into a kiln would be a disaster. Living next to Edith triggers twisted scenarios that churn in my head. A friend comes to save the day. Dian makes a surprise visit from Fort Wayne.

I leave my studio work at UCLA to drive her two hours north through the mountains, into the high desert, across the flat to the Poppy Reserve to see the wildflowers and Joshua trees that Greg and I discovered a few weeks ago. We descend into the desert valley. "Isn't it beautiful? Stark, but magical. At twilight, the Joshua trees come alive to dance in the changing light." Back in Fort Wayne, Dian and I often talked about magic in the natural world. We came up with a metaphysical connection between us in a past life—we were both priestesses in the Temple of Isis in ancient Egypt. It feels true.

"I can feel the energy of the mountains all around us," Dian says. "So different from the fields of green back home. Is this where you want to build?"

I nod, with my eyes wide like a kid on Christmas morning. I turn off the paved road and cross the California Aqueduct. Where the blacktop ends, the sand-packed road becomes indistinguishable from the surrounding landscape.

To stay on track, I follow tread marks left by other vehicles, using the realtor's hand-drawn map along with the aid of occasional street signs, one hand-painted on scrap wood. Cactus with outstretched arms cast their form across the desert sand, shadows dancing in the late day sun.

"What are we looking for?" Dian asks. The sameness of the sand muddles my memory from my excursion with Greg.

"When we picked up the map, we heard about a man in his 90s who owns most of the land around here. They said he won't sell to anyone he doesn't know. I figure if I could meet him, maybe I could persuade him to sell us a plot of land at a price we can afford." The cost of homes near Chuck made us recognize we have no hope of ever buying a place in LA. "We could put a mobile home on it until we could afford to build. I'm hoping we'll get lucky and run into this guy."

At the next crossroad, Dian points to the foothill rising from the desert in front of us backed by a mountain range. "See that house?"

My eyes follow her outstretched arm. At the crest of the foothill sits a lone house, with brush cleared around like a halo. Scrub oak, along with a bush of twisting red and white branches, cover the remaining hillside.

"What a view those folks have! Can you imagine? Looking out at the Joshua trees every day." My heart flutters. "They can sit on their porch every night to look up at the stars, and every morning, drink coffee with a sunrise."

Dian says, "Maybe it's for sale."

"It's a nice dream, but we can't afford a house. Only land."

"Look!" Dian yells. "There's a truck coming." A white truck, like what I'm driving, approaches us. "I wonder if that's him." Dian and I look at each other, eyes wide, lips turned up into grins.

"That would be a definite sign from the universe." I'm worried we'll get stuck in the sand if I keep going, so I pull my foot off the accelerator and slow to a stop. I'm a dozen feet from the other truck, which has also stopped. "I guess we'll find out." I gape at two men while Dian wears her Cheshire grin.

A lanky man in his nineties emerges from the driver's side and walks toward us. I rise out of my seat and walk toward his truck. Is he the one? *C'mon, Deborah. Your imagination is running away with you.* Why do I question the magic of the moment?

The man smiles. "Are you lost?"

"No, but I am looking for someone." I show him the realtor's map in my hand.

He turns his weathered face up and connects with my eyes. "Can I help you?"

I moisten my lips. "I'm looking for the man who owns this land to see if I could buy a plot."

His face brightens. "You've found him. But this land is not for sale —not right now." He turns, lifting his arm, revealing his baked skin, wrinkled from a near-century of exposure. "Would you be interested in a house?" He points to the house on the hill. "I've just finished building it."

With my heart in my throat, I look back at Dian. She has her head out the window, listening, and nods.

I turn back to the landowner, not wanting to tell him we can't afford a house. "Could we see it? If you have the time?" No harm in looking.

"Follow me." He returns to his truck.

When I slide behind the wheel, Dian and I look at each other, holding a hand across our mouths to keep from laughing, bending forward to hide it.

He backs up to a wider section and turns around. I'm relieved I won't get stuck in the deep sand. We follow in his tracks back toward the paved road, turning south before crossing the aqueduct. After we circle around a long ridge, we climb up the backside, next to a deep canyon.

I park on a flat next to the man's truck. Jumping out, Dian and I follow him up the covered walkway along the front of the house.

At the front door, he introduces himself. "I'm Al."

"Deborah." We shake hands. "This is my friend Dian, visiting from Indiana."

He walks us throughout the house, sharing his story. In the late twenties, he'd driven his Model T across the country from Michigan until he came upon this valley. Despite the Great Depression, he scraped together enough money for a down payment on a hundred acres of land, including the foothills, the canyon community, and the desert at the mouth of the canyon where we met. He points from the back porch to a house below.

"I built my home, divided the remaining acreage into ten-acre plots, and dropped the first of several community wells." Standing in front of the stone fireplace, he explains, "I chose each family to live in the half-dozen homes we passed on the way here in the valley." Horses dozed in fenced enclosures next to each house. "I call it Kings Canyon."

The house is lovely. Bright and simple. Well built. Isolated from the others. "I study art at UCLA, but I've dreamed my whole life of having a horse of my own."

"There's room for a horse up on the hill next to the water tank. If you like the house, I'll sell it to you for one hundred and fifty thousand."

The price is low compared to the cost of homes in Van Nuys on tiny city lots. None of them have anything close to an acre, let alone ten.

"I like the house—especially the view." I swallow hard. It's a long commute. Still, I want it. I feel like I belong here. He's waiting for an answer. "There's a lot to consider. I need to talk to my husband. And he'll need to see it."

After we exchange phone numbers, Dian and I head back to LA.

All the way home, we giggle about meeting Al. The magical serendipity seems hard to deny.

When I show Greg the house a few days later, he says, "I like it, but it would be a long drive for both of us. Maybe I can get into outside sales and work from home. Do you think you could manage the drive to UCLA?"

I nod nervously as my imagination soars. "The mortgage payments would be the same as the rent we are paying to Emily."

Greg rubs the ridge on his brow. "I don't know how we'll come up with the down payment. Let's think about it."

I let out a deep sigh. This isn't going to happen. *Let it go.*

But I can't let it go. I feel destiny pulling me to the high desert. "If we can't buy the house, maybe we can still buy some land and build a house later."

It's the Joshua trees—I can't explain it. They are calling to me.

CHAPTER TWENTY-NINE

HOME, LOST AND FOUND 1989

A few days later, I sit with Chuck on his new white sectional, listening as he laments about the insurance money he collected from Don's death. Two hundred and fifty thousand dollars.

"It feels like blood money," Chuck complains. "I don't want it." Instead of looking at me, he stares out the window at a bird hopping on his lawn. "I want Don." Tears well up in his eyes. "This house feels empty without him." He drops his head. "I feel him sitting next to me…or imagine him in the kitchen, cooking dinner." Chuck peers through the galley kitchen as if at a ghost. My heart breaks for him, but I can't help. No one can.

After a few minutes of eerie silence, I ask him, "What are you going to do with it?"

"I'm giving it away to friends who need it. I enjoy helping them."

My brother is too generous for his own good. I knead his statement in my mind. "But what if you need it later?"

"If that happens, I'll deal with it. I may not be around for long."

"I hate it when you talk like that." When he gets sick again, how will I take care of him? I need a place far away from Edith. Maybe he might help with the house. *But how do I bring it up?*

He notices. "So how are you doing living next door to Edith?"

Squirming in my seat, I say. "I've been avoiding her. If she says something horrible, I'll lose it. It's adding stress to what's going on at school."

"She's been here taking what she wants." His face is blank, like he's checked out.

"Without asking you?" My rage flares, but I dampen it.

"I don't want to argue. They're just things."

"They're treasures that hold your memories. I'll get them back for you." My fists clench at my side, hidden from Chuck.

"Don't!" he says more forcefully than I expected. "It'll only make things worse."

I take in a labored breath. "I can't stand it. I'm having nightmares of her sneaking into our house, poking around my art, screwing up my watercolors."

"Are you thinking of moving?"

"I'm working on a plan, but I don't know how to make it work." I tell him about wanting to build a house in the high desert, about meeting Al, and seeing the house up on the ridge that he's just finished building to sell.

"What does Greg think?"

"He thinks it's great. The mortgage would be the same as our rent, but we can't come up with the down payment."

"I could give it to you. What do you need? Twenty Percent?"

To stop this moment in time, I hold my breath. I'm worried I'll regret this. *I shouldn't have told him about this house.*

I push my fingers into my temples. "I don't want your money. You need to hang onto it."

He looks out the window at his manicured front yard. "I'll just give it to somebody else."

Is that a threat? Or a manipulation. I'm torn. To protect him, I'll end up owing him even more.

"If we buy the house, there's an extra bedroom. We'll have a place for you to come and stay, but that is up to you." I shake my head. "Don't help us unless you want to."

I know my brother. If I push him to live with us, it will push him away. I don't want that. But I need to move. And buying this house would put us back where we were before leaving Fort Wayne but with a larger mortgage. Rent for our first year in LA used up all the profit from selling our home. It's more expensive to live here than in the Midwest.

I stare at my brother, waiting. He must decide.

"So this is it?" he asks. "The house you've always wanted?"

Cautiously, I nod. "You'd like it. It overlooks the Poppy Reserve."

"Don loved going out to see the poppies." He looks up as if seeing a movie of his past on the ceiling.

"I can show it to you. It's brand new with a beautiful kitchen and some land, more than anything we could afford here in the Valley." *Don't show him the house if you don't want the money.*

"That's for sure. You couldn't buy our house for that price." He looks around the home he'd created with Don. How is he even out of bed? If I lost Greg, I'd collapse in grief for months, if not years.

"At the base of the foothill below the house is a forest of Joshua trees. I never expected to meet the owner driving down the road. The whole thing is unbelievable. Full of synchronicity."

"I wish Don could have seen it. It's not that far from the cabin."

I nod, then stare at my folded hands in my lap. Is this destiny leading me again? Are we fated to buy that house? Or is my yearning to fulfill my childhood dream pushing me too far too fast? It's a risk, but one I'm willing to take…if Chuck agrees.

"Give me a couple of days. I'll have a certified check for you."

My mouth gapes. "You don't want to see it first?"

"No. If you're sure this is what you want, I'll give you the down payment. I just need the seller's name. It'll be a long drive," his face lights up, "but a pretty one."

Chuck gets such joy from giving. Over the years, he's found unique clothing for me that fits perfectly. I still have a halter sun dress he gave me five years ago. It's one of my favorites. If this gives him joy, how can I say no?

"I can't wait for you see it." Now I need to tell Greg. I hope he agrees. Chuck seems content with his decision. Maybe when Chuck is ready to leave this house behind, he'll stay with us, if only to see the poppies.

"I hope this makes you happy." Chuck leans back into the chaise that is part of his new sectional. "Someone in our family needs to be."

I'll be happy if I never see Edith again, and I'll have a bedroom for Chuck when he needs my help...but he's not ready to hear about that yet. I hug my brother, and he hugs me back.

By the time I'm out the door, I slump with regret. I'm about to go back and tell him I've changed my mind, but rejecting his gift now would be a slap in the face.

The high desert house is where I will take care of Chuck. My enthusiasm burns bright, but doubts remain.

Two weeks later, we close on the new house and move. On one of our trips, Greg spots a sign saying, "Free German shepherd puppies." He picked out a male to help keep Tania safe when coyotes come near, but when he brought me back for the final decision, a female climbed into my purse. We took them both, naming them Brandy and Alexander, Alex for short.

We're making our last trip down the mountains to Emily's house to clean the carpets, kitchen, and bathroom and get our deposit back. After scrubbing for two hours, we load our cleaning supplies and vacuum into the back of the truck. With Tania in the cab squeezed between us, we pull onto the street. Three blocks away, we pass a U-Haul parked on the street near Chuck's drive.

"Greg, pull over. Something's doesn't feel right."

He parks behind the U-Haul truck. I jump out, pushing Tania toward Greg to keep her from following me. The streets are too busy with traffic for her to be running loose. Chuck appears in the kitchen door. He's carrying boxes and doesn't see me until he sets them on the deck of the truck. I stand dumbfounded, confused, not wanting to believe the horror before me.

Chuck looks at me blankly. "There's nothing you can do."

His abruptness unhinges me. "What's going on?" I ask, even though I know in my gut.

"Isn't it obvious? I'm moving." Anger fills his face and fire darts out of his eyes.

"Why?" This doesn't make sense. He loves this house.

"Edith filed the quit claim deed. She owns the house. And she's selling it."

"Edith is putting you out on the street?" Hearing her name makes me want to vomit. "When?"

"Yesterday. No warning. She showed up with a realtor. Says she's giving me a week to vacate," he says, his eyes steeled. "She offered me some of the profit to help me move, but I don't want her money." He pushes the boxes into the van, making room for more. "I'll be fine. I want an apartment, anyway. This place is too much for me to keep. I want to simplify my life."

That sounds like Edith talking, not Chuck.

He leans against the truck and lights a cigarette. "Don is rolling over in his grave. I told him this would happen, but he didn't believe me. He believed her. She promised the house would be mine. She lied to her son as he lay dying." He seems about to cry but shakes it off.

"I'm going to stop this." I declare without knowing how.

"I don't care." He speaks each word hard, forcing it out from his chest then turns his back on me. He steps on his half-smoked cigarette butt, and heads toward the kitchen door.

I try to keep my voice steady, worried my rage will bleed through. "I'll talk to Edith."

He halts and turns to look at me. "No. I'm tired of fighting her. It just makes everything worse. She won't listen. Not to anyone. Not with Don gone. She only listened to him. Anyway, without him, it's just a house. She can have it."

Edith has fulfilled Chuck's worst fears. He loves his home and, while caring for Don around the clock, he has managed with the help of a gardener to keep it immaculate. Why didn't Don prevent this? Chuck gave him everything. I've never trusted Edith to keep her word, and neither has Chuck. Why did Don? How did his mother's demands trump his fierce love for Chuck? No matter how many questions I have, nothing will change what is happening.

When my brother appears at the door, I grab the box from his arms to load into the truck.

"I wish you hadn't given us that money, but it's too late to get it back. We've already closed on the house." I want to burst into tears, but I redirect it into anger toward Edith.

Chuck leans against the moving van and lights another cigarette. "It wouldn't have changed her mind. Edith doesn't need the money. She's loaded. It's her revenge on me for making her son happy. If it weren't for me, she could have forced him to marry and give her a grandchild. Don was all she had left from his dad—her only true love —who died in the war. Now they are both gone forever. I understand. I just wish she didn't hate me. It's like losing Don all over again."

I'm seething with hate for that woman. She's punishing my brother for loving her son. Maybe one day, she'll need help, and no one will answer her call. I hope she dies a lonely, miserable death. But that's no consolation for Chuck. He's not vengeful. I feel a crack in my reality, a gorge opening with no bottom visible in the blackness, yet I am tempted to fall into it to relieve this pain.

Chuck opens the door to the kitchen and a flash of tricolor fur squeezes out. Tania barks from inside our truck, slobbering on the window. Greg grabs her collar.

I'm watching Greg wrestle with Tania when I hear tires screech.

"Wolfie!" I'm screaming inside and out. "Oh my god. No!"

He's lying in the street. The car that hit him pulls over and a hysterical woman emerges. It happened in the instant between seconds.

Before I can move, Chuck runs into the street. Greg jumps out of the car, pushing Tania back in. He helps Chuck lift Wolfie's limp body into the seat of Chuck's car.

Chuck throws me his house keys.

I nod.

I check this kitchen for anything needing turned off or unplugged, switch off the lights, then lock the door. By the time I've closed the U-

Haul door, Chuck's car is out of sight. I tuck his keys into my pocket. Chuck has got a spare under a rock in front. I climb into our truck cab to hug Tania, holding her as Greg pulls onto the highway heading north.

First, Chuck buries the love of his life. Then he loses his home filled with the memories of their time together. Edith takes it all. Now he may lose his dog. How much more does Chuck have to take?

Chuck asks me to meet him at his vet's office a few days later. "I need help transporting him." Wolfie survived but must wear a cast on his broken leg for six weeks. Chuck's new apartment is on the third floor with only stairs for access. Wolfie can't do stairs in his cast.

The vet techs place Wolfie in my little truck on the seat next to me, his cast resting on the floor. I follow Chuck to his new apartment a few blocks over because he didn't give me the address. He pulls into the gated parking below, signaling me to park on the street. He reappears walking up the ramp. I leave Wolfie and I meet him in the street.

He says, "This building doesn't allow pets."

"Can't you find one that does?" Chuck loves Wolfie. How will he manage without him curled on the sofa next to him?

"This is the best I can find. I have friends to help me get settled." He glances at the guys standing near the building, lighting up. "You go home. Take care of Wolfie. He's your dog now."

He turns and disappears with his friends inside the building. Even with them, he's alone. He won't move in with us—not yet. He's determined to make his own way first. At least I'm helping by taking in Wolfie.

I want to go up and see his new place, but I can't leave Wolfie in the car alone. I note the address on the building and the street name, then drive away. With one hand reassuring Wolfie on the seat next to me, I drift into my thoughts. How do I deal with Chuck distancing himself from me? *Okay, Chuck. You do what you need to do, and I'll go create a beautiful home. When you need me, I'll be ready. We are only an hour's drive from here.*

CHAPTER THIRTY

A HORSE AND A HELICOPTER 1989

The spring poppies and Indian paintbrush are blooming in the high desert. We settle into our new home between trips for Greg's work and my school *down below*—that's what the high desert locals call LA. Most of our neighbors, working-class people, invest their extra time and money in their horses. When we stop to say hi to one at the end of his drive, we ask about his Arabians. He tells us they compete in endurance races, including the race they host in the community. *I want a horse in our backyard.*

A few weeks later, I'm in Lancaster ten miles away for groceries where I pick up the Antelope Valley News to search for a horse I can afford, maybe one retired from racing but with enough basic training to ride him through the foothills and maybe in a dressage clinic. Circling an ad for a four-year-old Thoroughbred, I call his trainer, Shae Rooney, and arrange to ride the gelding that afternoon.

I dig for some short boots in my closet, ones with heels that won't slip through stirrups, then drive twenty minutes to the far side of the mountain from our place in Kings Canyon to Shae's facility. The five-foot-two-inch blonde-haired beauty, who used to break and gallop Thoroughbreds, Quarter horses, and Arabians for the racetrack, greets me and walks me back behind her house to her horses. "Now, I mostly train jumpers and teach kids to ride." We walk to a shed where she has him tied.

"This is Lance," she says as she opens the gate to the stall. In the dim light, a bay gelding stands quietly in a halter with the lead rope looped over his neck and a saddle on his back. He's dark brown, almost black, with a black mane, tail, and legs. At seventeen-hands, his withers are level with the top of my head and his long neck stretches up from there, his ears nearly touching the shed roof.

Shae hands me a bridle with a snaffle bit. "After you bridle him, be sure to tighten the girth."

The last time I rode was in 1968 when I first moved to LA and tried to buy a horse before I even had an apartment—21 years ago, but I remember everything. I reach up to stroke his nose and he drops his head. When I raise the bit to his mouth, he accepts it, but is fussy when I pull the leather strap over his ears.

Shae says, "I've been working with his ears, and he's better now, but needs a gentle hand. They must have twitched him at the track." I'd heard of but never seen the torture device which controls a horse by twisting and torquing his ear. The pain endorphins make him stand still but have terrible consequences, like making him head shy.

I lead Lance out to the arena with jumps, and cavaletti—low cross-rails used in training. Shae hands me a helmet. "Put this on." She holds him while I mount, putting weight in the far stirrup as I pull myself up. "He has a nice walk if you give him his head." She steps back to watch how I handle him.

I let out the reins until they are loose and squeeze my legs gently against his sides. He radiates power from his long, slanted shoulder, even at an easy walk with his extended stride. We circle the jumps twice. "Now ask for a trot," Shae says, watching from the center.

Shortening the reins, I squeeze his sides with more pressure, stand in my stirrups, then sit in rhythm with his big stride. I feel him talk to me through the reins, his legs an extension of my own. I'm flying once again, only this time I'm not dreaming. Our connection is immediate. Lance is my soulmate.

I call Chuck and he agrees to give me the two hundred dollars I'm short to buy Lance. "I'll bring you a check this weekend." He hadn't let me visit his apartment. I was glad I'd created a reason for him to come see us. When he arrives, we serve beer and Mexican food on the deck to watch the sun set over the poppies and Joshua trees. Chuck is elated with our new home.

I couldn't bring Lance home without another horse to keep him company. "Horses need a herd," Shae says when I bring the money to buy him, "even if it's only a herd of two." She suggests we take the chestnut Quarter Horse, a mare named Liesta, on loan from her friend Ginger, who is in a wheelchair.

"You can have her on a feed lease—you pay for her food, the farrier, and any vet bills. She'll be company for Lance and a horse for Greg to ride. You can keep her until early next year when Ginger plans to breed her to a sassy black stallion."

Greg learned to ride as a kid by getting on farm horses with friends. He is eager to ride Liesta, confident his natural athleticism will compensate for the lessons he never had.

"I'll give him a brush-up on the basics," Shae says. She tells us where to buy hay and feed and who to call for shoeing and vet checks. When the hay arrives, she shows us how to check it for mold, and how to watch for symptoms of colic.

The following day, Greg and I use a posthole digger to drop round wooden posts two feet into the sand-like decomposed granite of this high desert. We wrap the posts with small square, wrapped-wire fencing recommended for horses, attached to three-sided shelters we built for each to create corrals on the hill above our house. When Shae trailers Lance and Leista to our ranch, she stays to take me on my first California high desert trail ride. We head down our sand-packed road on the two horses and up a path into the mountains behind a half-dozen ten-acre ranches that comprise our neighborhood. On this ride and many that follow, Shae and I talk about horses, art, and spirituality, bonding as soul sisters.

Every day when I come home from classes at UCLA, I work with Lance—brushing him, picking up his feet to pick out manure and any stones caught between the frog and hoof wall that would bruise the sole and cause lameness. Then I mount him from a wooden box to not dislodge the saddle getting on. With Greg on Liesta, we explore the road that winds around the foothills, through the small community of ranches, and to the flat desert where Joshua trees grow. We don't venture any further than the aqueduct five miles from our house where the mailboxes stand in a long row on the paved highway.

One day early in May, Shae tells me Ginger, Liesta's owner, needs a place to keep a Thoroughbred broodmare.

"Ruby is in foal to Ginger's Quarter Horse stallion, Dusty. She wants the foal, but after he's weaned, you can keep Ruby on a feed lease. Then you can breed her to the stallion of your choice for the baby you want to raise. Ruby is too broken down to ride, but she's a lovely chestnut with good confirmation and a nice head."

When Greg comes home from work, I tell him about Ruby. "She'll be practice for having our own foal. And she won't cost us anything for a year. Ginger will reimburse all costs." When he agrees, we add one more stall with a shed shelter and accept Ruby into our growing herd. Every fiber in my limbs dances. *I can raise a foal from birth.* But I'll wait to make plans until after she's foaled. She will be my teacher.

A month later, I wake up to the smell of alcohol and Pine-Sol. When my eyes adjust, I recognize the stark hospital room. My head hurts and feels disconnected from the lower half of my body. *Now what have I done?*

"I've been waiting for you to wake up." It's Shae, my friend with the face of an angel and the energy of a whirling dervish.

"How did I get here? I remember crawling into the house, some commotion, then the pain from a bumpy ride down our hill. Nothing much after that."

"You don't remember?"

"I was getting on Lance. I'd left the dogs outside. When they run in the pasture, the horses ignore them."

"Your neighbor Marge found you."

"Who?" I roll my head back and forth on the pillow but stop because it's throbbing. "I don't know her." *What a way to meet a neighbor.*

Shae smiles. "She says thanks for the helicopter ride."

"The what?" The racket made by the rotating blades resurfaces in my dulled brain.

"Marge said they saw Lance on the hill with his saddle and knew something was wrong. She found you unconscious…and alone. The medics said she should come with you. Her first time in a helicopter. She loved it."

"Shit. I need to feed the animals. Greg's not home. When do I get out of here?"

She glares at me. "The nurse says you have a concussion, a fractured pelvis, and two cracked ribs," she scoffs as she pulls a strand away from her face. "You were lucky you didn't puncture a lung."

"I remember Lance moved as I stepped in the stirrup. As I swung my leg over, he started bucking." I pause and draw in some air until I feel a knife-like pain. "The dogs barked and nipped at Lance's back legs." My chest feels on fire from just breathing. "He kicked at them as he bucked, but the dogs kept going after him."

"They thought they were helping." She hands me a cup of water with a bent straw. "Do you remember coming off?"

I grab at the memory to find nothing but more pounding behind my eyes. "No." I take a sip. The sucking smarts but holding the moisture in my mouth helps relieve my desert dry tongue. "Are the dogs hurt?"

"Marge says everyone is fine. Lance, Leista, and the dogs. Everyone except you."

"I clung to his mane." Details are emerging from the fog in my brain. "He bucked like eight feet high. I thought he'd never stop."

"He's a big horse."

"I was sprawled across his back with my legs behind me and couldn't get my seat. When I bounced, I kept hitting the pommel. I guess I fell under his feet."

"I bet your head bounced too."

This is a disaster. I can't be laid up; I have too much to do.

Shae sits in the chair next to my bed. "How's your head feeling now?"

"Like a beating drum. My chest aches. I hurt all over." I put my hand between my breasts where it hurts. "How did you know I was here?"

"Marge called me to sit with you. She went to feed your horses." The light sneaking through the blind glistens in Shae's platinum strands. "I'm not surprised to see you in here."

I stare at her. "Why?" I hope she doesn't regret selling me Lance.

"With the pace you've been going, something was bound to happen. You need to slow down. When you don't, the universe kicks your butt. It's taken a wreck for you to hear it."

The seriousness of my injuries sinks in when I can't lift my head.

"Does Greg know?" I mumble, turning my head away.

"No one knows how to reach him."

"He's in Fort Wayne at a sales meeting." *He's going to be mad.* I put my hand to my brow as reality breaks through the pharmaceutical fog. "How am I going to finish the work I'm doing at school this summer?" I try to pull myself up by grabbing the chrome rails, but the pain knocks me back down.

"Take it easy," Shae says, soothing me like I'm a nervous horse.

"I need to go home."

"Marge said to tell you not to worry. She's got it."

I let myself collapse back into the thin pillow. Shae picks up the room phone. "Now focus. Can you remember Greg's office number there?"

I rattle off the numbers as she dials. When he answers, she hands me the phone.

By the next afternoon, Greg is standing in my room, shaking his head. His brow is furrowed more than usual. "I'm okay. Really. I'll be on my feet before you know it. The doctors insist I stay for another couple of days, but all they can do is control the pain." I hope they send me home with a boatload of painkillers.

As I lie in the hospital, I imagine Lance standing in his corral wondering what happened to me. *It wasn't your fault, Lance. I will heal and we'll explore the desert and mountains again soon.*

When I arrive home, with nothing but a prescription for pain meds, all my chores are waiting for me. I can't rest with them staring me in the face. Greg has already pounded most of the steel T-posts on the hill to create a pasture, of sorts, for the horses. "I want to help run the hot-wire for a pasture fence to give them some room to run around. I promise I won't lift anything heavy. And walking is good therapy."

Needing the help, he reluctantly agrees. As he pops the insulators onto the posts to hold the wire, I hobble around after him, unreeling the heavy roll of steel wire while the horses watch from their enclosures. Even though the unstable sand wreaks havoc on my injured pelvis, I stick it out for two hours, then crawl back to the couch in tears.

CHAPTER THIRTY-ONE

THE PARTY BUS 1989

Dian, my massage therapist friend from Indiana, refers me to Eric, a local practitioner of Hellerwork, a deep tissue myofascial and structural integration technique. She raves about it and assures me it is just what I need to heal.

With Greg back at work, I drive the ninety minutes twice a week to Eric's office at the back of his house in Van Nuys. He, like Shae and Dian, warns me—if I keep ignoring my body's signals, I will take longer to heal. I'm my mother's daughter, caring for my family—both two and four legged—even when I'm exhausted, making me accident prone. I need to rest, but how—there's too much to do.

After four weeks of Eric's manipulations, my pain eases, my flexibility improves. I'm ready to break out of my recovery routine when I receive a call from Scotty. He's my brother's new roommate who we met the last time Chuck visited us. "I'm hosting your brother's birthday celebration—bar hopping to the top gay watering holes in Hollywood. Can you and Greg join us? I'm renting a van, so Chuck won't try to drive and wear himself out. He didn't want a party, but this way he can't refuse."

I eagerly reply, "Great idea! We'd love to."

On August 1st, the eve of his forty-third birthday, we gather with his friends in front of Chuck's apartment to pile into the back of a van. Sunny, who volunteered to be the designated driver, turns onto the Hollywood freeway, heading south. With the van's high top and bench seats along the sides, we're able to stand without bending to move about the vehicle. My hips are still sore, but after a beer, I'm feeling no pain.

Scotty sits next to me on the van bench seat. As we chat, I learn he's active as an artist and actor, despite having AIDS. "So, are you and Chuck together?" I ask timidly.

"No," Scotty says. "He's helping me as a friend, giving me a place to live." Scotty passes me a fresh cup of beer from the small keg and whispers, "Greg is amazing. He seems comfortable hanging out with us."

"Greg knows who he is and doesn't judge others. Since we first met, he accepted Chuck and Don as family. When we lived in Indiana, he came to LA on business and visited them. Chuck had friends over for drinks around and in the pool, and Greg joined the party. But he's never been to a gay bar."

"Don't worry," Scotty says with a Cheshire grin. "I won't let anyone bother him." He glances across at Greg. "We've made a plan to keep him safe."

Before I can ask what he means, we pull up to the bar where guys are making out near the entrance. We pile out and walk single file through the door, each showing our ID to the bouncer as we pass.

My eyes adjust to the dim light inside and focus on a well-muscled stud standing at the bar wearing a leather vest and chaps. I gasp. The guy is wearing nothing else. I can't take my eyes off his bare well-muscled derriere framed by black leather. I hope he's wearing a cup in the front.

At eleven, I first saw the bare bottoms of showgirls in Vegas with Mom and Dad. Friends took me to Chippendales on Ventura for my bachelorette party and we had a blast. But they were performers on a stage. This guy is a customer standing at the bar. When Chuck tended bar in the valley, the crowd was less flamboyant.

Chuck comes up behind me to see how I'm coping with the nudity. He should know by now his little sister doesn't shock that easily.

I lean over and whisper to him, "Doesn't he get cold?"

Chuck grins and wraps his arm around my shoulder, escorting me to the other side of the bar near the pool tables.

"If you don't stop staring, you may cause a ruckus. They're not used to women in here."

"Did Greg see that?" I look around for him.

"Yeah. It's nothing he hasn't seen in gym class."

"That's my Greggy." I glow with pride. Chuck escorts me to a stool at the bar and orders me a beer.

After shooting a game of pool with Chuck, I switch my drink to white wine spritzers and strike up a conversation with the bartender.

"I'm here celebrating my brother's birthday. We have a party van and we're hitting all the hottest clubs." I point to Chuck, his flaming hair easy to spot on the dance floor. "He's redheaded too."

"I haven't seen you in here before." He smirks.

Greg taps me on the shoulder. "Did you bring extra cash?" He's flashing his silly grin as he turns out his jeans pocket. "I've spent what I brought, and I want to shoot some more pool." I hand him a twenty from my purse. The bartender breaks it for him, and he returns to a far corner to shoot pool with Scotty.

"Is he part of your group?" the bartender asked.

"That's my husband." I watch as Greg walks away. The bartender looks baffled, then smiles.

"Lady. You're the most understanding wife I've ever met."

"Thanks...I guess." I don't understand what he means but decide not to question it.

On our way to the next bar, I tell Scotty what the bartender said. "Do you know what he meant?"

He bursts out laughing so hard he's gasping for breath. Greg, hearing my question, is wearing a silly grin.

I elbow Scotty. "What's so funny?"

"Just before you sat down..." He takes a breath to contain his laughter as it bubbles up, vibrating his chest. "I introduced Greg to the bartender," he looks to Greg, then blurts out, "as my lover."

I gape at him.

"We planned it…to take him off the market, so to speak. Greg is really cute."

While Greg was growing up, he and his brother pulled practical jokes on family and friends every chance they got, like piling all his uncle's furniture outside under the neighbor's carport when he went to the store. This role-playing with Scotty isn't a surprise.

"No wonder the bartender said I was the most understanding wife he'd ever met." We all laugh until our sides hurt. Sunny can't laugh and drive. He gives up the fight and pulls to the curb to let it all out. The rest of the night is a blur.

If Chuck's party is measured from the size of my headache the next morning, it was a success. Walking, standing, and bouncing in the van all night relapses my pelvic pain. To ease the throbbing, I take a pill and do some easy stretching. Greg suffers no ill effects other than sleeping late.

Before he goes off on a trail ride with Marge and Vern, I asked him how he liked our night of gay bar hopping. He grins, then shrugs and says, "It was fun."

Another reason why I married him, although I wish I could go riding with them.

I continue receiving Hellerwork from Eric. During one session, he suggests I use the time away from my art to read and rethink the meaning behind it. Classes resume in September, fourteen weeks after my accident. I'm still healing, but to avoid falling behind, I attend class the first day. The long drive and walking from where I park tests my weakened endurance, but I rely on my grit to manage the trek.

When I need relief from my hip and low back pain, I call Eric for another therapy session, rebuilding my strength as I begin my final year at UCLA. After the session, when he shows me techniques to use on myself, I tell him how I'm struggling to develop an idea for my gallery exhibition to complete my degree.

"Think of your accident as a gift and express your healing journey in your art."

"Learning to release holding patterns in my body to relieve my pain and free up my movement has changed the way I experience life, especially kinesthetically—it's opened me up."

As we finish up, he says, "Have you read *Black Elk Speaks* or *Goddesses in Every Woman?*" I shake my head and reach for a pen and paper. "They'll complement your reading of Joseph Campbell." One of my MFA committee members had suggested *The Power of Myth* to deepen my knowledge of mythology, along with the self-help and women's empowerment books I'd been reading. They help me explain my work in critiques. I need all the help I can get to build a body of work for my MFA and a career as an artist. Critiques at school continue to be brutal, pushing me to grow a thicker skin.

At home, I return to riding short distances, but never again with the dogs out. My connection to Lance and his movement become my alternative therapy. The spirit of the horse, my spirit cards say, teaches us to step beyond our limitations and self-imposed boundaries, to express ourselves, to dance and laugh with abandon, to take in all the joy the heavens shower upon us.

After Greg and I feed the horses in the evening, we stand among them on the flat, watching them munch hay from the piles we placed on the ground. As the light fades, I commune with Lance, Ruby, and Liesta in a setting of sage and scrub, and Joshua trees below. I've found the home of my dreams. All I need to complete my dream is to finish my degree, and witness a foal being born.

CHAPTER THIRTY-TWO

EMERGING 1989-1990

Sunday, early September at dusk, I trudge up the hill, as I will every hour throughout the night, with a flashlight to check on Ruby. Her teats have waxed up, and she bends her head around to check her belly, showing me she is ready to foal. Shae says exactly when is impossible to know. I'm home until Tuesday when I will leave for my next class at UCLA. Until then, I'm here working in my garage studio.

At daybreak, the foal still hasn't arrived. I head down the hill for coffee, passing Greg coming up to feed the horses. I'm in the kitchen pouring a cup of hot brew when Greg ducks his head through the door.

"He's here. If you hurry, you can see him stand up to nurse."

I spill my coffee, then leave it to run up the hill. A beautiful chestnut colt with a white *C*-shaped star and strip down his nose lies on the ground. Despite my disappointment, I'm thrilled.

We rub him with the towels Greg carried up to bond through touch and to help Ruby clean him up. When he struggles to rise onto his wobbly legs, we respectfully step back, in awe of his determination. I hold my breath until he finds his first drink of milk and colostrum which gives him antibodies for his immune system.

Greg and I are both smitten. He's a jewel, so we name him Topaz. Ginger and Shae like his name. We continue to handle him every day, bonding with him, stroking him from the tips of his soft ears, down his neck and back to his stubby tail then along all four of his legs, from shoulders to knees to baby hoofs, from pelvis to hocks and down. It's easy when he stands still, more challenging when he wants to prance and kick out with a mini-buck.

The following weekend, I join a group of women at the Devil's Punchbowl, a strange name for an indigenous sacred place near Pearblossom, an hour from home. A cross-cultural shaman guides us to construct a medicine wheel—placing stones in a circle with a stake at the center. During our ceremonies, as in my bodywork sessions, I form a deep connection with my higher self that saturates my skin and my bones with an electrical charge, more like a hum than a shock. Around the campfire that night, we drum, chant, and share stories.

The next morning, during a guided meditation, an ancestor comes into focus with symbolic gifts to heal me and to inspire my art. On this, and other inner journeys, and in my dreams, I meet animal guides and connect with my grandmothers—indigenous crone spirits who offer to help me reach my full potential. In return, I honor them by creating my installation.

At UCLA, I explore drawers of artifacts to research patterns and forms used by ancient cultures for inspiration, then work out my ideas drawing on paper and sculpting clay, using photos, my sketches, and my horses as models. Focusing on my spiritual rebirth; my physical, mental, and emotional healing; and on death as a metaphor for change, I design a circular room—a feminine symbol of place—to reflect my journey of empowerment and healing and to celebrate the person I am becoming.

I formulate my clay, then ordering a ton of it from a regional clay company. It's a special mix I tested to build 3-inch thick, high relief tiles for my eight-feet-tall mythic figures. When it arrives, I build a full-sized panel to test my design, and my idea for installing it into the gallery.

In the middle of my third year, I find two women on the faculty who agreed to join my committee and help me defend my vision of a sacred space representing my empowerment journey. My faculty advisors see the ambitious scale of the preliminary drawings and warn me, "Your project is too large for your available studio space and the finite time before the exhibition."

"I came to UCLA to scale up my work."

Adrian asks me, "Do you want to add a year to your degree to resolve all the challenges working in scale brings?"

"I can't afford another year."

"Then you need to change your design."

My inherited stubbornness kicks in. *I can do this.*

My ideas come together in a series of drawings—one for each panel. Creative energy flows through me, yet I worry I lack the skill and vision to bring these ideas to life. Nancy would tell me to quit worrying, to work with my hands and allow it to be born through me —but she's in Indiana. I haven't found that kind of mentor here yet. Whenever I need support, I channel Nancy's voice.

On the covered cement porch at home in between feeding the horses, Greg helps me build thirteen curved panels with lumber to form a circular room with eight-foot-tall walls. We cut a round portal out of two panels for access. Now all I need is to carve and glaze 234 tiles, each sixteen inches square, to cover the walls. Eric taught me some do-it-yourself techniques to keep my neck pain from flaring up, but since I can't reach my back, I use ibuprofen to manage that pain. I've dealt with it since I fractured it at 17, so I'm practiced at working despite the pain.

My two thousand pounds of the clay I ordered arrives at home and is stacked in my garage. There, I pound clay onto a curved panel form lifted to waist high on sawhorses and carve a bear, an owl, and a stag to represent power, wisdom, and innocence. As I work, I imagine dancing around a roaring fire with my guides.

I work with the earth between my fingers while I listen to tapes of women chanting on my tape player. Guided by my drawings, inspired by Jean Shinoda Bolen's *Goddesses in Every Woman*, and her Greek archetypes of empowerment, I sculpt Persephone, Hera, and Artemis for one side, and for across the circle, Demeter, Athena, and Aphrodite. I carve deep and build up to capture the details of each form—to bring them to life—then cut each four-foot by eight-foot-tall section into twelve clay tiles to install on the room's curved inner walls.

To symbolize a ceremonial medicine wheel, I carve panels using Lance as my model—eight-foot-tall rearing horses in high relief and glaze one each in red, yellow, blue, and white to serve as gatekeepers for the four directions. To complete the thirteen panels—a strong number in women's mythology—I design a panel for Isis, the eagle-woman goddess of ancient Egypt. In the center of the installation, I will represent Hestia's hearth with a small circle of bricks. I pound and manipulate hundreds of pounds of clay for each panel, mesmerized by the figures as they emerge.

By spring, 1990, we have bonded with Topaz and can't imagine ever letting him go. I call Ginger to persuade her to let us keep the colt.

She says, "I'm not surprised." For a moment, I can almost hear her thinking. "Okay, but I need Liesta back to breed her to Dusty."

Greg's been riding Ginger's Quarter horse mare for the past year on trails, discovering she's too bulky to compete in an endurance race. We need a horse who can give Greg the excitement he craves—an Arabian who can carry him on narrow trails up mountain switchbacks. He doesn't mind coping with horse spooks and unexpected branches snapping back, almost removing him from the saddle. We've been learning how, for centuries, Arabian horses traveled for days through the desert to carry soldiers to war, then after a night's rest, charged into battle.

"Until you can find a horse for Greg," Marge says, "he can ride one of our Arabians. They could use a few more miles to keep them fit."

Unlike Greg, I prefer riding in an arena, feeling Lance's legs move as if they are my own, communicating through the reins like my fingers were on his tongue—a subtle but intimate connection. If I breed Ruby to the right stallion, I will have another chance to witness a birth and raise a horse for me that is great on trails and built for dressage.

When Vern hears my plan, he says, "Check out Balladeer, a champion endurance Arabian and a sweet all-around performance horse. His owner may be willing to breed Ruby to his stallion in exchange for your work on Balladeer. He wants to win his next endurance race."

"And he's close," Marge agrees. "When Ruby comes into season, you can walk her down the hill to be bred."

Shae approves, too. "His offspring out of Ruby will be great in eventing, dressage, and endurance!"

When Ruby comes into season, I'm nervous because I've never seen a stallion mounting a mare. The first time I walk her to his ranch, Balladeer's owner assures me his stallion is gentle with all his mares. I don't know enough to start a young horse under saddle, but I have three years to learn and plenty of friends to help. We may be horse poor, but I'm finding ways to live the life I imagined as a girl playing with my imaginary horses.

Meanwhile, at school all the grad students are hustling to finish their work. We compete for access to kilns. My thick tiles need to be fired slowly. And I have more to fire than the others. With no referee, negotiations escalate into shouting matches.

With the support of a small grant, I buy a kiln for bisque firing and install it in our garage, making my sculpted tiles less fragile when transporting them to school for the glaze process.

With a wall panel set up on sawhorses I spend hours bent over the clay, refining the figures. Then I carve it into squares and lift each piece, weighing thirty to fifty-pounds, in and out of the kiln. After finishing one panel, my back cries out for me to stop. But I can't. I have twelve more to create. So I inhale ibuprofen, cappuccino, and dark chocolate to keep me working, especially at school. When I'm home, Greg helps with the lifting. Spending time with our horses and dogs restores me.

But my kiln blows its breakers in the electric panel, delaying my grand plan. Our handyman neighbor installed the wrong size breaker, and I don't have time or money to hire someone else. Instead, I move the unfired sections of goddesses and horses, dried by the desert air to their most fragile state, down the mountain to my space at UCLA. But the thick tiles soak up the humid ocean air, especially after the rain and fog move in. To dry the tiles before firing, I set the gas kiln on the lowest heat setting with the door cracked open, but I run out of time and must rush the process, praying a slow fire will allow them to survive the transformative process.

But in some, the remaining moisture turns to steam and explodes the thick tiles. I must replace them.

Shae hears of a young Arabian for sale down the street from her house. She's busy with her farrier and can't join us, so she directs us to a ranch in the foothills above her place in Three Points.

We arrive to find a guy about Greg's age holding a saddled two-year-old gelding who he calls Ben.

"His real name is Nimr el Masri. He's a registered desert Arabian with old bloodlines."

Ben is all white (properly referred to as *gray*) and seems gentle. His low-slung back is a confirmation flaw, reducing his price drastically to be within our budget. Greg mounts the gelding and walks him along the sandy lane between fenced paddocks. When he comes to a wider area, he walks him in a few circles, then picks up a trot back to where I'm standing with Ben's owner, who says, "Take him out on the trail." He points past his house to the entrance of a trail hidden by spruce and scrub oak trees.

Greg looks at me. I nod. They take off at a fast trot and soon disappear.

A few minutes later, Ben comes galloping back, the saddle under his belly, with no sign of Greg. I scream silently inside my head as fear knots my gut into a double pretzel. Will this be another ambulance ride? Or worse?

The owner grabs the reins and releases the saddle, setting it aside. Ben stands, quivering.

I head toward the trail to search for Greg when he comes strolling up.

I rush toward him looking for a gash or a limp but see none. "What happened?"

"The damn girth wasn't tight. When the saddle flipped, there was no way to stay on."

The owner says, "Damn horse. He must have sucked air in and let it out on the trail." That happened to me the first time I rode Lance, but Shae stopped us and tightened the girth, preventing a mishap. I guess Ben knows the same trick.

Greg shrugs. He doesn't have formal training—only what he's learned riding the steep trails with Marge and Vern. *Ben is too young. I can't let him get hurt. We'll have to keep looking.*

He pulls me into a huddle. "I want him." I'm surprised, but I don't argue. When Greg decides, there is no changing his mind.

We negotiate a lower price of $500, which is a steal for a horse of Ben's breeding. Shae offers to trailer Ben home for us to join Lance, Ruby, and her foal Topaz. Our herd is growing.

When we tell our neighbors Marge and Vern about buying Ben, they show us videos of them climbing Cougar Rock when they rode in the famous Tevis Cup, furthering our education in endurance. "It's the toughest 100-mile race on the planet. Horses have died from riders pushing them too hard. We condition our horses for years before entering to avoid harming them."

My jaw drops as I watch, knowing I won't be doing any 100-mile races on Lance. Greg asks lots of questions, enthusiastic about riding Ben with them into the foothills and across the desert flats.

I only join the ride when I'm sure they won't be taking the steeper mountain trails. But I never miss one of the Natural Horsemanship clinics Marge and Vern host on their ranch when watching is free.

Afterward, they serve a burger and bean dinner. We eat outside their small A-frame at picnic tables. They tell the story of when they lost a beloved member of their herd to colic, vividly describing how the mare went down and wouldn't get back up, thrashing and rolling. They explain how we need to watch for mold in the hay and to keep our horses hydrated.

Throughout the spring, our neighbors Marge and Vern teach us how to *talk horse*—to translate what it means when Lance jerks his head up, the positions of his ears, and when he licks his lips. I practice on Lance the techniques I learned from Eric—the flat of my fist and the length of my forearm to release the binding of scar tissue. His body language guides what depth of pressure to use as I ease his cycle of pain accumulating since the racetrack.

To help him stand still, Marge and Vern show me how to grab the crest of his neck and rock him from side to side, shaking his head until his nose drops to nearly touching the ground. Then I bend his nose to his girth with the lightest pressure to teach him to release his resistance and holding patterns. Trust is hard to establish and easy to lose. I watch Lance to understand what he's saying, then respond with my body language. Each tip of his ear or lick of his lips signals an increased level of trust.

I submerge myself into the calming energy of the high desert and spend time with Lance. Like me, my equine companion lives every day in pain from injuries at the track and on the jumping circuit. One day, Shae shares how he went nuts in his first race, hitting his head on the gate, nearly knocking himself out. He repeats this pattern of terror whenever we load him into a trailer to go to a dressage clinic. He throws up his head, nearly knocking himself out or cutting his head on the ceiling vents. I stop trying to trailer him to events until I can borrow a trailer at least seven feet tall.

Standing with Lance in the paddock, I soften my voice, my breathing, and my body language to help him settle before I can start the myofascial techniques I've learned from Eric. As I work, Lance stretches to help lengthen his bound-up tissue and moves into the pressure of my fist or forearm. He confirms the release I feel under my fingers when he sticks out his tongue and licks the air.

One day, our neighbor Marge, who gets paid to train other people's horses, watches me work. "I can see the effect of your work in his demeanor. Would you work on some of our Arabians, maybe in exchange for attending our clinics?"

I agree with a smile. I'm sculpting horses' bodies like I do clay—softening the tissue with the heat of my hands, then lengthening it—and get paid while I learn on different horses. Within the week, more neighbors call wanting me to work on their horses, offering fifty dollars a session. It's a start. After working on most of the horses in Kings Canyon, the word of my work spreads.

My faculty committee must approve of my work for me to graduate. Two of the men assigned to my committee don't understand my symbolism using the goddesses and are confused by my personal expression of the feminine in my fire, water, and air sculptures. A third, the Chair of the Art Department, who encouraged me to read Campbell when he came to my studio, is unable to attend my meetings until the end of the term.

I sit back and watch the two women—my new committee members—explain my imagery to the male faculty during my next critique session. Still, the men don't believe my audience will understand. To appease them, I agree to describe each figure on my invitations to the opening that I will mail ten days before the event. Then I tune out their objections and return to work long days glazing and firing.

I fear deep in my gut I won't complete my work in time. If I don't, I won't graduate with my class. We don't have the money to keep me in school another year.

Work harder, Deborah. You can't let them be right.

Two weeks before the opening, I lose an entire panel—a week's work reduced to shards that I must sweep out of the kiln for the next person in line to fire.

I want to scream, but I'm too exhausted. To complete my empowerment project, I ignore my doubts and demons, garner my courage, and charge forward into the abyss.

For some damaged tiles, I don't remake the entire panel, but instead, sculpt replacements, measuring them to fit with existing pieces that survived, praying it matches after the fire gods contort everything. Clay comes alive in the kiln—it shrinks and moves in the hot kiln, mostly during the first firing. This close to the deadline, I must accept whatever comes out of the kiln. *I must surrender to the creative process.*

I don't like glossy glaze. So, I create unique matte-finish glaze formulas with the assistance of our lab tech. I add powders for bright colors, testing them on sample tiles to be sure they melt and fuse, ensuring a good *fit* to the clay. It worked fine on my sample tiles. Now, when I apply it to tiles with deep carving, the glass surface cracks. There's no time to figure out a reformulation. I adjust the kiln temperature incrementally for the next firing, but it doesn't fix the problem. I fire some tiles three and four times to build up its too-thin glaze to repair the flaws.

I walk around campus, a zombie from lack of sleep. My teachers see me but withhold judgment. When I can, I crawl into a sleeping bag on the department's office floor behind the classroom, waking to check multiple gas kilns throughout a twelve-hour firing. I beg for firing time, I end up running back and forth, simultaneously firing kilns in our department and in the sculpture department across the atrium.

The first day arrives to install our work in the Wight Art Gallery on campus, and I'm not ready. When staff assigns my space, Greg and I install the walls we'd built to support the tiles. But the two of us can't move all the tiles here in time.

My brothers come to my rescue. Mike and Chuck arrive to help install the tiles inside the circle. Chuck wants to help despite his illness. We give him small bricks to place in the circle as a base for the walls. Greg promises to look after him while I return to the clay department to unload a kiln. Mike says, "Let's get this done. Judy's home with the babies. They are a handful." They'd just adopted a boy and a girl, only a month old, from Honduras.

We move finished tiles from shelves in my studio onto a cart and up a cargo elevator into the gallery space—a twenty-minute round trip. I'm using industrial Velcro to attach the sculpted tiles to the wall to facilitate removal after two weeks. I had tested the Velcro on several panels, and it worked, but some of these latest tiles are heavier, and I'm worried it won't be enough to keep them in place on the vertical walls.

Can't change it now. I cross my fingers and push forward. After unloading the last kiln, I join my family to lift the remaining tiles into place.

It's the evening before the opening. We stand in the circle and look at my creation. Greg and my brothers nod their approval. It's all up, all but one panel: the last rendition of Isis blew up days before we began erecting the installation with no time to replace it. My teacher tells me to paint the wood black and leave the space blank. Before my family leaves, I thank them for their help, wishing I had a better way to show my gratitude.

On the way home, I pop pain killers while fretting over the installation's shortcomings. After fitful dreams of Isis haunting me for being left out, I wake up at five in the morning. I have nothing to wear. On the way to UCLA, I go shopping and find a royal blue cotton dress that matches the glaze in the autumn horse. I dress in the store. The salesgirl clips off the tags.

At the campus gallery, a mass of people waits for the doors to open. I find Greg in the crowd, standing with the rest of my family. He whispers, "Your dad is here."

"Really? He actually came? I didn't think he'd make it."

I look but can't find Dad. Someone calls my name. It's Danny. He's gallery staff.

He approaches to whisper, "There's a problem. You need to come with me. Now!"

Danny grabs my arm to lead me through the museum into my space. With pedestals supporting four armless goddess figures in the Ante Room, I climb three steps into my installation, crunch through the four-foot-wide circular opening, and then down three steps more into its center.

I'm facing my worst nightmare. I stand, frozen.

An entire panel has collapsed and shattered on the floor.

I don't know what to do.

Danny's quick thinking saved three others from collapsing by nailing two-by-fours vertically to hold the tiles in place. It looks ghastly. My heart cracks, splitting like the earth when it's torn apart from within.

Danny says, "The wood is helping, but I'm not sure they'll let anyone in to see it. More tiles may fall. It's too dangerous for the public."

My heart drops to my feet. A year's work. Ruined. No one will ever see it in its fullest wonder. I nearly collapse …but I can't.

I climb out and return to my family, waiting outside. "A panel collapsed. Tiles are shattered on the floor. They've closed my room to avoid getting sued. The entrance is boarded up. You can peek through the opening, but it's only a partial view."

The crowd pushes into the Wight Art Gallery, visiting the rooms of each graduating student. I return to my space and send my family off to see the other work. I'm expected to greet the public. How do I explain this?

Adrian, the head of the clay department, comes up behind me and puts his arm on my shoulder. "I think it's done falling."

I follow him inside. Danny has swept up the clay dust and shards, leaving the larger pieces on the floor but pushing them closer to the wall. Only Adrian can overturn the decision to open my circle to the public. I hold my breath, trying not to cry, afraid he'll say no.

Adrian says, "I think it's safe enough now to let people in."

My jaw drops. "Thank you."

"It's quite powerful. I don't want them to miss out on seeing it."

I return to the anteroom, where my three elemental spirits—fire, water, and wind—along with the empowerment figures, dignity and humility, stand guard on three-foot-tall pedestals. When a spectator approaches, I hand them an invitation describing the symbolism of my creation, and reassure them it's okay to go in. I'm in a daze, unable to register their compliments. After thirty minutes, with people going in and out, a woman sticks her head out and asks me to come inside. I set the invitations down and step in.

"I love the *horse of death and transformation* broken on the floor. It's like an archeological dig." A recording of women chanting goddess names, on a loop, plays in the background. "It gives me chills—like I'm in an ancient sacred space."

I hadn't noticed which panel had fallen, hadn't remembered its symbolism. As I listen, my skin electrifies as joy erupts outward. My audience understands—better than me. I dance inside as my destiny survives another test of fire.

A few hours later, Dad finds me outside in the plaza. "I'm proud of you."

It's the first time I remember hearing it. I wait for a criticism to follow, but it doesn't come. Instead, he whips out a business card with the title of Doctor of Metallurgy below his name. My heart sinks. He can't have a daughter with more education, so he has elevated himself one level above my degree.

I know it's a lie. Both my brothers say Dad never completed his bachelor's degree, let alone a doctorate. All the companies he's worked for just accepted his resume. I guess they didn't check in the 40s when Dad claimed his engineering degree.

It boggles my mind how he gets away with it. Dad can take one evening class in metallurgy, read some periodicals, then do the work of a degreed professional. I feel sorry for him. All my life, I've wanted to be like him, to make him proud, but *I've been a fool.*

As the evening wanes, a new fear settles in. What am I going to do now? I need a job. But there are no open teaching positions near where we live. *I won't move—not ever again.*

I return home with the degree I've always wanted, but I worry I'm no better off.

A voice whispers in on the wind. *Don't worry. Everything will be alright.* Even though I know I will face all my worries again tomorrow, I release them to my spirit guides tonight and drift into a deep sleep.

In the fall, Greg enters an Endurance Race and rides Ben twenty-five miles through the Tehachapi Mountains. I act as crew, helping with food and water at vet checks. Vern arranges for me to do a demo of myofascial techniques on a stressed Arabian mare after she wins the fifty-mile version of the race. I'm led to the center of a crowd of riders and spectators where a man hands me a lead rope to his mare who stands braced, head high, eyes wide, shaking all over.

Before touching her, I calm her through my breath. As a herd animal, she will naturally mimic me, which allows me to help her. After three deep breaths, I exhale with a loud sigh. On the last one, she drops her head and stops shaking, building the first step to trust. Using techniques I learned in my sessions with Eric, but adjusted for a horse's anatomy, I work through layers of her eleven-hundred-pound body to relieve the knots that had built up over time.

A half-hour later, her grateful rider leads the mare, nearly asleep, to his trailer while I answer tons of questions and schedule three new customers. By manipulating equine muscles with my fingers like I do clay, I'm continuing my journey of empowerment and healing while earning money to buy horse hay.

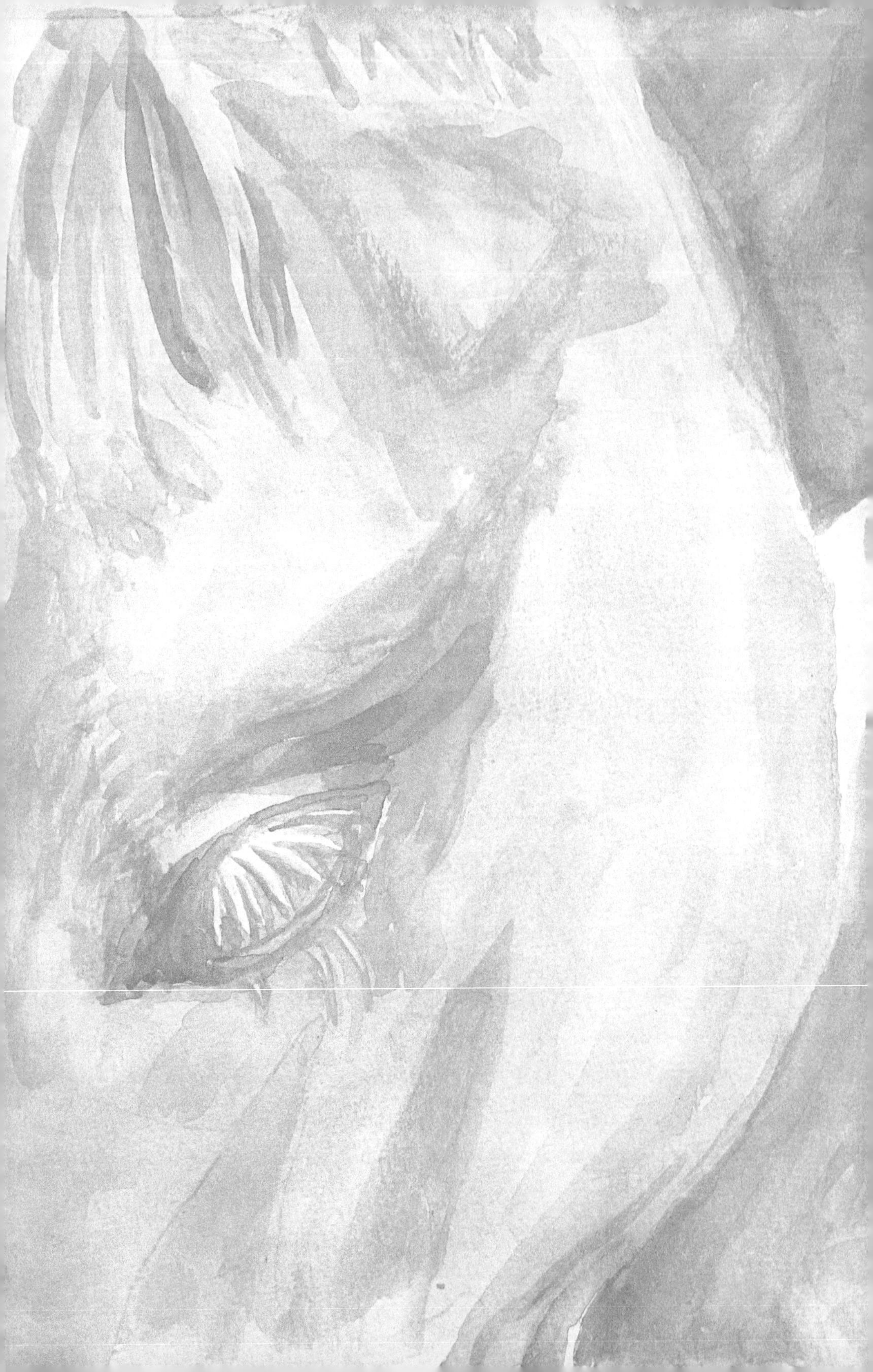

PART 3

HEALING WITH HORSES

Miracles surround us at every turn,
if we but sharpen our perceptions to them.

— WILLA CATHER

CHAPTER THIRTY-THREE

HELLERWORK 1990

I sip coffee on our covered porch as the morning light casts my shadow onto the boxes Greg and I moved home after my MFA show closed—sixty in all stacked two high behind me. He's making breakfast while I squirm in my chair to keep my spine from locking up after all the lifting. I skipped commencement yesterday, too depleted to attend.

Only my family and I saw the ceremonial space when it was intact. The room, braced by boards, stayed open for one week. When it closed, we packed my installation into cardboard boxes and brought it home. I look at my installation in pieces, packed tools, and bags of raw clay, and I want to cry. With no energy to restore it, and no money to build a foundation to install it, the piece to which I have devoted a year of my life will remain boxed for now—as long as I am plagued with back pain.

After selling *Fire* for $1500 out of the exhibition, I don't have a gallery to sell my art like I did in Fort Wayne. The few colleges with teaching positions open are too far away to commute, especially when I'd be responsible for firing kilns. But I need income to support our horses.

One night, over a spaghetti dinner, I discuss my options with Greg.

"I'm not ready to approach a gallery to sell my art. I don't have enough work even if I did have the confidence."

"But you've worked so hard." His brow crunches, and his frown line deepens.

"Working on horses is healing for me and the pay is good. Shae, Marge, and Vern continue to refer horse owners to me. Business is picking up."

Greg says, "If that's what you want. As long as it pays for hay, hoof trims, and vet bills."

"It will…" Shae's been encouraging me to work with horses and I love doing it, but I've stopped working in clay. I look over at the shelves above the tv, at my sculpture of the elemental water goddess, her head seaweed floating in the ocean. And *Wind*. Her waves glazed in white bring me calm. *I'll make art again once I get my life under control… and my back pain.*

A fender bender in the Valley after a session with Eric, triggers my decades-old neck injuries. The headaches make it difficult to work, drive, even sleep. At my next session, Eric explains, "Your repeated traumas, falling off horses and car accidents, have accumulated in your tissues. We'll need to release it a layer at a time."

I exhale and imagine the pain leaving my body. "When I work on horses, they stretch and breathe intuitively the same way you've taught me." He smiles and nods.

At the end of our session, Eric says, "A Hellerwork training is starting soon. You should sign up. You would be great working on people."

I sit up to catch his eyes. "Seriously? For working on horses, I studied books on equine massage and took a course to learn anatomy by layering clay muscles onto a model horse skeleton. Are you saying I could help riders, too?

"Yes. And you'd improve your horse work by seeing movement patterns and how they reveal past traumas."

"In my dressage training, I learned how a rider's body, when out of balance with gravity, throws their horse out of balance. The horse must compensate so he doesn't fall over and becomes crooked himself. Are you saying I might help the horse by working on the rider?"

He nods, offering me a hand up and a phone number on scratch paper.

I call when I get home, and an instructor explains the program. "It's a rigorous eighteen-month training that will change your life. During a two-week-long training session at a high desert retreat, you'll learn a series of ten bodywork sessions, each focused on a different part of the body. You'll be taught to release and rebalance the tissue one layer at a time, like peeling an onion."

"That's like my work with Eric."

"Yes. He called and recommended you for the program."

Wow. Eric really believes in me.

"For the year after the first retreat, you'll practice the series on friends or family and attend monthly meetings in LA with your class.

I'm ecstatic about the potential to help horses and riders heal while earning enough to keep the horses. *But can we afford it?* When Greg gets home from his weekly trip to see customers, I tell him about the training. "I'd be gone for two weeks to start. Then I'd work from home.

"What about teaching?"

"There are still no openings. Even if I could, teaching won't work. Someone has to be home for our animals. I already have horse owners asking for sessions. I'll work on horses, get certified for people, and care for our animals while you travel. If I work full-time, at a hundred dollars per hour-long session, I can pay feed and vet bills. The upfront cost of the training is the problem—two payments three months apart."

Greg shrugs. "What will you do?"

When I tell Chuck about it, he is eager to help. I apply for the next class that starts after Christmas and purchase a massage table to get started.

On the morning I'm due to report to class, I stand on our porch soaking in the desert's calm. The horses have been fed, my bag is in the car, and I'm ready for the two-hour drive east. Greg plans to drive me. A week ago, I tried to back out of the training. I'm taking pain meds to cope with severe headaches from my last car accident, but the Hellerwork instructor convinced me I could wean off the meds with the sessions I'll receive at the retreat.

I follow Greg into the kitchen, leaving the dogs outside, and glance at the wall clock. "The dogs need fresh water before we go. We need to hurry." I'm nervous about going and the thought of arriving late makes it worse.

I hear the dogs bark and dash out to drag Alex, the biggest of the three, and Wolfie, who's a smaller Australian shepherd mix, inside to prevent them chasing a coyote roaming nearby. I hear the two girls, both good-sized shepherds, on the far side of the garage, out of sight. When the commotion intensifies, I race out to yell into the wind, "Tania. No." I round the corner to find them entangled in a brawl. "Brandy. No." I call back to Greg, "The girls are fighting," praying he hears me and comes to help.

Their prior scraps have been only a nip or a snarl, but this fight is escalating. Tania, who we've had since Fort Wayne, suffers from severe pain in her lower spine. Despite the painkillers we give her, she's become sharp and ornery with the other three dogs.

The girls are going at each other hard. Instead of taking Tania's abuse, Brandy, now full-grown, is fighting back. I reach into the fierce tangle of snaps, growls, and bared teeth with saliva and blood flinging in every direction, hoping to grab one of their collars. I come up with Tania's and twist my wrist to tighten the strap so she can't slide out. It's my only hope to restrain her.

Greg comes up behind me and I yell, "I've got her. Get Brandy." He reaches but misses her collar. She comes after Tania with teeth bared. "Brandy, no!" I attempt to pull Tania to the ground, but with a twist and a leap, she is free to defend herself. The fight resumes, even more fiercely.

Terrified that they will kill each other, I scream their names at the top of my lungs and dive back in. When I grab Tania, she slips out of her collar. My hand ends up in her mouth as her teeth sink into my flesh. Ignoring my pain, I drop to the ground and wrap my legs around her, desperate to stop her. But they continue to fight.

At last, Greg somehow pulls Brandy off and drags her into the garage. When he comes back out, I'm still on the ground, out of breath, with Tania between my legs. Blood runs down Greg's arm. "You're hurt."

"Look at yourself. You're covered in blood," he says, approaching cautiously.

Shit. Now, I'll never get to my training.

Tania's injuries look worse than mine. I grab her by the scruff of the neck—one of the few places without an obvious wound—lead her to the porch and plop onto a lawn chair. I dare not let her go, not yet, even though she's returned to her docile self.

Greg brings me a damp towel, taking care to keep Alex and Wolfie in the house.

"How's Brandy?" I hear her whine behind the closed garage door.

"A few scratches, but she'll be fine." He hands me three ibuprofen and a glass of water. "Your adrenaline will wear off soon."

Holding Tania between my legs, I pop the pills, then use the cloth to wipe Tania's face. After cleaning her biggest wounds, I wipe the blood from my hand. "Greg! It won't stop bleeding." I begin to cry. My chance for a new career is shattered.

"Let go of her and come in the house."

"I can't move." The last of my energy has drained out of me. I look up, wishing to reverse time, to undo this day.

"I'll get you a clean compress."

He returns, pulls a chair up close, pressing the cool cloth to my bloody hand. "Both of us need stitches and tetanus shots." He hands me the cordless phone he'd set on the table. "We can't keep doing this."

I punch the keys, as my injured hand grows stiffer by the minute, to dial the vet. When a tech answers, I describe the deep gashes in the skin around Tania's face and neck. "We're coming now." We leave

Brandy, whose wounds appear superficial, in the garage so she won't bleed on the carpet.

It's twenty minutes to Lancaster. As Greg drives, I study his face, his frustration a dark cloud enveloping him. The same dread imprisons me. At a stoplight, he turns to me and holds my eyes. "We can't leave the dogs alone anymore."

I shake my head, ready to melt into a mushy mess. "I'll skip the training." I stare at Tania in the back seat, bloodied but contrite. Her jaw drops into a hapless smile.

Greg glances back, then returns his eyes to the road. "Maybe he can give her some stronger pain pills. Or surgery. We'll do what needs to be done." But we can't afford surgery.

We drop Tania at the vet, then rush to the hospital emergency room. With the excruciating throb in my hand, I've forgotten about my head pounding and the spasms in my neck.

As the doctor stitches the wound, I rewind our life to when Tania was a puppy. This isn't like her.

With our wounds bandaged, we leave the ER for the vet, hoping for good news. We've always left the dogs outside when we're gone, but now I worry Tania might attack a deliveryman or a neighbor. How can we trust her?

The vet says, "There is nothing I can do. Surgery won't help her degenerating spine." He points to her x-ray. "Her pain will only increase." He looks down and away. "I'm sorry." He strokes Tania's head then leaves us alone in the room.

Greg lays his uninjured hand on my shoulder. "She's in pain. We can't ask her to live with it every day." He turns his hand to show me his stitches. "And we can't go through this again. How would you make art? How would you handle Lance without your hand? What about your work?"

"I'll stay home." *I owe it to her.*

Greg stares at me. "Not go to the grocery or to the doctor?"

"A kennel?" The picture of her trapped, clawing to get free tears at my heart. "No. We can't. She's never been caged."

We have only one remaining choice. Tears stream down my face, but I don't wipe them away. I fall with them as they rip open the earth beneath my feet. "How can we?"

Greg puts his bandaged hand around my shoulders and pulls me into a hug. "It's the right choice." Tears stream down his face too, like I've never seen before.

The vet returns. Tania lies in my arms on the cold metal table. I hold her face as the vet injects the medicine. "I love you, my beautiful girl."

I stop breathing when I feel the life leave her body. *She's gone.*

Greg helps me to the car because my legs alone won't carry me. I peer through the glass, watching him and the vet's assistant carry her blanket-wrapped body and place her on the back seat of our truck.

We bury her on the point just past the house. When Greg drops the last shovel of sand to cover her, we add stones to deter scavengers. I shake the rattle I use in ceremonies to awaken my spirit guides. *Take our beloved dog to where she is free of pain, to play with Duke, Tina, and Greg's King. We release your spirit.*

Greg says, "If you still want to do the training...we need to leave soon."

I look up at him, wanting more time to grieve. Instead, I just nod.

After a two-hour drive, Greg drops me off at the desert retreat. I'm late by half a day. My head pounds. My whole-body aches. *I shouldn't be here.* Perhaps this group of healers can help relieve my pain, but not my grief. Poor Greg. He must travel to see customers and will come home each night to a dark house without Tania or me to greet him. I will call him every evening to tell him how much I love him and share what I've learned.

During the two-week retreat, I learn how the pain we store in our bodies, if left untreated, can accumulate, causing lifelong distress. At twilight on the last night of the retreat, I walk in the desert by moonlight, talking to Tania's spirit. I feel the grace of her presence and her forgiveness for not saving her. I call on my spirit guides to help me not fail and to help people trust me with their horses and their own pain.

Four weeks after the rigorous and glorious retreat, my graduating class continues our Hellerwork training at our instructor's West LA office. Once a month, we gather for an evening to discuss each of the ten sessions of bodywork for different parts of the body—and to learn about other modalities, such as craniosacral work, to use in our practice. I'm protecting my hand, but it is healing fast.

Joseph Heller, the founder of our school, joins us when he's in town, encourages us to integrate anything that helps the client heal. I'm giddy when, in one class, Joseph compliments my work. I now understand why I've been in pain most of my life and know how to manage it. Helping others with their pain is exhausting but satisfying work.

One evening, we learn a new trust exercise and ask questions that arose with various clients. When we finish, it's after ten o'clock and I'm anxious to get on the road for my two-hour drive home and take the elevator downstairs. As I approach my truck parked on the street, I reach in my purse for keys but come up empty.

My keys are in the ignition of my locked truck. I return to the classroom for help.

Someone calls for a tow truck that will take an hour to arrive. Daniel, our instructor, says, "I can unlock it faster with a coat hanger." Billy, a classmate, offers to help. Returning to the street, we each take a turn feeding the elongated hanger through the top edge of the window. Despite a broken streetlight above, we can see to work in the starlight once our eyes adjust. It's not the safest part of town. I'm focused on wiggling the wire to catch the lock release. I almost get it open, unaware that an older Impala has stopped in the street twenty feet away. Shadows of people inside are unrecognizable in the dark. When someone exits from the back of the sedan, I assume he is coming to help and keep working on the lock.

Then I hear, "Give me all your money." And after a pause, "I've got a gun." I glance over my shoulder. A young man is standing on the sidewalk about six feet away with his arm behind his back. I turn to make out his face. He's not holding a gun. It's a hammer.

"Don't," I yell out, but it's too late. Daniel has already tossed the stranger his fanny pack, carrying his driver's license, keys, and some cash. Billy is backing up in terror, inching toward the office.

Growing up with two older brothers, I had my fill of teasing from them, like when they tried to tickle me or when Mike tried to dunk me in a pool, and I learned to fight back. If someone was going to mess with me, they had better be ready to carry it out. This guy can't. I run at the stranger and grab Daniel's fanny pack by the strap, determined to retrieve it. The robber holds on too. *I'm in a tug of war with a thief.*

Working with horses, I've built some strength, and I'm not about to give in. I don't let go even after he swings the hammer at my face and hits me in the eye. My glasses shatter. The glass and wire rims go flying into the street. I'm hurt, but I stand my ground until the would-be-thief lets go. He runs back to the car, and they drive off. None of us catch a license plate number. Maybe they didn't have one. Billy runs upstairs to call the police. Daniel sits with me on the curb. I hold one hand over my injured eye and proudly hand over his fanny pack with the other.

He says, "Why did you do that? What if he'd had a gun?"

I turn toward him. "I saw the hammer." It's still banging inside my head. "Where are my glasses?"

Daniel finds them twisted with a broken lens. He turns his back to me. I hear him weep.

"I'm okay, really."

"I'm glad, but that's not it. My wife and baby are at home. My fear put them in danger." He drops his head. "Inside were my keys and my address. I wasn't thinking when I threw him my pack. What would have happened if you hadn't rescued it? You've saved us all." Quivering like a child, Daniel gives me a tender hug.

The police show up, take a report, and say I must go to the hospital for an x-ray. I want to go home, but Daniel insists. Billy drives me to the ER and tells me how he responded. "It's not like me to be afraid. It's just that, this morning, when I broke up with my girlfriend, she threatened I would be harmed for breaking her heart. You know, karma? I was sure he'd kill me."

As we wait for my x-ray results, I comfort him. An hour later, I learn my orbital socket is undamaged, but all around my eye turns purple and midnight blue by the time Greg picks me up.

He says, "That's a helluva shiner."

"Hmph." I hurt too much to laugh. We leave the truck.

I return two nights later for the truck and to attend a women's circle with Carolyn Conger, a psychic healer. She led an energy workshop as part of my Hellerwork training. When her group sees my shiner, now black and violet, everyone wants to hear the story. I edit the tale but add, "I've told this story to everyone I encounter, even at the ER. All the men, including my dad and brothers, say I shouldn't have risked my life for a fanny pack. But the women cheer me on as their warrior."

Carolyn says, "There is more to this story. The young man connected you to his grandmother when you confronted him, or he would have kept pounding you with that hammer. And why the others in the sedan didn't come after you with a gun. That young man must deal with the shame of letting you thwart his robbery. But yes, Deborah. You have every right to own your power. We have no idea what we will do in an emergency until we are faced with it. Now, you know."

CHAPTER THIRTY-FOUR

KINGS CANYON 1991

Carolyn Conger's words echo in my mind as I resume my work at home. I practice all ten sessions on Greg and, with my horse anatomy research, apply it to Lance, and Greg's new horse Ben, especially when I crew for him during the Tehachapi Endurance race.

After most of the horses are in, Vern announces Ben has won third place and Best Condition. They want me to demonstrate my techniques at the reward ceremony. We walk to the front of the riding facility's offices, where the event organizer has gathered a crowd. A gray Arabian mare, the horse with the fastest time, is led into the center. She pulls back on the lead and throws up her head. The owner hands her to me and backs away.

I can't work on her if she continues her nervous dance. She needs to stand still—willingly. Horses are herd animals. They follow whoever is leading. Maybe she will breathe with me.

I take in deep breaths, making loud sighing sounds as I exhale. Once, twice, three times. The mare watches. On the fourth breath, she drops her head and releases all her air in a big sigh. The crowd gasps.

She's putty in my hands...as long as I don't work too fast. I begin with gentle strokes down her neck, inching deeper to release the knots in her muscles. She tells me with her mouth, ears, and body movements—it's working. An hour later, I hand her, mellow as a purring kitten, back to her grateful owner.

In April, Ruby shows signs she's ready to drop her second foal. I stay up all night hoping to witness the birth. Like when she gave birth to Topaz, Ruby waits until morning, when I go to the house for coffee and a bathroom break. I return to find a filly already on her feet, searching for her mother's teat.

I watch her nurse for a while before I head back to the house to fetch my camera. As I hold the door for Greg, all three dogs sneak through and race to the flat, barking the whole way, to where Ruby is standing with her new foal. I chase after them. Greg follows with leashes.

"Brandy! Alex! Wolfie! Come! Right now!" I yell.

My skin quivers. What if one of them nips the foal's legs? It would cripple her. Can Ruby protect her? I crest the hill and see the foal come out from behind Ruby and face the dogs. *No!* The dogs slow and approach with caution.

The filly, only an hour old, splays out her front legs, drops her head down to eye level with the dogs…daring them to come closer.

The dogs freeze a few feet away from her to inspect and sniff the new arrival, then turn and trot back to me. I help Greg put the leashes on before he takes them inside.

What a feisty filly! She stands up for herself. With her self-confidence, she'll be a handful.

The chestnut filly is the spitting image of her mom and her half-brother Topaz. A thinner white strip runs down her face from her star to her nose. Her fine legs, short back, and sculpted head reflect her Arabian father. Born fearless, we name her *Red Sonia* after the movie about a fierce woman warrior.

Sonia's the horse of my dreams, born from a borrowed mare. With her dad's versatility, she'll be a great all-around horse.

As the word spreads about my healing on horses, I get a call to work on a racehorse at Santa Anita. Another horse bumped him during a race and now he's lame. The big bay Thoroughbred responds to my work, stretching and yawning like Lance.

Two days later, the client who recommended me calls. "His lameness is gone, and he's running great...but they won't have you back. They don't like women knowing more than they do, even though it could help their horses win. Sorry."

Requests come in for demos at dressage clinics, endurance rides, and riders who want to learn how to DIY. In a clinic with a group of riders, I teach basic horse anatomy using bones Shae helps me collect in dry washes where a creek once flowed. We gather scattered skeletons of dead horses left to rot for decades by absent landowners. I tell my clients, "Once you locate your horses' pain, relieve it with easy strokes using your fists and forearms." Greg is shooting video to document what he calls *my dog and pony show*.

One evening, I hear a horse screaming. I run up the hill to find Lance on the ground, thrashing, his eyes wild, while the others keep their distance. He stops rolling and looks at his belly, then rolls again...and again. He lifts his head and neck, then pounds them back to the ground. He strikes at the air, then pulls himself over. He's too dangerous to approach. I wait, soothing him with a low voice.

He gets up, bucks, screams, then goes down, and thrashes again. *It's colic. I'm sure.* He's had it before, but never this bad. A twisted gut will kill him.

He pulls himself up and strikes the ground, his hoof like a sledgehammer, too fragile for the force of the pounding.

I throw some hay into the stalls for Ben, Topaz, and Ruby with five-month-old Sonia. Eating will help keep them calm.

On the flat below, Lance takes a break from his thrashing. He lifts his head from the ground and stares at me, imploring me to make it stop—the pain evident in the widening circles of white around his dark eyes. "Easy boy." I stroke his face. "I'll get help."

Fear knots my gut. *I can't lose Lance, not after losing Tania.* I steady myself, eyeball my path down the hill in the dimming light to rush, taking care not to fall.

The sound of Lance striking the ground behind me sends shivers up my spine. I call back to him. "Hang in there, boy." Once I hit the flat, I run to the patio door and yell for Greg. He pokes his head around the corner from the living room.

"It's Lance. Colic. It looks bad." I grab the phone on the counter and punch the speed dial for the vet. He's an hour away, so he lets us keep emergency medicine in our fridge. I describe Lance's symptoms, and he tells me what dose to inject into his neck. The vet says, "Keep him up and walking. I'm on my way."

I retrieve the medical supplies from the fridge. Greg grabs a long lead rope and heavy leather halter in extra-large from the tack room.

Lance, on the ground, bends his neck to look at his belly. I buckle the halter on him and encourage him back onto his feet. Greg holds him while I shoot the medicine into his trapezius, the largest muscle in his neck. I listen for gut sounds with a stethoscope even though the deep rumbles would be audible with an ear to his side. Walking him in circles eases his pain, but not for long.

Since horses eat with their heads down, evolution removed their ability to regurgitate. Gas produced by anxiety or a bit of mold in the hay or grain can twist a gut. The folded intestine cuts off blood circulation and kills essential tissue. Colic kills many horses, especially when the vet can't get to them fast enough to tube oil down their throat to release the blockage. When that treatment is not enough, they try surgery at an equine hospital, that is, if the horse lives long enough to trailer there. Horses, despite their power and size, are immensely fragile.

Greg watches as I walk Lance in circles, then holds him when I lift and massage his belly. I put my ear against his flank to listen for gurgles and groans. It's dark when the vet arrives. Greg opens the gate to let him drive onto the flat, then follows him with our truck to illuminate the flat with the headlights. Walking Lance feels like a death march. I push the thought out of my mind. *We'll get through this.*

When I hand over the lead rope to the vet, Lance goes crazy. He rears, then strikes the ground with his front hooves, first one, then the other, so hard I fear the crack in his hoof will extend to the hairline, making it impossible for him to stand, let alone walk. The vet pushes me out of the way and hands the lead rope to Greg. I stand aside, angry and scared, knowing Greg and the vet are just trying to protect me. *But Lance is my horse.* I can handle him better than anyone. With my jaw clenched, I stand back to let the vet work—for now.

The vet shoots more pain killer and muscle relaxants into Lance's neck vein. Our neighbors, Marge and Vern, show up to help. Greg must have called them. At endurance races, they've seen more than one horse die of colic. Like the vet, they look worried. Greg does too.

Once the tranquilizers kick in, Lance has a moment of calm, but the waves of pain soon return. The vet says, "I can't give him anymore. With what I've given him he should be totally out." He stares at the ground. "See if he gets through the night. Call me in the morning."

Marge and Vern say, "We need to go home and feed our horses, so good luck."

Lance is lying on the ground, covered in sweat. Every few minutes, he raises his head to look at his gut. I walk over to Greg, who is standing next to the truck. "I'm staying with him."

"I know." He gives me a hug. "I put the sleeping bag in the truck with a thermos of hot coffee." On his way down the hill, he looks back. "Need anything else?"

I return a half smile, grateful for his support. All the meds the vet injected will help, but I can do more. I call to him, "A bucket of warm bran mash?" That's our go-to remedy for gut problems. When he's almost to the house, I yell, "I need more towels too."

The desert nights are cold in October. I rub him dry with the towels. I'm more worried about Lance getting chilled than me. Still, Greg returns with my heavy coat. He brings two containers of hot water and a bucket of bran to make the mash, and more towels. To be sure it's the right amount of warmth and moisture, I mix the mash with my hand then stretch out a handful to Lance, who's on his feet again. He takes a mouthful, letting most of it drop onto the sand. I sigh. It's going to be a long night. "C'mon, son. You need to eat some more."

As the hours pass, I walk Lance in circles and add water to warm the mixture in between loops. I feed him handfuls of mash, as much as he'll eat. When he's down and quiet, I take a nap in the bed of the truck. When he's up, I do belly lifts with my hands and long strokes alongside his spine, pressing my fingertips into his butt muscles to release the knots. Whenever he stirs in the night, I jump up and use every technique I know to stave off the next round of painful spasms. If he rests, I rest, knowing it won't be long before we start all over again.

In the morning, Greg comes up the hill with hot coffee and a bagel. I'm sitting on the tailgate half asleep with Lance's lead rope in my hand. He's standing with his head down, nibbling on a flake of hay. The bucket of bran is empty. We made it through the night.

A week later, we are out with Shae for lunch when we run into the vet. I offer to buy him a beer to thank him for coming out late on a Sunday night. He says, "I didn't think he would make it. A horse in that much pain—I've never seen one survive. I don't know how you got him through it. You must have an angel on your shoulder."

His compliment turns into a jinx. A week later, we call him back for our two-year-old colt Topaz, who has stopped eating. After injections and a blood draw, the vet diagnoses a bacterial infection of some kind. He's my first baby horse, not quite three. I must save him too.

CHAPTER THIRTY-FIVE

GRIEVING AND GIVING THANKS 1992

In January, Topaz relapses. After more tests and another round of injections, the vet has done all he can and recommends we take him to the vet school in Sacramento. I arrange for my client and friend, Sharon, to transport us six hours north to the equine hospital. Topaz barely loaded into her trailer, but he survived the grueling trip. For me, the worst was the last hour of driving through pea-soup-thick fog. Sharon drives the whole way, steadfast and steady through it all. At the large animal hospital, I give Topaz a hug and leave him in their capable hands, begging the doctors to heal him. I cry for most of the long trip home.

Two days later, we get the call. Topaz has Valley Fever, an ancient fungus that comes out of the soil. *Did I make my baby sick…when I had the hilltop bulldozed flat for riding?*

I can't let him suffer. We give our consent to have him euthanized and used for medical research. They're just beginning to research for a cure. It's some consolation that our Topaz will help them treat other horses in the future. Having his half-sister Sonia is comfort too, though I worry she may get sick next.

I tell Ruby her son won't be returning. As I hug her neck, my tears drop onto her shoulders. She's been lethargic, with eyes drooping and a tightness in her lips. I think she knows. Animals have a kind of psychic wisdom we often discount. Ruby drops her face into my hands. Sonia, who clings to her momma's side, nuzzles her baby nose under my arm. Together, we silently mourn.

A month later, Greg hears a rumor that the company where he's been working for three years is being bought out by a large conglomerate. The word is the new owners plan to layoff the entire sales force. Greg starts job hunting, and in the fall, accepts an engineering sales position in Utah.

We'll have to move. That fact of life becomes more acceptable after we drive to Salt Lake City and find a lovely house with ceramic tile floors throughout and a big barn that will be perfect for our horses. On our return, we trade in my little truck that we bought from Dad to buy a Ford F-350 dually super cab—a four-door with a bench in front, a full backseat, and four wheels on the back to carry loads up to one ton. I'm ready to haul the horses with a rented horse trailer as soon as our Kings Canyon ranch sells.

Just as we list our house, the California economy crashes, including the housing market. Our realtor shares some wild stories of people in posh LA neighborhoods who can't sell their enormous homes for anything near what they owe. Their banks refuse to work with them, instead foreclosing on the properties. Before vacating, the owners trash the million-dollar homes, breaking sinks and toilets with a sledgehammer, then use it to put holes in the walls. I could never do that to a home I've cherished. Surely our home, with its amazing view of the poppies each spring, will sell quickly.

Unfortunately, our ceramic-tiled kitchen and baths and a spectacular view of Joshua trees and poppies don't entice a single offer. Only one person came to look. Our realtor explains buyers are getting better deals on properties closer to the city. We drop the price, but it's too late. The housing market hits bottom. We're stuck with a home we can no longer live in and can't sell.

In August, I stay behind, hoping to find a buyer, while Greg moves to start his new job. He rents a room in a house with three other guys.

"I'll come to see you as often as I can—at least twice a month. We'll talk every day." Somehow we'll get through this.

With Greg gone, I struggle to care for our animals while maintaining my practice—driving hours to some of my appointments. When I next talk with Chuck, I tell him about Greg's job and our trouble selling the house and ask if he would help by caring for our dogs so I can work. He says, "I'm moving again. Maybe we can help each other."

A week later, when Greg is home, Chuck arrives in his Camaro, followed by Mike driving a loaded U-Haul truck. He moves into the guest room with his queen-sized bed and dresser, and, for my living room, brings an antique sideboard and China cabinet with a rose marble top filled with his crystal and Mom's wedding dishes. I even accept the white sectional I didn't want him to buy before Don's funeral.

That evening, Chuck plops onto the sofa and gives me his wry smile and arched brow. "I told you so." The sofa fits perfectly and replaces the one I had from my first marriage, now shabby from cats' nails and dogs' paws. When we moved it to the trash, we discovered mouse droppings inside the base, a consequence of living with nature, something we didn't mention to Chuck.

Everything we own, even our cars, is secondhand—our only purchase, a used four-piece mahogany bedroom set for $200. Our house now contains more of Chuck's furniture than our own.

Two months later, the family gathers at our house for Thanksgiving with turkey and all the fixings. Mom and Dick drive over from Santa Barbara, Greg down from Utah, and Scotty up from LA. Mom's sister Dee and their younger brother Tom fly in from Florida. They haven't seen Chuck in years and are careful to conceal their shock at his yellow skin and haggard condition.

Tom, with long tangled blonde hair, always has a kind word for me and helps clean up dishes before I ask. With his fair skin, weathered from too much sun exposure, he looks like an innocent caught in a war zone. A free spirit, Tom once lived on a mountain, made furniture from tree trunks, and greets everyone with a smile. He and my brothers, all born a few years apart, hung out together when we lived in Michigan, but I was too little to join them.

After hugs all around and some catch-up chit-chat, Chuck, Scotty, Mom and Dick head out to the covered porch to enjoy the view complete with desert wildflowers, while Dee, Tom, Greg, and I stay inside. Tom holds up the empty blender pitcher. "Do we have time for more margaritas before dinner?"

Greg closes the oven after checking on the turkey. "Go for it. Dinner won't be for another hour."

"I want some more too." I pull the mix out of the fridge and the ice tray out of the freezer and place them on the counter for Tom, who's already pouring the tequila for the next batch.

While Mom and Dick are outside smoking, Chuck who pulls out his pain management joint to share with Scotty. I'm okay with him smoking it on the porch, but not inside. I refresh the snacks on the counter that divides the kitchen from the dining room, then join Dee who's sitting at the table looking out at the valley through the closed sliding door.

Dee says, "Debby, he looks a lot thinner." She only knows me by my childhood name, so I let it slide.

I join her at the table. "He's lost a lot of weight, but he's getting stronger since I've been driving him to the gym for a swim. When he left the hospital, he could barely stand, but he wants to bowl again. Now, he's walking short distances with a cane. I drive us into town to swim at the health club pool three times a week. It's an Olympic size pool, and he's already up to a hundred lengths."

"You're kidding," Tom says, joining us with a full pitcher and fills our glasses. "I couldn't do that."

"He swims very slowly. When I come back from my workout in the gym, he's still at it, determined to increase his stamina to go bowling again."

After the family devours the turkey and fixings, Mom and Dee serve coffee with pie, and I clear the table. Dick slips into the kitchen to add some hard liquor to his coffee. *Damn it.* I hope his drinking doesn't spoil another family gathering. I wish Mom would leave him at home. She used to be more self-reliant, but the older she becomes, the more she surrenders to his control.

Mom needs someone to take care of. It's who she is. It used to be Dad. Now, it's Dick. Greg and I have always taken care of each other and take care of the animals together—at least we did until he moved to Utah. But now, I have Chuck living with me. Caring for him is the least I can do. And I do it all.

By the time we finish dessert, Dick's speech is slurred, his words abusive. I stand up to him, making *me* his favorite target. He points at me. "You think you're smart, but you don't know anything."

Instead of speaking up in my defense, Mom usually pleads with me to cut him some slack. I'm startled when she says, "Please, Dick. We're all having a good time. Don't spoil it."

He shrieks at Mom, "I'm under attack, and it's your job to defend me. I want another drink." Mom shrinks back.

I stand up and point, "Dick, if you don't stop, you need to leave."

The room becomes dead quiet. Everyone looks at Dick to see what he'll do.

"I know when I'm not wanted. Let's go, Carlie. We're leaving." He grabs the half empty whiskey bottle and storms out the door.

Mom says, "I'm sorry, honey. I have to go."

"I know, Mom. I just wish it could be different." She kisses everyone goodbye and walks out the door.

Without Dick's drama, those who remain settle in for an evening of cards, conversation, and spiked espresso.

CHAPTER THIRTY-SIX

AND THE RAINS CAME 1993

Time drags on. I sit at our butcher-block table paying a stack of bills, weary from driving long distances to do bodywork on horses and people, then home to help Chuck and feed the animals. Greg has lived on his own in Utah for four months. When he comes home twice a month, petty arguments erupt about how I'm spending money and who he's having drinks with after work that threaten our marriage. How will we get through this?

It's a chilly January. After paying what bills I can, I move to my twenty-year-old black enamel desk and my secondhand Mac SE in the living room. I'm writing my first book, *How to Massage Your Horse,* then print pages on a mini-printer to edit. I had a publisher interested, but it fell through.

The house is quiet. Chuck went to his doctor in Van Nuys for a checkup. All three dogs are sleeping nearby with one ear perked in case I decide to move. After treating myself to a few recorded episodes of Oprah, I head to my desk to work on my book. I'm typing away, lost in my thoughts, when the phone rings. It's Chuck.

"Are you busy?"

"Just writing. What's up?"

"I'm at the hospital." My heart quickens. "It's Scotty. He's in a coma."

Scotty has become a friend of ours, too, since Chuck's birthday party, and when he came with Chuck to see the horses. Scotty and I talked about art and theater. Before Greg left for Utah, we watched him perform in a Shakespearian play at the Hollywood Bowl.

Chuck says, "They don't expect him to come out of it."

Shit keeps flying. Chuck has lost many friends to the disease. "Is there anything I can do?"

"Can you come down and see him?"

"I'll feed the animals and be there in a couple of hours. Sherman Oaks? What room?"

"Room 308. Don's room the last time he was here."

My body tenses. The nurses Chuck worked with at Sherman Oaks hospital are like family. After four years, the memory of Don's death is still raw…even for me.

"I'll be there as soon as I can."

"Can you bring some crystals?" he asks.

"Sure."

After throwing hay to the horses, I select a handful of the smaller crystals Chuck had given me over the years, grab my keys, and drive to Van Nuys.

Crystals are a part of my healing practice. I've worked with shamans, Native Americans, and Caroline Conger, the psychic healer who taught us techniques at the Hellerwork retreat to heal with energy. Chuck doesn't believe in crystals as much as I do, but he's desperate—he can't face losing another loved one.

When I walk into the room, Chuck is talking to Scotty who's deep in coma. Whenever Chuck speaks, Scotty's eyelids flutter. I move to the opposite side of his bed, pull out a velvet pouch, and set my purse on the floor. On the sheet over Scotty's heart, I place an energy-charged stone and another on the pillow just above his head.

Trust, Deborah. There is no right or wrong. Focus on your intention.

With Scotty's hand in mine, I visualize the energy flowing from my heart, down my arm, and into his body, reaching with my mind to connect with his consciousness.

Scotty, if it's your time to leave this world, I honor and support that. But if there is still work here for you to do, drink in the healing energy I am sending you through my body and return to us. Come back to us. Open your eyes.

I meditate for a few more minutes, then place his hand on the bed. When I turn, Chuck is watching me. I pull my chair close to his.

"Thanks for coming, Sis. I knew you were the right one to call."

"I don't know if Scotty wants to come back," I explain. "It's up to him."

Chuck shakes his head. "He has big family issues only he can resolve—he hasn't told them he's gay, because they're Baptists. He was afraid of losing them, so he returned home to Georgia and stayed for years, hiding his true self. We met when he moved back to LA."

"Are his parents on their way?"

"Yeah. The doctors called them. I warned the staff his parents don't know he has AIDS and Hepatitis B. The nurse told them he's in a coma, and they needed to come now. They'll tell them more once they arrive." When Chuck drops his head, a flop of red hair falls forward, concealing his eyes. "He's so afraid, he'd rather die than face them."

"I hope he finds the courage. And I'll pray they find the compassion to accept him for who he is." With a deep breath, I send more energy to Scotty.

"It's sad he could never be honest with them," Chuck says. "Not even his mom. They may not get the chance to say goodbye." I don't respond, giving Chuck the space to wrangle his feelings.

After a moment, I tell him, "I believe Scotty will come out of this. Don't give up hope."

Hope is rare on the AIDS floor. Doctors, when faced with the inability to change the outcome, try to ease the patient's pain. Most families just want the suffering to end.

"Do you need anything?" I ask.

"I could use a break. Can you sit with him while I run down to the cafeteria?"

"Sure. Take your time. I'll leave the crystals, giving them time to work." I feel another rock in my bag and place it on his abdomen.

Chuck stares lovingly at the emaciated form, once full of life. "Scotty would like you using crystals. He started collecting little ones that fit in his pocket. I helped him as much as I could when he needed money." Chuck drops his head, fighting back the tears.

I put my arms around him, giving him a bear hug like Dad gave us growing up.

"Get something to eat. I'll watch over him."

When Chuck returns, I head for home, leaving two crystals behind, one in Scotty's palm, the other under his pillow.

The next evening, I receive a call from my brother.

"You're not going to believe this," Chuck says. "When Scotty's family arrived, the doctor told them in the hallway he would never wake up. When his mother went in to see him, Scotty opened his eyes and spoke. The crystals worked!"

Tingles run up my arms. "Did you meet his family?"

"Not exactly. His mom asked me to leave. She's taking charge of her son's care. The doctors told them that Scotty has AIDS. I guess they figured out I'm gay."

"They kicked you out after all you've done for him?" Heat flushes my cheeks. Scotty's family needs to hear the truth.

"It's okay." Chuck's voice soothes with its softness. "They didn't walk out. After learning he has AIDS, they're still here. I did overhear they're in denial about him being gay, but it's a start. Perhaps now, he will build a new relationship with his family. One based on honesty. I'm so happy for him, I feel like I'm going to burst."

I hear him softly cry; the sound sucks the intensity from my anger, and a chill runs up my spine. I shiver and shake off my resentment for how they've treated Chuck. I hope Scotty is content being with his family, despite losing Chuck. "I'm happy for him too."

Since Greg left for Utah, the recession has only deepened. No one has looked at our house even though we've lowered the price twice.

Despite my thriving Hellerwork practice, it is not enough to maintain two households.

In February, the rain comes in torrents. Greg's in Utah and Chuck's in the valley visiting friends. I'm on my own. Rainwater runs down the slope of our drive narrowing into a river, carrying away tiny granules of granite, creating a gully along the edge of our road.

I don my red vinyl poncho to walk down the drive in the downpour, with the hood up and my head tucked to keep my face dry. Halfway down the hill where the road curves, the rushing water veers across and plummets down to the gorge below. Wary of heights, I stand back as I peer over the edge to the stream, transformed into a rushing torrent far below me. I'm exhilarated by its power despite my fear.

The canyon edges our property and is a dry bed most of the year. When mountain top snow melts in spring, the gully becomes a lazy narrow creek but is still easy for cars and horses to cross.

Now, it's a fierce river crashing against cliffs, our home set back at a safe distance from the edge. The fast-moving water dislodges boulders and carries them downstream like shifting pebbles and cuts off access to Marge and Vern's, our neighbors downstream. After decades, they've learned how to prepare, using a four-wheel-drive truck and a tractor to go around, and a loader to shift boulders off the road. Once the rain stops, they'll need to bucket sand back in for cars to cross without getting stuck.

The rain comes down harder now, as I attempt to minimize the damage to our road. The gorge widens and deepens—my only tools: a shovel, a pickaxe, and the strength in my arms. I must divert the path of the water, guiding it along the edge to stop it from cutting me off. While imploring the rain to stop, I build a berm of sand, praying the stream will honor the boundary. I push up my sleeve and wipe my face to see the time.

It's almost eleven at night. I've been working in the dark for hours, piling up sand into a wall high enough to redirect the flow. It's raining harder, washing away my efforts. Exhausted and chilled, I drag myself back up the hill and fall into bed without eating dinner. A nightmare of rushing water destroying my berm robs me of restorative sleep.

In the morning, I gulp down my coffee, grab a shovel and head down the hill. Halfway down, I stop dead in my tracks and gasp at the display of the water's immense power before me. A fifteen-foot-wide V-shaped chasm severs my road as it flows to join the river thirty feet below. I'm cut off from the outside world. Stranded and alone. Thankfully, Chuck stayed in town with friends.

The rain is still falling. All I can do is trudge back to the house and find the money to repair the road. Within the hour, a dozer shows up, answering my call for help. The unknown neighbor spends the day pushing loads of sand from a dump truck into the crevice to replace what the rain has carried away. At mid-morning, the rain stops falling.

Chuck comes home the next day after the road reopens. Shocked at the level of damage, he helps me gather several thousand dollars to pay for the repair. I don't call Greg until it's over, because there's nothing he can do.

That summer, Chuck goes on a month-long road trip with Scotty to visit his family. They buck his family's demands by taking Chuck's Camaro to Georgia. After a visit with his family, Scotty shows Chuck all his favorite places near his home. Chuck didn't lose his friend after all. His love for Scotty gave them both the strength for this last journey.

Chuck paid for the nicest hotels, and the best restaurants. "They were courteous," he told me after returning home, "but never welcoming." Scotty didn't become the lover Chuck hoped for, but he gave Chuck the tenderness and companionship he needed to heal from losing Don.

However, the trip took its toll. To recover, Chuck resumes swimming lengths at the pool in Lancaster. "I have to drop back to ten lengths to start," he told me, instead of the hundred he swam before.

A few months later, Scotty checks into a hospice facility where I visit him only once before he dies.

Winds roll tumbleweeds across the road as I leave the desert on my way to Topanga Canyon for Scotty's memorial. I turn into the drive beside the mailbox of the address Chuck gave me, entering a narrow break in the wall of trees that line both sides of the road. The heavy brush opens into a clearing shaded by weeping eucalyptus trees that wave in the light breeze. Parking my dually truck with a dozen vehicles, I walk down the dirt path, drawn by the sound of music and laughter. Inside a hidden glen, I find a group in casual dress chatting around tables of food—a charming 60s flashback celebration of Scotty's life.

We sing songs in a circle and share stories of Scotty's adventures. Chuck tells the tale of their trip to see Scotty's family. I share the birthday van story and how Scotty became my husband's fake lover. Everyone laughs. The circle breaks to enjoy wine, fresh fruits, and cheese, then more stories. Driving home, I process the visceral fear of losing Chuck triggered by the memorial. Losing Scotty feels like a breaking point. I go home alone where dread shadows my days and invades my sleep.

CHAPTER THIRTY-SEVEN

IMPOSSIBLE CHOICES 1993-1994

In December, Chuck comes out of his room carrying his gym bag for the pool in town as I hang up from talking with Greg. I reach for my coffee on the kitchen island and suck in a deep breath, mentally prying my jaw open to get the words out.

"Chuck. We need to talk."

He walks past me and pulls out a Coke from the fridge, popping the top and chugging down a third. Diet soda used to be all he drank, but he needs calories to help him gain weight. After a few more gulps, he sets the can on the counter and leans against the wall.

"What's up?"

"Greg needs surgery." I brace for his reaction.

He pushes off the wall, leaning into the wave of bad news. "Car crash?"

"His Achilles tendon snapped in half while he was playing racquetball." Greg never gets sick and never complains about pain. For the eleven years we've been together, he's never been in the hospital. "He stretched before the game. All it took was one step, and wham, he went face down."

When Chuck shakes his head, his golden red locks swish across his forehead. "Is he in much pain?"

"No. Not right now. He's in a cast and on crutches until they operate tomorrow." My breath quickens when I think of him going into surgery alone.

"When are you leaving?" Chuck knows me. I want to hop in my dually and rush to Greg's side. But I won't make it in time.

"It's an eleven-hour drive. I have things to do before I can leave. They'll keep him overnight after the surgery. I should be there when he gets out. After that, he'll need me to drive him back and forth to work."

I lift my head and look straight into my brother's eyes to find some clue that he's deciphered what I am saying. Their color hasn't faded from the onslaught of his illness. They remain provocative, specks of gold unexpected in the mud brown, reflecting his compassion for others out of his own pain.

"We can't afford to keep this place when I move to Salt Lake City, so we're giving the house to the bank."

He sucks down the rest of his soda then holds the can with both hands. "I see."

"You've been saying you want to move closer to your friends and healthcare. All I do is drive you to the pool and buy groceries for the days you are home." I'm calling this place home, but it won't be for much longer. "I don't have a choice."

His long lashes flutter. "There's always a choice," he says, "though we may not always like our options."

"You have friends. Greg has no one but me. He needs me more than you do right now. We've been living apart for 16 months and we're barely hanging on. Our finances are at the breaking point. No one is coming to see the house let alone make an offer. I have to walk away from this house before the bank takes it and before I lose my marriage."

Chuck won't look at me. He walks to the glass door and peers out for more than a moment. I am frozen in time, holding my breath, waiting for him to tell me he'll be okay.

"It's fine." He turns to face me. "What are you going to do with the horses? Can you keep them?"

"I'll find a place somehow. Our realtor says the bank will accept a short sale for the difference if we drop the price again. It'll be a huge hit on our credit, but I want to avoid foreclosure. If I move into a cheaper place, we can save up for the down payment, and maybe, in a year, buy another house."

"You're losing your down payment on this place? All of it?"

I nod with my eyes squeezed shut.

"I can't stop it." I am mortified. "I had planned to pay you back when we sold this house." Being honest with him is making things worse.

"It's a shame. You're losing a fabulous place. Someone will get a real steal." Chuck looks away. "I hope you've enjoyed the time you've lived here. I know I have."

"I will pay you back, somehow." I brush my face with my arm, like I'm swiping at a fly, pushing back my remorse. Before I can call the bank, I have to pull it together...then ask the neighbors to watch the horses while I'm in Utah looking for a house to rent. I'll need to borrow a horse trailer too. Greg will be on crutches for three months. *Can I move four horses by myself?*

"Don't worry about the money," Chuck says. "I'll take it out of your portion of my death policy. I've kept it even between you, Mike, and Mom."

"Stop talking about death benefits!

"Debby, you're leaving, so I'll say anything I want." He shakes his hands in the air.

I hate when he calls me that, but I don't dare correct him. "You've gotten strong again, especially for when you took Scotty on that trip home, driving all over the south."

"That was a great trip. But I'm tired ever since we came back, and then he died. All my friends are gone." The gold seems to fade in his eyes, the brightness replaced by melancholy.

"I may not know them, but a lot of those people at Scotty's service are your friends. Being closer to them may help." Chuck needs to be involved. "What about AIDS-LA? You speak to groups there. And you have your bowling league."

"Don't worry about me." He pauses for a swig of soda, then brushes his hair off his brow. "But you're right, I do need to move closer to my doctors."

How can I leave him after I promised to care for him? Greg needs me too. It's an impossible choice—one I wish I didn't have to make. I hold my face in my hands.

"I'll be okay. I'll get an apartment. You can keep the sofa. I want a new one, anyway. I'll take my new queen bed and dresser. You keep the king…"

Greg and I are prepared to give it all back—except the bed. We've been sleeping on it—the bed Don died in, an antique Chuck purchased early in their relationship, with its marble finial balls topping each corner of the brass head and footboards. Chuck offered it to us after he lost his house. I smudged it with rosemary and cleansed it with crystals. If Chuck did want it back, we'd end up sleeping on the floor. Good thing he's letting us keep it, and the sofa too, even if it is white. Our last sofa was mouse-infested so we tossed it.

He scans our living room. "And keep the antiques. I don't want them."

The softball in my throat keeps me silent. I feel like a junkman collecting his castoffs.

Chuck interrupts my thoughts. "Hey, this'll be fun. I get to go shopping for furniture again. That always makes me happy." He disappears down the hall to his room, closing the door behind him.

His positive turn makes me feel worse. I can only hope Chuck will eventually understand. I'm not keeping the promise I made to take care of him the way he cared for Don. A black hole opens in the center of my chest where my heart had been, sucking up all hope for achieving my dreams. *You'll see. I'll be there when you need me, and I will fulfill my promise.*

I call the bank, and they agree to a short sale. It's the new standard since the housing market collapsed—we sell the house, and the bank accepts whatever we get, then close the loan with only a minor hit to our A+ credit rating. But they won't put it in writing. "That's how we handle short sales," the loan officer assures me. "After the house is sold and we have all the numbers, we'll send you paperwork." I have no choice but to trust them.

I'm riddled with guilt not being at Greg's side, even though he told me not to come for the surgery. When I fell off Lance in the middle of his business trip, he flew home.

Breathe in the desert calm. Take it one step at a time. There's much to do before I can leave. Greg is okay in the hospital. Finding a house we can rent for our dogs, cats, and horses will be the hard part.

I work the next two days to earn some cash before leaving. Chuck offered to look after the dogs and cats until I return. Then he'll move out. Marge and Vern will take care of our horses. After I say goodbye to the animals and Chuck, I jump in my truck and hit the road.

Greg is released from the hospital before I arrive. I pick him up at the room he's renting and drive him to the follow-up appointment with his surgeon with my questions. *Huge mistake.*

With one look, the surgeon scowls, "So, you're the wife. I wondered why no one came for his surgery." *He's saying I'm horrible.*

This doctor has no idea what Greg's injury has cost me. "I'm here now."

Greg turns to me and says, "She just arrived." The surgeon's judgment softens when Greg declares, "I want my wife to do my rehab."

The house Greg's been living in with four other guys is shabby. His dark little room with a single bed leaves barely enough room for a crappy dresser and a TV to fight the boredom. Coming was the right decision. Chuck's not answering our house phone back in LA and I am worried. He's probably apartment hunting during the day. He'll disappear into his community again, but this time, I know none of his friends who are helping him move. *Have I lost him forever this time?*

For two nights, I barely sleep sitting up in Greg's recliner. He needs rest to heal. I insist he sleep in a narrow, lumpy bed. The door won't lock. To bar any intrusion, I prop my overnight bag against it.

The next morning, after not much sleep, I mess with the knob using a pocketknife. The house owner installed the door handle backwards. I fix it, surprising Greg. He hadn't figured it out after living here a year.

The next morning, I drop Greg at his office and start looking at rental houses. One in the south end of the bowl that cradles the city might work but for its spiral staircase—impossible for Greg on crutches, though he could access a kitchen, living room, and two bedrooms in the upstairs house that faces the street. I creep down the steep dirt hill beside the house to see the lower level. It has a door and a picture window facing the backyard with the same rooms as above, but smaller.

The owner says, "We build for two generations of Mormon families who live together." As he leads me up the stairs, he adds, "With an additional deposit, I'll allow your dogs and cats."

The layout is odd, but I can make it work. "Any place we can keep our horses?"

"For another two hundred a month, you can use the three acres off the backyard, but you'll have to fence it."

I bring Greg back to see the house after work. He hobbles through the upstairs on his crutches then, since he can't manage the spiral stair, I drive him around to see the lower level.

He says, "The rent is as much as our mortgage."

"If I'm going to drive you to work every day, we need to live in the city."

We explore an adjacent structure that might work to store my ceramic installation, and its support walls. I'd left them out in the sun and rain back in California with only tarps as protection. If it gets wet and freezes, it will shatter into shards, like my heart when I think of Chuck.

"Would that include the garage?" I ask the owner.

"For another fifty."

I turn away to speak with Greg in hushed tones. "It would cost more to board the horses, and I'd miss not having them near, especially with Fashion close to foaling."

Greg and I exchange telling glances, then I turn to the owner. "We'll take it."

Since Greg's employer won't move the horses, I set aside money to rent a trailer. We'll transport them ourselves. The horses will board at the farm we had hoped to buy until we can put up fencing. With Greg on crutches, Shae says she'll fly up and pound T-posts with me if I will drive her to Park City so she can go skiing when the work is done. She'll be leaving her husband to care for the horses, dogs, and cats to help us bring our horses home from the boarding facility—something only a best friend would do. She knows she'll be skiing alone because I don't ski.

I drive with Greg back to Kings Canyon to prepare for the movers. We find Chuck and his friends loading the last of his boxes into their cars. Mike, who's moving Chuck's furniture, already left with his bed and dresser in a U-Haul. I give Chuck a hug, with moisture gathering in my eyes and a cool breeze between us. I can't deal with that now. I'll mend this wound later.

Greg on his crutches gets in my way as I pack. But I'm glad for his comfort at night.

We rent a horse trailer from a neighbor. When the movers leave with our furniture, we load three dogs into the backseat of the truck, three cats into kennels in the trailer's front compartment, and four horses into the rear—Lance, Ben, three-year-old Sonia, and Fashion, a majestic Thoroughbred broodmare we rescued last fall. She hadn't been able to carry a foal to term and was heading to slaughter. We bred her with another trade-for-bodywork to an all-around champion Arabian stallion, hoping for an offspring built just for dressage, and return Ruby to Ginger as agreed.

When we stop for gas, Greg hobbles on crutches to walk Brandy in the grass while I handled the other two, giving them exercise and relief before closing them back in the truck. Greg heads to the men's room while I open the drop-down feed doors for the horses to stretch their necks. I give each a drink from a bucket and fill their hay nets.

The cats get water and a quick pet. As soon as Greg returns, I run to the ladies' room, then climb behind the wheel to continue our trek. We get waves as we leave, from people who were watching.

Twelve hours later, we descend into the bowl of Salt Lake City, drop off the horses at the barn, then head home to sit with our dogs and cats on the living room floor and wait for the furniture to arrive.

CHAPTER THIRTY-EIGHT

THE NORTHRIDGE EARTHQUAKE 1994

It's mid-January when Shae flies in to help me build the horse fence. She reaches up from her short stature to bring Lance's head down next to her face. "How you doing, boy?" Her blonde ponytail and fair skin remind me of a palomino.

Six new inches of snow camouflage a stack of T-posts and rolls of wire. Shae and I put on work gloves and slide a cold metal tube onto the top of a 60-inch post, each holding a vertical rod handle. We slam it down, again and again, hoping to force the bottom foot with its stabilizing diamond shield beneath the surface of the grass.

"It's not working. Damn it!" The post refuses to sink more than a few inches. I pull off my gloves to rub and warm my fingers.

Shae says, "The ground is frozen. It won't yield."

"How do we do this?"

I'm in a hurry to build the fence because the horses don't have heated water buckets at the barn where they are being boarded. The girls who take care of the horses place two buckets in Lance's stall, but they freeze within ten minutes. If he finishes the first bucket, he either knocks over the other one, or it turns to solid ice. "I offered my heated buckets, but they don't have power in the stall at that barn. I have to get this fence up and bring them home. Without enough water, he will colic."

Shae rubs her hands together and stomps her feet to warm them under the fur-lined mukluks she's wearing. "How about hot water? We could pour it in the hole as we pound in the post to defrost the ground."

"You're a genius." She grins.

Once the posts are in, we work through the afternoon, running wire to create an enclosure around two large run-in sheds made from pallet wood, big enough for all our horses. The landlord tractored them with his pallet fork a quarter mile to shelter our horses against the biting wind and snow.

The sun warms the air, making the day pleasant by the time we finish. The mountains, framed by blue sky, seem close enough to touch, a backdrop behind a stage. We plug in the extension cords to the fence and water buckets before walking up the hill for a hot cup of tea.

While the kettle heats on the stove, I phone the barn to tell them I want to be there when they load Lance, but I'm told they're already on their way.

A horn honks in our drive. Shae says, "They're here."

With the horses settled in munching on the hay, all that's left is to drive Shae up to the ski resort tomorrow.

The next day, a six-point-eight magnitude earthquake hits Northridge, its epicenter near both my brothers, worse than the two I experienced while in LA. When I try to reach them, I hear, "All circuits are busy at this time." Shae calls her husband outside in the brisk morning air for the best cell reception. When she comes in, I hand her a cup of hot coffee with Baileys added.

"Is anyone hurt?" I'm worried about her dogs and her horses.

"Everyone's fine. The animals are nervous, but they'll settle down. A rockslide destroyed the rusty old tractor he wanted to restore. Andy is perturbed, but I'm glad it's gone."

"Are you leaving?"

"We won't be able to mend trails until the aftershocks stop; the broken jumps can be repaired later too. I want to ski. Can you drive me up to the slopes?"

"Okay if I don't stay? I don't ski, and I have tons to do here."

"As long as you pick me up." Shae, who's gorgeous and smart, will fit right in with the beautiful people at the resorts. After dropping her off at Deer Park, I return home and continue calling my family. Just before lunch, Chuck answers.

"I'm okay. Mike, Judy, and the kids are living in their van in their driveway. With all the cracks, their house isn't safe."

"Have much damage inside?"

"Mike's clown pictures all crashed to the floor, spreading shattered glass everywhere. When the kids screamed, he ran in pitch-black down the hall, cutting his feet. The bloody footprints he left in the hall scared them worse than the quakes. The first shock left an enormous crack in his pool and splashed out most of its water."

"Oh my God. What is this? Your third earthquake?"

"If you are only counting the big ones."

"The news says the freeways are a mess."

"All of LA is a mess."

"How about you? Do you have damage?"

"My TV inside my new armoire crashed to the floor. Pictures fell too. One hanging over the bed dropped on my head."

"Do you have a concussion? Go to the hospital."

"I'm a nurse, remember. I'd know if I had a concussion. I don't."

"Then I'm coming to help you clean up." *And to watch him through the night.*

"You can't get here. The highway is closed. Debris on the roads hasn't been cleared either. They won't let anyone into the city—not until it's safe. Wait a couple weeks." My pounding heart drops into my stomach. *I should be there.*

I stay glued to the news, feeling the same dread when moving as a kid—afraid of being left behind, feeling unsafe in each new place—everything and everyone unfamiliar. We almost lost Mom to a tornado. When I was four, we stood in the street a few miles away, watching the twister drop out of the sky onto where she was shopping. All my terror-filled memories emerge and bind my core like a straitjacket.

Shae flies home the following day. I continue unpacking, filling kitchen cabinets, and hanging my art, making it the best temporary home I can.

Weeks pass. Then months. Our Kings Canyon house doesn't sell. The bank calls, and I negotiate to settle our loan. Greg asks, "So?"

"They'll get back to me." Our finances are a mess. I keep busy, hoping to push back the dark cloud of depression that hovers over me. I make calls to drum up some new clients. I subconsciously punish myself for abandoning Chuck by dropping things on my foot and walking into walls.

After it stops snowing, I go down to the garage to check on my clay installation. Instead of whole tiles, I find chunks and shards. In another box, more damaged tiles are cracked like Mike's home from the quake. I created my own catastrophe when I left my home in the canyon, overlooking the poppies and Joshua trees.

I've lost more than my home. Don is dead. Scotty too. Chuck is next. He's in danger, and I can't get to him. My empowerment circle is destroyed. *Instead of dancing through the flames, I'm being consumed by them.*

Three months after the earthquake, Interstate 5 opens again. My nerves set my skin on fire as I pass the devastation heading to Chuck's. When I told him I was coming, he said I can only visit for a few hours, just long enough to see his decline. He's gaunt, his skin a light shade of jaundice. And he's taking too many painkillers.

He sends me to pick up his prescription. After waiting in line, the pharmacist says, "Tell him he needs to see his doctor if he wants more Percocets."

I look at the pill bottle. "It says he has two more refills."

"I know he needs it for pain, but he's taking too many. It's a controlled narcotic and can be dangerous."

"Dangerous how?"

"He's taken a month's worth of pills in just over a week. Like morphine, it can shut down his organs—his kidneys and his liver."

My jaw drops. "I'll talk to him. But can you give him a few just to get by." He nods with reluctance. As I wait, I wonder. *Is my brother trying to kill himself? Does he have that much pain, or is this a symptom of his depression?*

In the apartment, Chuck is in the kitchen wearing loose-fitting shorts, a white tee-shirt, and has bare feet. He leaves his cigarette burning off the edge of the counter as he fills a glass with water—no ashtray. He'd never do that if Don were alive. The vibrant, muscled body he once worked to maintain has disappeared, devoured by his illness, leaving him emaciated. He hasn't even bothered to tan. The paleness of his skin is stark in contrast to his unkept mop, still red but without the luster of shampoo and conditioner.

He doesn't care anymore. I shiver. This is against his very nature. His will to live has always been powerful—a stubbornness we inherited from Dad and the determination to survive at any cost from Mom.

"The pharmacist said you can't have more Percocets without a new prescription." I try to catch his eye, but he won't look at me. "Why are you taking that many?"

"I take them because I'm in pain." He holds the cigarette butt under the tap, then tosses the soggy remains in the trash under the sink. He passes me as he returns to his sofa. "My legs are on fire. You can't imagine. This disease eats away the sheathing of nerves, exposing them."

"Are you swimming?" I walk behind him carrying his water glass as he shuffles across the room, lowering himself into a pile of extra pillows.

"I can't." He pops two pills, chasing them with water, and lights another cigarette. He takes a long drag, then places it in the nearly full ashtray on the glass coffee table. "I still go bowling with my league occasionally. When someone can't make it, they call me to fill in. But I can't even do that anymore."

"What are the doctors saying?"

"They've trying everything. I can't take AZT. It's worse than the disease. If that's the only way to live, I'd rather die. Anyway, it costs hundreds of thousands of dollars a year. Most patients can't afford it unless they get on a program."

"Are you running out of money?"

"I'm okay. I sold the cabin."

"No!" I can't imagine him giving it up, especially after losing the house. He loved walking among the pines, with squirrels scampering, deer grazing, and hawks soaring above.

"The money is in the bank for when I need it. None of you can help. You're all broke."

Shame slams me in the face. A silence expands, creating a chasm between us. He's right, of course. Greg and I will be lucky to sell our house for what we owe. Since the earthquake, Mike's house is destroyed, and his family is sleeping in the van. Mom and Dick, and Dad too. We're all broke and broken.

"I get why you feel that way." His cigarette burns up in the tray, like a prophecy of all that is to come. "I'm sorry."

"Hey, don't sweat it," he says, making light of it.

He needs to hear the truth. "Chuck, I'm worried. You're not taking care of yourself. You're depressed. Are you seeing a counselor?"

"Once in a while. When I need to. It's part of the AIDS LA program. Don't worry, Sis. I've got lots of people looking out for me. My doctors. My friends. Though I don't have many of those anymore. I don't want to even think about it."

"What can I do?" I want to help because I love him. But also out of guilt.

"There is something you can do…when the time comes." He looks at me with eyes wider than I'd seen all day. I could lose myself in his brown eyes—deep, murky pools.

"If I get bad, well, you know what I mean, I want to end it fast. If I can't, I want you to help me. Will you do that? Promise me."

I nearly fall over, using the sofa to balance. "Chuck…I don't know if I can promise. Are you sure you want to end your own life?"

"When I'm not me anymore, I want to be set free…to be with Don."

I swallow hard. "Are you *sure*?"

"All my friends are dead. Everyone I've loved. Don. And Scotty. I'm tired." He runs his hand through his thinning hair.

"I'll try. That's all I can promise."

I pray that day never comes. Would he take his life? Could I? If it saved him from suffering? Is that what he truly wants? Or is this depression talking?

I push the tortuous thoughts out of my mind and return to the moment. "How can I help you today?"

"Clean my bathroom. I haven't had the energy." He reaches for his cigarette, almost burned to the filter, takes one last puff, and snuffs it out.

"I'm on it. Why don't you lie down while I work?"

Chuck drags his feet over to click on the small replacement TV, dwarfed in the cabinet now tethered to the wall in case aftershocks increase. Curled up on the sofa, he pulls up his blanket to watch Jeopardy like he did with Don when they competed for the right answer; Don usually won. He perks up as if Don is with him whispering answers in his ear.

I take the overflowing ashtray on the table in front of Chuck, exchange it with the clean one, then step into the bathroom. Cigarettes aren't good for Chuck, but he'd argue, "How much can they hurt?" As I turn away, I close my eyes, unable to accept the inevitability of my brother's downward spiral.

In the bathroom, I clean a glass ashtray like the ones Mom had all over the house when we were young. I gave up smoking at twenty-three. Greg did too, right before I met him.

The air tastes sour in the two-room apartment. It's too cold to open the window. The heat, set at eighty, is almost unbearable for me as sweat covers my back and brow. But it's what he needs to be comfortable. His pain fills the room, lands on my skin, and enters my pores. My muscles tense to resist it.

With his cleaning supplies, I scrub the sink and toilet and polish the counter until the bathroom sparkles. After an hour, I run the vacuum in both rooms, then join Chuck on the love seat. I grab sodas for us both, then I eat too many mini-Snickers from a dish on the coffee table. The stimulants will keep me awake for driving. When he tells me, "You'd better go," I beg him to let me stay longer. But he's made up his mind.

I leave after dark and head up to Lake Hughes to spend the night with Shae. The next morning, after a breakfast of fresh chicken eggs, I tour her barn to say hi to her horses, calming my agitated nerves before starting my long drive north. My worry for Chuck has ballooned and feeling helpless with no action plan grates on my bones.

CHAPTER THIRTY-NINE

ONE BORN, TWO RESCUED 1994

In Salt Lake, I establish a rhythm to spend time with each of our animals. In between Hellerwork clients, I reassemble my shelving units in the lower level and unpack my clay tools and watercolor paper to inspire me to return to making art.

As spring nears, Fashion's belly swells. She's carried him for nearly a year and is ready to drop her foal. I missed seeing Ruby birth both her foals—Topaz, who died when he was two, and Sonia, who's now three. Fashion is my last chance to witness the miracle of birth. When I took her on, she'd had too many problems keeping a foal to term and no one else wanted her.

That evening, when she shows signs of labor, I grab my sleeping bag and coffee thermos, and settle into the corner of her shelter. I keep my cell phone ready to call the vet in case the mare or her foal exhibit signs of distress. We'll need the vet to visit anyway to give the foal his first vaccinations.

I stay awake all night in the cold shelter, watching. At first light, I run up to the house to use the bathroom and grab some coffee. When I return, the foal is lying in the mix of shavings and hay in the shelter —a bay colt. Fashion is up to lick her newborn, cleaning him and stimulating his muscles, nudging him to stand for his first suckling. I help dry him with a towel, moving from his face down his neck to his chest, then down to his tiny front hooves, still soft from being inside the womb. In the dim morning light, I notice his feet curve backward.

When he tries to stand, they curl under, throwing his weight onto his ankle joints instead of the bottom of his feet. His knees buckle forward, and he falls to the ground. I stroke his neck to reassure him and gently run the tips of my fingers down the back of his legs to stretch the tendons to straighten the colt's legs enough for him to stand before the vet arrives. A slight curve remains. Despite that, he reaches under his mother's belly for his first drink—milk full of antibodies.

The vet arrives, checks him out, and giving him shots, then says, "If his legs don't completely straighten soon, I can cut the tendons." I shake my head, determined to lengthen his tendons with my hands to avoid surgery.

The sun rises in a blue sky, revealing how lovely he is. A bay like his momma, the only white he bears is in the center of his forehead, the shape of a small star. His eyes are soft and kind, but he's feisty too. He kicks out his hind legs in the small enclosure, missing me by inches. I want to name him Charles Frederick after my brother, and Greg agrees. We call him Charlie, taking pictures to send my brother, even though they will never meet.

After I tell Shae the colt's arrived, she congratulates me, then says, "Ruby's in trouble. Ginger placed her with some people who are keeping the mare in their backyard fenced in with other horses, and she isn't getting enough to eat. These people know little to nothing about horses and Ruby's at risk."

When I tell Greg, he says, "We shouldn't take on another horse."

"But she's given us two foals." I scrunch my brow. "Ruby is family. I have to save her."

I call Ginger, arrange to borrow a trailer from a neighbor in Kings Canyon, and head to California to pick her up.

When I arrive, she's standing in the corner of a fenced yard, her ribs and spine protruding from her once massive form. A dozen healthy horses in the corral must be getting all the food. I call out to her. She whinnies a greeting and drops her nose into a halter. I hold her face in my hands and kiss her face.

"Poor baby. You're coming home with me. This time, to stay." I hug her neck and whisper, "We'll get you healthy again." With no one around, I swing the gate open and lead her into the trailer. She limps up the ramp and steps in without resisting.

At home, we give her plenty of feed to fattening her up, but her belly remains distended. I'm worried, so I call the vet. He examines her and tells me, "She's in foal. To grow a healthy baby, she needs her feed increased, and prenatal vitamins."

When I break the news to Greg, he's not happy. Why should he be? We're struggling financially, living in a crap rental house in an alien culture.

Despite all the abuse and neglect she's suffered—her withers and hip were probably broken at the track—she's mostly sound, even lively, enough to live a happy life and give us one more baby. Horse owner clients will see how effective my work is. *How do I convince him to help me keep her safe?* "Greg, I can't abandon her now. Her baby will be a full sibling to Topaz, like him being reborn into our lives. It's synchronicity."

When my tears flow down my cheeks, he holds me and says, "We'll figure it out."

My joy with Fashion's new colt and rescuing Ruby evaporates when a mortgage officer at the bank in LA calls. "We're rescinding your agreement for the short pay and are foreclosing."

But they promised not to. Now, our credit will be ruined. I stare into space for hours. When Greg walks in from work, I haven't moved from the sofa with the dogs at their post by my feet.

He rushes over. "Is it Chuck?"

"It's the house. The bank lied." I fill him in without tears—I'm all dried up. "I've kept all our bills paid. Why are they doing this… just as my business is picking up?"

"Make some more calls. Figure out our options."

If Greg sees my fear, he'll get scared, and then we'll be really screwed. But I'm unable to drag myself back to work and rearrange the week's appointments to give me time to cast off the hopelessness. *Pull it together, Deborah.*

We're in this mess because of circumstances beyond our control. Greg was laid off during a recession and could only find work out of state. Keeping the horses doesn't help, but I couldn't live with myself if they landed in an abusive home like where I found Ruby…or worse in a slaughterhouse where Fashion was headed when we took her in. I'm making good money, my calendar nearly full, with bodyworkers from the massage school downtown. It's essential they receive regular massages to continue their work on clients.

We're climbing out of our financial hole created by the collapse in the housing market. That's all moot because the bank won't be reasonable.

Will we ever find a home I can hold on to? *I can't give up. Not ever.* I'll figure it out—whatever it takes to support Greg and the horses. They are my family.

Our California realtor suggests bankruptcy to give us a new start— after seven years to get past the black mark. Greg and I meet with the attorney before deciding. He says professionals with much higher incomes were caught like us in the recession. I crunch the numbers, trying to avoid filing, but we don't have a choice.

No matter how atrociously the bank has behaved, I will make one last trip before giving them our home—where I thought I would live for the rest of my life—to clean up any trash we left strewn while coping with movers and wrangling animals, and to say goodbye to all the memories created in that magical place.

After cleaning for hours, I pause at the bathroom mirror to stare at my reflection, noticing lines around my eyes and mouth, and a deep crease in my brow. I don't know what lies ahead, but I will endure whatever comes.

I pack bags filled with things we'd left behind into my truck: a garden hose, rags, t-shirts, and socks that were hiding in the back of our closet. In the front seat with my cooler, I squeeze in my bucket of cleaning supplies and the vacuum. Sliding the glass door closed, I turn for one last look at the view from my covered porch. *Goodbye, Joshua trees. You have inspired my art. Goodbye, Manzanita bushes.* I've collected some of their old, broken branches, twisted wood of rose and blonde, to inspire me, along with the horse bones Shae and I found on late night excursions in dry desert washes. These magical desert remnants I carry with me to wherever we land, reminders of the place where Topaz and Sonia were born. On the point overlooking the canyon, where Tania, our first German shepherd, lies buried, I place a few more stones on her grave to protect her from coyotes. *Goodbye my sweet girl. I miss you so much. Your spirit will always be in my heart.*

Goodbye to my friend Marge, who came to my rescue and rode in a helicopter with me, and to Shae, whose friendship has helped shape the person I've become. She taught me to talk with horses—an essential part of the work I hope to carry on. I've become a healer, but I'm not yet healed.

I start my truck, crank open the windows, and blast country music as I drive down the sand-packed road leading out of Kings Canyon for the very last time.

At home in Salt Lake, with my emotions in overdrive, I catch every virus floating around. My doctor prescribes antidepressants to break the downward spiral of my depression, but after taking a little pink pill for three days, I become disoriented while the world spins around me.

My calendar is filled with clients; my future business and our financial survival depend on me showing up to all of them ready to work. I stop taking the pills. The few meds I did take help me until I find a natural replacement. I'm in the first year of my too-early-onset of menopause and too sensitive for most traditional medicines. I try acupuncture. After they stick tiny needles all over my face and body during several sessions, my hot flashes ease, and my sleep improves.

One day, after working on a horse, I visit a health food store and meet Mary, a massage therapist who recognizes the horse manure aroma on my boots and starts a conversation. Her husband trains and breeds Thoroughbreds for the track. "Unlike most in his industry, he believes in hands-on-healing for horses," she says. "I'm not trained to do it, but I'd like to learn."

"I'd love to meet him." I call Greg to let him know I'll be late, then follow her home to their ranch near Park City. We swap bodywork sessions, and I get a tour of the barn. I offer to demo my techniques on his stallion. He's impressed with the results, enough to pay me for full sessions.

"How about in exchange for a stud fee?" The big bay has great conformation, good feet and is as smart as they come. Watching him move takes my breath away—just what I want out of Fashion, if I can get her to carry another foal to term. He offers to pay for a few sessions to cover my gas and promises referrals to other horse owners. I eagerly accept, excited to foster an important relationship. I'd earn gas money and get a new baby out of Fashion. If my business continues to grow like this, maybe we can rent-to-buy a house with a proper barn.

Greg agrees with the potential opportunities to work with race-horses and helps me trailer Fashion to their Park City ranch. Mary and I become friends, talking as we continue to swap therapy sessions. She teaches me about Ayurveda, an Indian philosophy of food as medicine. "Why don't you join me for a lecture series based on Dr. Christopher's herbal cleanse formulas?"

Needing to lose weight and improve my energy for my ten-hour workdays, I sign up.

For six weeks, I learn about natural healing, start a regime of herbs he formulated, drink only organic apple juice and water, and only eat vegan one day each week. Greg says, "I hope this does what you believe it will," but otherwise keeps his opinions to himself. By the end, I've become a vegan, not because of some philosophical belief, but because meat tastes like raw flesh. Even the smell of Greg's cooking meat makes me want to puke.

"I've lost ten pounds." I twirled around in front of him with my hands in the air with a wide grin and a twinkle in my eyes. "Can't you tell?" My blue jeans are loose and slip down,

With Thanksgiving around the corner, I buy two vegetarian cookbooks and research how to prepare a vegan feast. "I've picked out six recipes. Sweet potatoes with apple slices, carrots with a peanut butter sauce, a sumptuous stove-top stuffing made from scratch, a vegan version of your favorite green bean casserole, mashed potatoes, and broccoli with an Asian sauce."

I show Greg the full color pictures of each recipe as I make a grocery list. "I'm off to Whole Foods to buy organic."

"Does this mean I'm eating tofu-turkey?" He's not smiling.

I kiss him on the cheek. "Don't worry. I'll still fix you some meat. How about a turkey breast?"

"I'm glad you like being a vegetarian, even happier you aren't trying to convert me."

I know better. He's a Midwestern meat-lover through and through. He flashes his lopsided grin. Greg's happy when I'm happy. I love that about him.

On Thanksgiving Day, I undercook the veggies to enrich the flavor and maintain the crunchy texture, adding sumptuous sauces, and have no desire to pig out on white bread or turkey. We eat on TV trays while we watch an old sci-fi movie, then gather and carry the dishes to the kitchen.

Greg puts the TV on hold. "There's something I need to tell you."

I glance back. "What's wrong?" I can hear it in his voice.

We stand face to face in the kitchen, surrounded by dirty pots and pans. "I'm flying to Chicago on Monday."

His eyes reveal his angst. "And?"

"I...we...are being transferred. To Chicago."

I take a moment to process his words. My business is thriving. Next week, I'm to work on a horse bound for the Olympics. Still, Salt Lake will never feel like home. And I know Illinois. I finished high school in Peoria. The winters may be somewhat colder than here, but I'll no longer feel like an alien being surrounded by Mormons. They seem nice, but it is like living among Martians.

I speak up. "Okay."

His brow goes up.

I lift my left brow and ask, "When do we leave?"

His jaw drops. "You're not mad? The last time my job forced us to move was horrible. It's taken you a year to unpack."

He's right. I had just emptied the last box of art supplies downstairs, organizing them in cabinets and on shelves. I'm ready to get my hands back into clay. "Are you asking me if I can start over again?"

"I expected you to be rattling off a list of reasons why we can't move. What gives?"

I shrug. "I want to settle, but not here. This city doesn't feel like home. And even if it could, houses are too expensive. I can take my work anywhere." I cock my head. "So, yes. I'll move—but *only once more.*"

"What about Chuck?"

"When he needs me, I'll fly back."

"So, we're moving again," Greg says, in disbelief.

"Yep. We need to find a new home for us and the horses."

"The company will fly us out twice to look, but they still won't move the horses. The company policy says horses are agricultural, not personal property."

"Having them transported that far will be expensive. Maybe we can buy a used trailer." My planning wheels turn. "I'll research horse properties in Illinois, but first, I better get this kitchen cleaned up."

"You dry, because you know where everything goes." Greg flashes his big grin. "I'll wash." When he picks up the dish scrubber, I give him a bear hug, then grab a dishtowel to dry.

CHAPTER FORTY

FINDING HOME 1995

The realtor pushes me and Greg to make an offer on any property she's shown us over the last two days, but none are quite right and all cost more than our budget. We haven't told her about our bankruptcy. Even though we can't get a bank loan, Greg makes a good salary. I believe we'll find an owner who will carry the loan or let us rent-to-buy until our credit improves, just like how I met the man who sold us the Kings Canyon house.

I hate not being forthcoming with the realtor but fear she won't show us anything if she knows. If we find something affordable that will work for all our animals, then we'll work it out with her. Right now, it seems impossible, but I can't lose faith. Somehow, somewhere, we'll find a place to live.

We'll rent if we have to, but after our experience in Salt Lake, I'd rather not. The landlord won't return our deposit, and we really need that money. We fulfilled the one-year lease, but he doesn't like the fencing we put in for the dogs and plans to tear it out. He claims our cats bent a ll the mini blinds, but I found only two with minor damage needing to be replaced. I thought he'd appreciate all the landscaping we did for him, putting in stone steps for safer access down the steep hill to the lower level plus adding rose beds in the front yard. But in Utah, landlords are all powerful.

As I look at houses, I feel like Goldilocks. The first one is small with little land. The second is crowded against the street and crammed between neighboring houses. Late in the day, the realtor shows us a farmhouse and dairy barn with concrete aisles sitting on a busy road where animals can get run over. I won't make that mistake again. Where is my *one that's just right?*

Day two is a bust; on the third day, when our agent is busy with a closing, we take her sheet of listings and a map to drive by on our own. One she crossed out as too far to commute, catches my eye.

On the country road, we see houses surrounded by hundreds of acres of cornfields. We miss the address on the listing and backtrack to find it. "Is this it?" I ask. "Slow down. Nope. Wrong address." Greg wants to give up and head back to our hotel, but something is driving me to find this property. "It's got to be here someplace."

Greg parks across the road from the only *For Sale* sign for miles. Nothing matches the listing—not the realtor, nor the house number— and there's no house in sight. A chain blocks us from driving down the gravel lane to find it, but I won't be deterred. I jump out to remove the chain, but it's secured with a lock, so I step over it and start walking.

Greg calls out, "Where are you going?"

"Over that hill." I glance back. Greg is following me, shaking his head. I trudge up the gentle slope.

He jogs to catch up. "Put this on before you freeze. It's the middle of December." He holds my coat as I slip it on and zip it up.

"Thanks." I give him a sheepish grin and pull up the collar against the brisk wind. Brushing the hair out of my eyes, I walk on, an old growth forest on my right and truncated cornstalks poking up through a snow-covered field like lined-up yellow soldiers on the left. "The exercise will help me wake up." Running through different scenarios for moving the animals kept me awake last night.

At the top of the hill, we don't see a house, only another hill.

He hands me a fresh tissue for my running nose. "Do you want to keep going? You've got a cold and I'm freezing."

I love how he takes care of me, but I won't turn back. "I'm warming up."

He slows, falling behind my pace.

I turn to face him with my back to the wind. "Please? Just a little further. I have a feeling about this place."

When he catches up, I take his gloved hand in mine, and we continue the trek.

At the top of the second hill, still a distance away, a baby-blue two-story house comes into view. There's a huge barn at the end of the lane, its roof ridge slumped like a broken-down horse with huge holes where long sections of sheet metal are missing, probably stripped away by the wind.

"The picture doesn't match." Greg stares at the realtor's list. "It says it's occupied. We better turn back."

Despite his caution, something urges me on. "I don't see any window coverings. Maybe they moved out."

We circle to the far side of the house through weeds, using a cinderblock to step onto a covered front porch. Through the windows, we see large rooms, empty but for construction materials leaning against the walls and piled on the floor. "I love the big rooms."

Next, we investigate the barn. It reeks of hog manure piled everywhere, inside and out. Three haphazard storage buildings built with creosote poles line up toward the north from the house, the first with one side open like a makeshift garage, all three covered in rusted sheet metal. The largest on the end filled with pig shit stinks too. Sections of old farm equipment tangled with weeds dot the uneven ground around the buildings. In the backyard, excavated piles of dirt as tall as me hug the house on two sides.

Clumps of long green grass peek through the snow everywhere. "We can make it safe for the horses if we clean up the junk. We just need some hot wire fencing." I point to the biggest storage building. "There's room to store my installation so, in the spring, I can repair it." The place is a mess. If we had any sense, we would run. "Maybe he'll lower the price."

The next day, the realtor shows us inside. I ignore the disrepair and half-ass fixes, and instead, focus on the possibilities. Measuring every room, I sketch a floor plan on my yellow pad to estimate renovation costs at a home improvement store and gather samples. "To start, we'll make the kitchen and bath functional."

In every fiber of my body, I know we're supposed to live here, but I don't tell Greg. He needs to figure out if this is home.

With my rough estimate of repairs, we calculate an offer and submit it to our realtor. The owner, who we learn is in his eighties, refuses the offer. She says, "He's in no hurry to sell, so he won't budge on the price." Will my plan turn to ashes? *No. I have to find a way.*

It's a week before Christmas and we're running out of time. The company won't pay for another house-hunting trip, but they want Greg right away.

At dinner in the hotel, I nibble on my salad and meatless pasta dish as we discuss our options. "The blue house best meets our needs. I know it's a mess, but we can make it beautiful." It's the only house I measured throughout. With my sketch, I envision all the changes I'd make to open up the downstairs. Greg doesn't see it yet, and may, I fear, want to settle for a house requiring less work. Or worse, he'll say I have to give up the horses.

I can't. I've already lost too much.

With his company paying, Greg had ordered a steak; he forks his last bite but holds it over his plate. "We'll be living in a mess while we work on it."

"I get that." To fill my queasy gut, I eat too much pasta. "What else can we do?"

"You could stay in Salt Lake, and we could keep looking."

"Living in two places? I'll never do that again." I breathe in positive energy. "Which house do you like best?" I wait for him to speak. He doesn't, just shrugs. I place my fork on my half-eaten plate of pasta and interlace my fingers at the edge of the table. The restaurant is quiet, half empty. It's late. "The realtor showed us everything in our price range. Waiting will cost more...and we may not find anything better."

I rub my ice-cold fingers.

He shrugs again. "That's true."

"The blue house down the lane is a one-of-a-kind property. Isolated. With a view of farmland and forests in every direction. It's all about location, right?" Under the table, I touch my thumbs to each of my fingers. "Should we bite the bullet and pay the owner's price?"

Greg tilts his head. "He'd need to carry the paper until a bank gives us a loan."

Our realtor hasn't asked yet, but I believe the owner will. I see it in my mind.

"She said he has for his other properties. We can explain how the California bank screwed us on the short pay." I can't sound desperate.

Greg reaches across the table, takes my hand, and holds my gaze. "Okay, call the realtor. Tell her we'll take it...if he agrees to the loan." He does. Now, all we need to do is move.

CHAPTER FORTY-ONE

MOVING TO ILLINOIS 1995

Back in Salt Lake, Greg supervises the packers from the moving company while I shop for a used horse trailer. I take the truck with the bumper-pull ball-hitch to look at two trailers an hour north. We need one big enough for Lance. The last time I unloaded him from a too-short trailer, he threw up his head, slammed it into the ceiling, and came out dazed and wobbly, with a nasty gash between his ears from a ceiling vent. I vowed, never again.

At a trailer lot, they direct me to the trailers in the ad, but everything is too short. Before I can leave, a guy in the shop yells, "There's a steel one out back. It's got some rust, but it's big."

I pull up my hood against the rain and wander toward the back fence. Tucked behind smaller trailers, I discover a slant-load gooseneck, abandoned to the elements for what looks like decades. I pull down the creaky ramp and step inside. The steel sides look okay. I lift the torn rubber mats to examine the wood floor for rot. *It's solid.* I pull out my tape to check the height. It's large enough to hold all our horses except Fashion, who is staying behind anyway to be bred.

The guys weld a gooseneck hitch to the bed of my truck, hook me up, and send me off, pulling the first horse trailer I've ever owned.

Greg takes one look at it. "We need a mechanic to check it out."

At a shop down the road, the owner tells us the brakes need major work; plus we'll need a new set of tires and new wiring for the lights. When I pay the bill, I'm still under my budget of $1,800 which is less than the cost of shipping one horse to Illinois. We're lucky so far.

After another week of packing, we prepare to move the horses. The dogs go to stay with the vet while the cats stay home with food and water. We've arranged to board the horses a few miles from the new house in Illinois. It's inexpensive and close enough to check on them. The middle-aged couple have a pasture with a spring-fed pond for water but know nothing about horses. A few ponies, with burrs in their manes, are boarded in an enclosed pasture. The only shelter is a shed, open on one side with a cement floor—not a good place for Ruby to foal. After our next trip, we'll add fencing at home, repair the barn, and move them before the baby comes.

On the day we load the horses, a biting wind spooks Sonia. She refuses to walk up the ramp, so we hold her back. Once Lance, Ruby, and Ben load up, Sonia calmly follows. Charlie, only six months old, rides in the slot in back where saddles usually go. We hang hay nets for each, latch up the ramp, and say goodbye to the cats. Wired from coffee, I convince Greg to let me drive first. Otherwise, I'll drive him crazy with my nervous chatter.

As we snake through the mountains around Salt Lake, big snowflakes smash into the windshield, freezing on the road. I wish Greg were driving, so I exit to get gas and switch, but the truck's wheels spin on the slope halfway up the snow-packed ramp. The weight of the fully loaded trailer isn't enough to lend me traction.

"We're not going to make it!"

"Keep going," he reassures me. "We'll be okay." He adds, a bit too harshly, "Don't gun it."

The momentum from our highway speed carries us forward, but we're slowing too much to reach the top. The tightness in my gut wraps around my chest. *I'm going to kill us all.* Horse trailer wrecks on icy roads are the worst—can even be gory. If we backslide, we'll jackknife and tip the trailer onto its side. Catastrophic for horses.

I've transported horses in the desert, but not on ice and snow. My knuckles are white from gripping the wheel, my arms ache. Like my mom in the chaos when I was a kid, I stay the course.

One foot at a time, we crawl our way to where the road levels out at the stop sign. I gently tap the brakes, holding the wheel steady to not swerve. *Whew! We made it!* But when we pull into the gas station, my wheels spin on solid ice. Then we slide sideways, all forty-feet of truck and trailer—out of control. "Shit." I suck in air and hold it. "I can do this." A bit of sand gives me enough traction to pull the rig alongside a pump, thankfully without ramming into it. When we come to a complete stop, I turn to Greg. "Your turn."

With Greg behind the wheel, I focus on being a good copilot, which gets easier when the mountains give way to plains. I check mile markers and estimate the distance to the next gas station.

It's after dark when we pull into the fairgrounds in Grand Island, Nebraska, where we booked overnight stalls for the horses. Rocking inside the trailer all day takes a toll on their legs. Using flashlights, we lead them to five box stalls bedded with pine shavings and stocked with fresh hay and water. They seem relieved to be on steady ground and quickly settle in for the night.

We pull the empty trailer down the road to a motel and collapse into bed. After only six hours of sleep, it begins all over again.

Before dawn, we pick up breakfast at a drive through and return to the fairgrounds to load the horses. Sonia refuses to load into the dark steel box, so we tie her while we load Lance, Ben, and Ruby and lock their dividers in place. Sonia still refuses to load. I tell Greg, "I know what to do. Load Charlie and close the back doors."

Sonia's eyes fly open. We named her after the Red Sonia movie for her courage as a newborn—a quality she needs today so we can hit the road.

After a few minutes, we reopen the tailgate. Greg unloads Charlie and I lead Sonia to the ramp. She looks around then walks in, her struggle evident with every twitch in her body. Greg reloads Charlie and we close the trailer. While they munch on hay from their nets, we gas up the truck, reenter the highway, then eat our cold breakfast sandwiches.

At eleven that night, we arrive at the farm where the horses will stay. Greg and I are tired from too little sleep and the long drive. The horses are weary, too, from the vibrations and turns, scrambling on their feet for a second long day. We drop the ramp, and Charlie leaps off, but Sonia slips and falls to her knees. *Damn it. I forgot to check for ice. Earning her trust again will be twice as hard.*

We release them into the pasture. They frolic and kick up their heels, scattering snow into the moonlit sky. When they drop their heads to munch on hay, we drive off to find a nearby motel for the night. I look back, hoping they'll be okay until we return.

In the morning, we close on the house, then drive down the long lane for a quick look. Whether it will be a disaster or a realization of a dream, I'm not sure, but it's ours. After lunch, we drive straight through to Utah , pulling the now-empty trailer. The dogs give us lots of licks when we pick them up. All that's left is to clean the rental and supervise the movers loading two long vans. We check on them, load our trailer with steel pipe corral sections, tack, and boxes of red clay needed to restore my broken installation.

Sunday, our last day in Salt Lake, we place the cats, each in a carrier, in the trailer's front compartment. Our three dogs jump into the backseat of the truck. With improved weather, we hit the road, hoping for an uneventful last leg of our move.

Late that night, somewhere in the eastern plains of Nebraska, the truck wakes me out of a shallow sleep with its clanks and grinds. "Do you know what's wrong?"

Greg switches the transmission out of overdrive. The sound continues. "I'm not sure. It's not shifting right." Panic seeps into his voice. "I'd better pull over."

Before he hits the brakes, the truck slows on its own, independent of the engine's revolutions. Greg eases us to the side of the road. "The transmission is shot."

I'm working at not panicking. The fear sinks into my bones. "I have no idea where we are." With map in hand, I search the horizon below the starlit sky for any city light to give me some bearing. "Wasn't there some kind of highway emergency phone at the last mile marker?"

He nods. "I think so."

"You stay with the dogs. I'm going for a walk." He hands me a flashlight he had stashed under the seat. I pull my coat around me against the bitter night air. It didn't seem like it would be this far, but I've been walking for eight minutes.

I arrive at the mile marker to see a post. There a highway phone was once installed, but it is gone now. Shit! I turn around and walk back. As I near, the dogs bark, either in greeting or because they didn't expect a figure to emerge out of the blackness.

"No luck," I say as I crawl up to my place on the bench seat. "It's okay, babies," I say, half turned, reaching to calm the dogs in the back-seat. "Now what?"

Greg says, "Why does this always happen on a Sunday night?" He points to my purse lying on the floor next to my feet. "You think you can raise anyone on that mobile phone?"

I hadn't wanted him to buy the clunky brick phone, but now I'm glad he insisted. "I'll try." I dig into my purse for the right number and dial our insurance company. I'm surprised when someone answers.

"We're broken down in the middle of nowhere." She asks me to hold on. I turn to Greg, my throat tightening, diminishing my voice. "The phone battery is low. I hope she hurries."

I sweat bullets over fifteen minutes until I hear her voice again. She has located a tow truck big enough to pull our rig with our fully loaded horse trailer to Grand Island, but it is a hundred miles away. I tell Greg, "They're on their way, but it might take a while." She stays with me on the phone until my cell phone dies. To calm my nervous energy, I check on the cats in the trailer. They are doing great, especially with the mild tranquilizer the vet gave us.

Next, I walk Brandy, and Greg takes Alex and Wolfie through the ditch to a grassy area until the dogs have relieved themselves. We return to the truck and wait in the silent darkness. The landscape from our view looks eerie. I start talking about what I want to do with the farm and the house, even though I know my list making and planning drive Greg batty. He only wants to know what is next. I plan far into the future. I'm Aquarian.

The minutes crawl by as we stare at the stars, glorious this far away from city lights, then brainstorm what might be wrong with the truck. Some scenarios scare me. How will we pay for repairs?

An hour later, flashing red lights appear and grow out of the blackness. The oversized truck passes, turns around, and backs into position. After a few words with Greg, he climbs behind the wheel. They lift the front axle of our super cab dually high in the air, throwing us back against the seat, our feet level to our heads. *Weird.*

Greg reaches for my arm. "It's okay."

After some full-throated barking, our dogs nestle into the backseat and fall asleep. Our cats stay in the horse trailer, snug in their carriers. When Greg waves we're all set, the tow truck enters the highway, pulling us to Grand Island. It's 10:08 pm.

With up and down askew, I'm stuck on a rollercoaster, rocking high in the air, terrified of the drop to come. We stare out our respective windows in silence, mesmerized by the pricks of light splashed across the immense blackness. I worry about the cats but can't do anything. Thankfully, the boxes of raw clay in the back aren't stacked high, avoiding a rollover.

When a rare pair of oncoming headlights breaks our monotony, it illuminates our comedy show, trapped and tipped, traveling down the highway.

At midnight, the tow truck pulls us into the rear lot of a motel. Its sign says they allow pets. We don't tell them we have six. Greg pays for a room. I walk the dogs on a strip of snow-covered grass along the blacktop, out of sight. Greg unhooks the trailer. We stand together without speaking as we watch our truck disappear into the night, not knowing how long we'll be stranded nor how much the repairs will cost.

The next day, our fears are confirmed. The transmission is gone.

Dead. Destroyed. The mechanic will order parts for the rebuild—three days and two thousand dollars. Without knowing where we'll get the money, we say yes—fix it. We have no other option. *It's getting harder to be brave.*

I stay with the animals while Greg walks to the nearest cafe. As a vegan, I don't want to eat cheese, but there is nothing else available for protein. I alternate between a sandwich and a baked potato. We give our dogs and cats, who remain well-mannered, free run of our small room. I worry one will sneak out into the cold, and we'll never see them again. To keep from going stir crazy, Greg and I watch television and play cards while worrying we'll miss the movers and, with the house locked, they'll leave, taking everything we own somewhere else.

On the fourth day, we wake up to a call saying the truck is ready. After calling Mom to beg for help, and a long, excruciating pause, she agrees to send us half. I manage to cover the rest, leaving us financially vulnerable in the extreme. We load up and are back on the road by late morning.

We arrive at our new home at two the next morning, carry the cats in their carriers inside the cold empty house, and sit wrapped in blankets on the floor, huddled with the dogs to wait for moving vans to arrive.

CHAPTER FORTY-TWO

MAGGIE, CHUCK, AND OPRAH 1995

The sun reflects off the snow, a blinding white, as we begin work on the pasture fence. First, we pour boiling water into the starter hole, like Shae and I figured out in Utah, then slam our steel tube pounder down onto the T-post top until the stabilizing shield slides below the surface. *Why do we always move in winter? I* long for Shae's help, but she's a thousand miles away. Greg helps when he can, but by the time he makes it home from the office, it's too dark to work outside. So, during the day, I pound T-posts alone, one at a time, gripping the cold pounder until my fingers go numb. When my hands quit working, I go inside to stack trim-boards left in every room from the unfinished renovation before I can unpack another box.

On weekends, we ball up barbed wire and remove rotting wooden posts, then replace it with electrified wire strung between posts. Inside the barn, in places where the roof doesn't leak, we create makeshift stalls using left-behind scrap lumber, then connect our six-foot-long steel pipe sections for three outside runs—not enough, but it's a start.

We want to bring the horses home before Ruby foals. The shelter where she's boarded is so low, she can't lift her head. After resting, when she struggles to get back up, she scrapes her legs on the concrete slab, drawing blood. Any straw bedding we spread inside their shelter is carried away by the wind.

In early March, I find Charlie lethargic with fever from a puncture in his neck just below his right ear. After a quick search, I find the culprit—a bent out broken wire in the hog panel fence. I call a vet.

"The wound is infected," the vet warns, and he gives him a shot of antibiotics. "If it spreads to his brain, he'll die."

I gasp, horrified. "What can I do?"

"Clean the wound twice a day, give him these meds, and call me if the fever gets worse."

Greg and I use truck headlights to finish our fence that night. The next day, we trailer our horses home. I'm reassured to find Charlie's fever has broken. Once they're settled in, I think of Chuck sitting in his apartment alone. But it is not time yet, so I do what I can here to get everyone settled in. I'll be ready to leave when Chuck needs me.

In April, my friend Dian visits from Fort Wayne just as Ruby goes into labor. We bring out three chairs and coffee to watch. Dian birthed two sons—she's my expert.

With the foal's front legs sticking out, Ruby pushes herself up.

"Oh, no!" I screech. "They'll break."

"It's okay," Dian says. "They're pliable." She touches my arm. "She's adjusting the baby's position. Trust me. Ruby knows what she's doing."

I watch, gripping my mug until the filly is born and pulls herself up onto her wobbly legs. As a full sister to Topaz, the Universe is returning what's been lost.

Dian suggests we name her Maggie, short for Magdalena, a woman, according to myth, who bore witness to the death of a loved one. Greg and I rub Maggie dry with towels and touch her all over to bond with her. Once she's nursing, I ask him, "Promise me we'll never move again." He replies with a hug.

The bankruptcy and truck transmission repair stretch our finances to the limit, leaving nothing for renovations—for now. Seeing our home for what it can be, I gather my creative ideas into a design on paper. After I tear out a few walls and open it up, Greg will see it too.

Exhausted from unpacking boxes and building fences, all I want to do is sleep. Eight weeks after our move, I'm out feeding the horses when Mom calls.

"Chuck had a bad fall."

I return to LA on May 22nd—Mom's birthday. Shit. I forgot to buy something. Mom looks worn out when she picks me up at LAX. Thankfully, she left Dick at home. She's relieved when I offer to drive. Chuck's ground-floor apartment is easy to find—right across from Sherman Oaks Hospital. *That's handy.*

When I enter his apartment, I'm confronted with an enormous fish tank as tall as me, perched on a black lacquer cabinet. A light in the lid illuminates colorful fish darting in and out of tiny castles. Across the room, Mike and Judy sit on a new sectional sofa—white again. *It doesn't matter.* My family is together, the first time in a while—except for Dad.

Chuck comes out of the bedroom, leaning on a cane with Mom at his side. "Hey, Sis. Glad you could make it for Mom's big day."

"You falling upside down in the tub has nothing to do with me jumping on a plane."

He arches one brow, revealing despite the gauntness, the brother I've always known. When he sits on the sofa, I notice his thighs, smaller than my forearms, his pallor, a familiar jaundice yellow. I swallow my distress.

"Did you see my fish tank?" Chuck brightens. "Isn't it great? I watch the fish for hours. They're mesmerizing."

The fish swim through the obstacle course of bridges and castles while bubbles ascend out of the pink and purple gravel floor. "I can see why."

Mom asks, "Can I get anyone something to drink?"

Mike jumps up. "Relax, Mom. It's your birthday. I'll get it."

"I'll help." I follow him into the kitchen. Within minutes, Mike comes out carrying sodas. I'm right behind with Mom's birthday cake ablaze with candles, which she easily blows out.

Everyone settles on Chuck's sectional to eat cake off paper plates.

I positioned myself next to Chuck. "How exactly did you fall?"

Chuck shrugs. "I'm not sure. One minute, I'm combing my hair. The next, I'm upside down in the tub. I guess I lost my balance. It happens." He nibbles his cake. "This time, it was harder getting out." He lifts his shirt to show the bruising wrapped around his side.

"This has happened before? Mom didn't tell me." *Maybe she doesn't know.* Chuck keeps secrets. He doesn't want to be forced into hospice.

He put his finger to his lips and looks around the room. "Don't tell Mom. It'll spoil the party. Let's just enjoy this time, okay, Debby?" He puts his hand over his mouth. "Oops. I mean Debby-rah." Then he laughs. I couldn't help but smile.

When Mike and Judy leave for home, a helper shows up to check on Chuck, who just went to bed. *At least he ate a few bites of pizza and cake.* Mom makes up the sofa with sheets and a pillow for me and for herself. I can't sleep. The long plane ride aggravated my body pain from work at home. I lie still and listen for signs of distress from Chuck.

The next morning, Chuck rallies...like he has so many times before. He and I play cards on the edge of his bed while Mom gets her hair done. Another skilled helper arrives. Chuck says, "They come in daily." Everything seems under control.

I left Greg alone to manage all our animals. I'm ready to go home, but my return ticket isn't until Sunday—four more days.

Mom, back from her appointment, calls out, " Debby, you're wanted on the phone. It's the Oprah Show."

I'd requested a ticket for her weight loss show after losing thirty pounds, adding brightly colored flowers to the envelope with markers to stand out. After not hearing, I'd given up. *Greg must have given them this number.*

Since 1986, I've raced home to imagine being a guest or in the audience for nearly every episode. Watching Oprah helped me battle emotional binging. I want to thank her, for that and so much more. With Chuck's phone to my ear, I listen, making notes on a pad. "Can you hold on for a minute?" I ask, then turn to Mom and Chuck. "They have a spot in Oprah's audience. If I fly back tomorrow, I'll make the early Friday taping." It would cut my visit short by a day. I swallow hard. "What should I say?"

They say in unison, "It's Oprah! Say yes!" Mom and Chuck watch her too.

Greg picks me up at the airport shuttle just after midnight on Friday. After each taping, Oprah greets everyone in her audience. I've dreamed of her buying a piece of my art, encouraging me to publish my story of healing horses and write another one about myself. I can't be late, or I'll miss it all.

With three hours of sleep and a shower, I drive into Chicago for the first time to meet my idol. The man who sold us our house said, "Take Route 64. It's the best route to Chicago from your house." *What a mistake!* With heavy traffic and road construction delays, I'm an hour behind schedule. I arrive at a warehouse on an abandoned corner, soaked in nervous sweat, and knock on the metal door below the HARPO sign. A staff member tells me, "You're too late."

I panic. "But I left my sick brother and flew across the country to be here." After checking with someone, she lets me in. Minutes after I find a seat, Oprah rides in on an elephant.

I'm flushed with energy as we all scream, then go silent on cue. Oprah says, "The elephant symbolizes the weight this audience has lost. Congratulations!"

After the epic show, we line up to meet Oprah. She shakes our hands as her staff shuffles us to the exit. I have no chance to share how Hellerwork helped me overcome decades of pain, leaving my hope of touching fame trampled like yesterday's newspaper. This ego feeding event does nothing to get me closer to publishing the horse massage book I wrote a year ago or selling my art. Maybe I should give up on both.

I took my shot at touching fame, but at what cost? What if Chuck's rally fades? Should I have stayed? Or should I bide my time? The turmoil of not knowing when he will need me churns in my gut, my head, and my heart.

CHAPTER FORTY-THREE

SECOND TRIP TO CA 1995

Six weeks later, I'm in the pasture with Lance when Mom calls. "Debby, he can't keep food or medicine down. And he won't go to the hospital." I scheduled a flight the next morning.

Uncle Tom, only a few months older than Chuck who had flown in from Florida, picks me up at Arrivals in Chuck's Camaro. He tells me, "I had to see him…before it's too late." They'd been raised like brothers, especially when we lived near Detroit.

"How's he doing?" I ask.

"Carleen is with him." He always called his sister that, instead of Carlie. "Chuck's been waiting for you."

I study my uncle's face, drawn and sullen, his pain palpable.

"I was shocked when I saw him." Tom turns away and wipes his cheek. "Sis is at her wits' end. She wants to be with him all the time, but Dick keeps calling her to come home." He pulls up to the curb in front of Chuck's Van Nuys apartment and turns to me. "He's the best of us. Why him?"

"I don't know, Tom." My travel fatigue morphs into sadness, swirled with anxiety and doubt. *You can't fall apart.*

When I walk in, Chuck's sitting in a wheelchair holding a pan in his lap. "In case I throw up again." He looks up, his eyes imploring. "Could you push me over to the ER?"

"If that's what you want, sure, Chuck." I turn to Mom, "Why don't you and Tom drive his Camaro over while I push him across the street?" Before leaving, I speak to his doctor on the phone to tell him we're on our way.

We're halfway across the bumpy boulevard when Chuck throws up in his pan. I stop, but he waves me forward. "Keep going." He wipes his mouth with the towel, then uses it to smother the odor in the pan.

In the ER, I'm furious when they make us wait for an hour because his doctor forgot to call in the admit order. They won't treat Chuck's vomiting until his doctor arrives.

I scream at the staff, "Help him!" channeling Aurora from *Terms of Endearment*.

By the time he's taken to a room, I'm vibrating with excess energy but ready to collapse, an odd feeling. Chuck, drugged into a mush-mouth state of la-la-land, thankfully is no longer heaving, so the three of us return to the apartment. Tom curls up on the floor while Mom and I make our beds on two ends of the sectional. I can't sleep. I'm still fuming about Chuck suffering for an hour needlessly because of paperwork.

The following morning, Chuck's doctor, a friend of his from his nursing days, stops by my brother's room to tell me, "All Chuck needed was antibiotics for a simple kidney infection that was so bad it could have killed him."

"You know my brother. He hates hospitals and doesn't want to die in one. He is his own worst enemy. But with his nurses' training, he knows what's coming."

"He seems to listen to you. It's good you're here."

What happens next time? He won't listen to Mom. *I need to stay.*

The following morning, while Mom sleeps, I drive Tom to the airport. He says, "Thanks for taking over his care. I can't handle watching him wither away."

"Remember that winter when I followed you, Mike, and Chuck to that dog racetrack to check out the beavers?" It was one of the few fond memories I had with the three of them.

Tom grins. "What were you thinking? You were in what, first grade?"

"I wanted to see the beavers too." The memory lifted both our spirits, but only for a minute.

After dropping him off, I rush back to the hospital to catch Chuck's doctor on his rounds. Chuck is still out of it, so I share what I know with his doctor and ask him, "What should I watch for?"

He gives me concise answers and his number. "Call me if you need anything."

For the first time, a medical professional is listening to me, taking me seriously, helping me give Chuck the best care, working as a team. Most want AIDS patients to give up and die, thus ending their suffering and that of their families. Despite battling this disease for years, my brother still has fight in him, so I will help him stay alive.

Over the next few days, Chuck improves enough to wheel him back to his apartment. I send Mom home to Santa Barbara for a much-needed break. Jerry is Chuck's daytime caretaker, provided by an AIDS support organization to relieve weary families like us. With his support, I settle into a routine—giving Chuck his meds and watching him sleep. Jerry is thin but looks healthy. I'm not sure how he came to this work, but he's well suited, demonstrating unending patience and an unflappable calm. He comes to see Chuck five days a week, four hours each day. Different guys cover the weekends.

In the weeks that follow, Chuck declines from the harshness of his new meds and the wicked persistence of his illness. When he sleeps, I sit in a chair dealing cards to play solitaire on the edge of his bed like we did as kids. I flip the cards, placing black on red and red on black for hours, watching his chest rise with each breath. I study his brow, seeing brief moments of peace amid the prevailing viciousness of the pain. He described it as every nerve in his body being on fire. I've known pain from car and horse wrecks, but nothing like what he describes. I weep inside.

When Chuck becomes unable to eat for days or keep his pills down, his doctor orders Compazine to be administer rectally. Chuck had done this for others but becomes embarrassed when I act as his nurse.

I put on surgical gloves from the box. "This is nothing," I tell him. "Our vet talked me through putting my hand up Lance's rectum to feel for a blockage when he was colicking."

"Don't do that to me!" We both laugh.

After I've administered his medicine, he's able to keep down liquid meal replacements he drinks through a straw. I urge him to take a few more sips whenever he wakes to help him regain strength. The sun is shining out the window, but I have no interest in going outside to enjoy it. I won't leave Chuck's side, so when Mom returns from Santa Barbara, she runs errands for me.

With her at the pharmacy and the helper finished for the day, the stillness is unsettling. Chuck, with his irresistible laugh, always has dozens of friends around him. Now, it's my turn to be here for him.

The next morning, Jerry knocks twice at the front door and steps in. Chuck had given him a key. When Jerry enters Chuck's room, I tell him, "He stopped breathing. For four or five seconds…then gasped for air." I take a shallow breath. "Is this it?" The knot in my throat makes it hard to speak. "I've never been with someone when they died."

Jerry says, "It could go on for hours. Even days." He studies Chuck's face, then turns back to me. "Everyone dies in their own time. We're here to help him pass over when he's ready."

"In case you're not here, what should I do?"

"All you can do is keep him comfortable. Feed him ice chips and use the swabs on his dry lips. When it's time for him to go, it's important that you tell him it's okay."

Like what Chuck did for Don. He didn't want to let him go. But when the time came, he somehow found the courage.

I share stories with Jerry about Chuck when Don was alive, how together they threw the best parties, and took us camping in Yosemite.

"That's amazing for two gay guys to be the center of their straight families. It's rare."

I hear Chuck stop breathing again. We watch in silence. I glance at my watch, waiting for his next gasp for air, wondering if it will come. "Six seconds that time."

Jerry asks, "Are you ready?"

I close my eyes and shake my head as I watch my brother struggle for breath. "I don't know. He's a fighter. He's fooled the doctors so many times, fighting his way back to return to his bowling league. Not to bowl every week, but at tournaments when they needed a sub. He loves bowling, and he's good at it. Once, he threw a three-hundred game at a tournament. He makes them all laugh with his antics."

Jerry nods.

He's a good listener. "Why did you choose to work in hospice?"

"I'm honored to support the families. It's such a terrible disease." Jerry is an old soul, put on this earth to usher the suffering to a place of peace. He asks, "What can I do to help you let him go?"

Chuck's red hair is tousled against the pillow, his cheeks hollow, his lips crusty and chafed. But yesterday when he opened his big brown eyes, his charm and stubbornness remain—what he uses to get his way. *Will he ever open them again?*

I turn to Jerry, barely breathing. "If today is the day, I will let him go and be glad he won't suffer anymore." I sit straight and face Jerry. "But if he wakes up, and his fight is back, I'll fight for him. It's not for doctors or nurses or insurance companies to say when he should die. It's up to him."

Jerry nods. He hugs my shoulders. I lean my head against him, accepting a moment of respite.

When Chuck turns over and falls into a deep sleep, Jerry stands up and gathers his things. "It looks like he's going to fight for another day. It's time to leave. I'll see you next week."

But I never see Jerry again.

The following day, I call an ambulance to take Chuck back to the hospital. Then I call Mom in Santa Barbara to meet me there.

When she arrives, Chuck mumbles a few words, fighting his way back.

An hour later, a social worker we'd never met, orders us into a private room, then closes the door behind us.

She blurts out, "You can't keep doing this."

I narrow my eyes. "Who are you?" She haughtily hands me her card with MSW after her name. I show it to Mom.

The social worker says without pause, "I understand you don't want to let him go. But you must. Both of you." She looks like a stern teacher slapping a ruler in her hand. "He needs to go into hospice."

Mom shrinks back in her chair, overwhelmed by the certainty of losing her son, and starts to weep.

I fold my hands in my lap to process what she's telling me, comparing it with what Chuck has told me he wants, and what he's taught me through example. Her assumptions are wrong. She doesn't know us.

Chuck talked about this when Don was in the hospital. She may bully families because she thinks that's her job, but she won't bully us. Not Chuck. Not Mom. And not me. *Why is she pushing him out? Do they need the bed? Is insurance no longer willing to pay?* It's all about money. I channel my pent-up rage. She's a few feet away when I hold my rage near and stand up to reply, my voice projecting a quiet power.

"I will fight for my brother because he told me he's not ready to give up." I put my hands on my hips. "So, no. I won't let him go. Not until he is ready."

I take a step closer to the social worker. She leans back, her eyes big. I guess she's never had anyone push back. I feel as tall as my brother Mike, who's 6'3".

"Do you understand me?" I lean in. "Not until he is ready."

The social worker responds, her voice squeaky. "Well, you need to move him *someplace*. He can't stay in the hospital. The insurance won't pay." Her eyes jerk from side to side as she scrambles for a solution. "He's not strong enough to go home. He should go into hospice."

"If he gets another kidney infection, will a hospice give him antibiotics?" I already know the answer.

"No. Only palliative care."

"Then I'm not sending him to hospice, not until he's ready." I maintain my authority but, remembering she's just doing her job, I soften my demeanor.

"Here's the list of hospices in the area. Pick one."

At that, she leaves.

Mom is wrung out. "Debby, whatever you decide. I can't..."

"I know, Mom. I'll take care of it."

With Chuck still out of it the next morning, I decide to placate the social worker by visiting three of the facilities on the list while Mom stays with Chuck.

By the time I return, and I walk into his room, he's responding to new medication and is alert. I report on what the social worker said and show him the list with the three I visited circled. "There's only two I think you would even consider, one that is in a West Hollywood neighborhood that's closer to a home environment."

He shakes his head. "Debby, you have to fight this."

Mom catches me in the hallway. "I just talked to Dick. He saw an article in the Santa Barbara paper about a local AIDS facility—a care center that's not hospice."

I call the number scribbled on the corner of a newspaper page from the hall paid phone and learn it's worth exploring. I tell Mom, "I'll go check this out."

"You go, honey. I'll stay here." She moves toward the door to his room, seeing Chuck has fallen back to sleep. "You'll know what's right for him."

I drive up the coast to Santa Barbara in Chuck's Camaro with his music blasting. The break recharges my batteries. When I arrive, I learn the Sarah House is a not-for-profit supported by the community, designed for AIDS patients, and allows full medical care—perfect for Chuck. But will they have a bed? The first of two facilities is a house divided into mini apartments with full-time nursing. I like the coordinator, but she doesn't know when she'll have an opening. She sends me to their other facility ten minutes away, newly constructed, open for six months.

The director, Debbie, who's a delight, shows me around. The entrance of the one-story structure opens to a central community room with residents playing board games, watching tv, and eating with family members in an adjacent dining room. Individual rooms for residents, off two divergent hallways, open to the community garden of roses through a patio door. "Chuck would love the rose garden," I tell her. Around the garden perimeter, a six-foot block wall muffles traffic noise from the nearby highway.

"My brother wants to receive medicine if it will help," I tell her.

Debbie says, "We give access to whatever medical care our residents need. We have a resident who just came back to us from the hospital. We're here to help, not to tell them what they should do."

This is a solution Chuck can live with, and it's located only miles from Mom's home.

After Chuck's records are faxed to Debbie, she says, "We have an opening, and we'll accept him immediately." She shows me the room, which contains a hospital bed.

"Can we bring Chuck's queen-sized bed?"

She says, "Bring whatever makes him comfortable. We want this to be home."

Chuck is going to love her.

Later that day at the hospital, I share all I've learned with Chuck. His eyes brighten and he nods.

I tell the hospital staff, including the social worker, about the facility that has a bed for Chuck only two hours away. They say they've never heard of it. *How can that be? Is the healthcare system that broken?* When I ask about transportation, they say, "Insurance won't pay for an ambulance. You need to drive him."

Managing Chuck's needs while driving scares me.

In Chuck's room, he looks tired. "Can you manage riding to Santa Barbara in your car?"

"Let's do it," he tells me.

The next day, I help Mike load a rental truck with Chuck's bed and his fish tank along with an antique dresser and some of his art. He leaves to set up Chuck's room in the Sarah House. When I get to the hospital to pick up Chuck, he looks tired.

"I'm good. They gave me some really nice pain meds." He smiles his crooked smile.

As I drive on the 101, we listen to Chuck's favorite music and chat about game shows. When we arrive, Chuck walks into his new room to find his bed moved in and made up with his sheets. He climbs in and drifts off.

Mike says, "I left some boxes of knick-knacks for you to unpack."

"We'll unpack later, after he wakes. He'll want to tell me where they go." With Chuck asleep, I follow Mike back to Van Nuys to help clean out Chuck's apartment. By the time we've finished, Mike looks like his bones are collapsing inside his frame.

"Go home," I tell him. "Go see your family. I've got this." He hugs me and heads to his car. When he's gone, I grab some takeout to eat in the car on my return to Santa Barbara. Mom's relieved to have Chuck close. I am too. She won't need to drive so far to see him. Her trips to LA have taken their toll.

After sleeping in Mom's guest room, I return early the next day to find Chuck sitting on the patio outside his room in a lawn chair, smoking a cigarette.

"Hi, Sis." His face is bright. *Must be the roses.*

"What are you doing out here?" I'm worried he'll overdo and relapse.

"They won't let me smoke inside."

"I'm surprised they let you smoke at all. Where'd you get the cigarettes?" I peer through the open patio door for the culprit.

"From the nurse who helped me out here." He knocks off ashes into a familiar glass ashtray balanced on his knee. I walk out to the patio. Chuck says, "The room looks great...but could you hang a painting and a woodcut, and buy me a table and two chairs? I need a place to entertain when people visit me. This chair is borrowed from my neighbor."

"What people?"

"I've had a dozen already—other residents, staff, even some volunteers. Some friends called wanting to drive up from LA to see me. I think I like it here." He takes a drag off his cigarette. "Where have you been?"

"Closing up your apartment." I lean against the open door.

His face drops. "So this is home. What did you do with the rest of my things?"

"Everything went to someone who needs it. Jerry dropped by and Mike encouraged him to take some things, from the kitchen, I think." I'm disappointed I missed saying goodbye. He took such good care of Chuck.

"I'm glad." Chuck nodded. With a flick of his head, he threw the hair out of his face, letting go of his old life. "Can you get me some high thread-count sheets? And some throw rugs for the floor in a green-blue palette?"

"Got it." As I turn to leave, I noticed the fish tank Mike had set up in his room was missing.

"Where are your fish?"

"It was too crowded in here. I had it moved into the community room. I can see it there. And Dan loves it. Debbie says he sits in front of it for hours."

"Are you sure? You love those fish."

"It's where it's supposed to be."

That's my brother, always thinking of others, still teaching me life lessons.

When all my tasks are complete, I leave Chuck on the patio surrounded by three nurses he has doubled over laughing, showing them the *slut ring* he bought while at a bowling tournament.

I don't join them because I've been here six weeks and I'm exhausted. I miss being home with Greg and our animals. After giving Chuck a quick hug, I check in with Debbie. "Keep me posted on how he's doing. Call me anytime, night or day."

CHAPTER FORTY-FOUR

THE FINAL JOURNEY 1995

When I arrive home, Lance is grazing on the flat outside the barn. He sees our car and lifts his head to nicker, saying, *where have you been?*

"Go ahead," Greg says, dropping me off near him.

Lance places his face against my chest. I hold his head, and we stand together in silence. When he lifts his head, he snorts, and I breathe into his nose. Then, he drops his head and presents his neck for massage—a command more than a request.

I press with my fingers, starting behind his ears, sliding down his neck to his back, to his rump. Using my elbow, I work deeper. He positions his body to show me where he wants my hands, shifting forward and back as I knead the knots.

I feel the tension in his body release and in mine as well, but the exhaustion from the last six weeks creeps in—an ache radiating from the base of my skull.

Lance turns around and presents me his other side. I chuckle. "Okay, a little more." I work a few more minutes until a wall of fatigue closes around me. "That's all for now." I turn to leave, but he blocks my path. I wrap my arms around his neck and let my tears fall. *I have nothing left to give, not even to you.* "Maybe tomorrow, after I get some sleep." He swings his head around, wrapping me in a horse-hug.

Three weeks later, I'm in the pasture when Greg steps out onto the covered porch.

"Deborah! You have a phone call." His voice echoes across the expanse like the beating of a drum summoning me for duty.

I twist in slow motion toward Greg on the porch, his hand bracing the glass storm door.

He says, softer than before, "I think it's time."

I'm not ready, but I dare not delay much longer.

I enter the house through the mudroom, drop into the nearest chair, and punch in the numbers for the Sarah House. Debbie, the Director, answers. "You need to come now."

I haven't been home long enough to recover, but my answer must be yes.

She adds, "And hurry."

With my travel plans set, I call her back with my arrival time, and Debbie gives me an update on Chuck. I ask, "Who's with him? Mom or Dad?"

"A staff member always stays with Chuck. I haven't seen Carlie yet today, but she visits often. As far as I know, your dad has never visited him." My heart drops. *Dad continues to disappoint him.*

I call Dad before leaving for the airport. He says, "I've been busy."

Summoning all my control to keep my tone even, I tell him, "You'd better *make time* to see him… NOW…or you'll regret it." He mumbles some kind of nonsense, so I hang up.

When I arrive at Sarah House the next day, Dad still hasn't shown. Chuck is sleeping, so I call Dad again.

"Where are you?" My voice is sharp. I'm tired from traveling and frantic with worry. Dad gets defensive. I ignore it. "You need to come. *Now!* I don't know how much longer Chuck will be with us."

He mumbles something about a meeting.

"You're running out of time." To make sure he finds his way, I give him directions, repeat my warning, then hang up. I have a long night ahead. I won't waste more energy on him.

In Chuck's room, several staff members have gathered around his bed, talking about Chuck's needs for the coming night. Chuck's eyes are open, and he's talking a little. The phone on the nightstand rings. Chuck reaches for it, but he's too weak to grab it in time. It stops after three rings. Debbie says, "They probably picked it up in the office."

Chuck puts his hand to his ear like he was answering it. "Hello? Yes. I understand." He's talking to his open hand as if it's the phone. He reaches toward me, handing me the invisible phone. "Debby, it's an angel. She's inviting me..." His voice trails off. His eyes close.

I nod.

The entire room grows still. Debbie gets it. Chuck was talking to an angel. *Heaven is welcoming him.*

Out in the hall, Debbie says, "We have a priest come from the Mission to give our residents Last Rites. Would Chuck want that?"

"Would they come here? Even though he's gay?" Chuck had been an altar boy, and it broke his heart when the church rejected him for being gay. *I loathe the Catholic church for that.*

"Oh, yes. They come here all the time. The monks are more liberal. Should I call?"

"Chuck would want Last Rites. Yes, please."

Within the hour, Father Vincent arrives. He places the anointed oil on Chuck's forehead as he chants. I watch from the opposite side of the bed in reverent silence. At the end, he holds Chuck's hand for a moment, then caresses his hair. I'm touched by his tenderness.

In the hallway outside Chuck's room, Father Vincent offers me his condolences. Then he asks, "Would you like me to do a service for Chuck?"

I'm bowled over by his generosity. He doesn't even know my brother.

"At the Santa Barbara Mission? You would do that?"

"We would hold it in an adjacent chapel. It's quite lovely."

I nod eagerly, struggling to believe it. Chuck will have the send-off he'd hoped for but never expected.

"We'll plan on that then, shall we? When the time comes, you come visit me and we'll talk about the service."

I nod, tears flowing. He opens his arms, and I step into them, overwhelmed with gratitude. Chuck will have a Catholic service. Mom will be pleased. And Dad. *But he hasn't come to see Chuck yet.*

I warned him. If he can't make time to say goodbye to his son, he will have to live with the guilt. *I can't help him anymore.*

The doctor comes in and hooks up a morphine drip. He explains to me how to squeeze the bolus for extra pain relief—every fifteen minutes. Chuck's face tells me when he's in pain. Others might not see it, but I know my brother. Maybe I can't read his mind, but I can read his body language.

I pull a sketch pad and pencil out of my bag. It's been a long while since I've made art, except for colored markers on the back of my letter to Oprah that got me in the audience. When packing for this trip, I tucked art supplies under my clothes. Sketching calms me and will help me through the night.

Sitting next to Chuck's bed, I set a small pack of watercolors and a brush on a side table and use them to create three portraits of my brother's departing spirit.

Debbie stops in and shows me a room next to Chuck's. "You can sleep here tonight, so you are close."

"Do you have an alarm clock I can borrow?" I need to wake every fifteen minutes to squeeze the bolus—if Chuck needs it. The law prohibits staff from administering morphine. Chuck can't, so when he shows distress on his face, it's up to me. I stay up, squeezing the bulb until 2am when I must lie down for a bit.

On the bed in the next room with the door open, I can hear Chuck's labored breathing. A volunteer sticks his head. "Come in. Please."

He says, "We'll take care of Chuck." He squeezes my hand. "You'll need your rest for tomorrow." I express my gratitude with a nod, my eyelids already half-closed. He switches off the alarm and pulls the door closed as he leaves.

Debbie wakes me at seven, interrupting a fretful dream. At the little sink, I splash water on my face and enter Chuck's room wearing the clothes I slept in. Barry, a retired physician and resident, stands at my brother's bedside. He and Chuck had grown close in the last four weeks. Debbie stands next to Barry with the on-call nurse just behind.

Debbie says, "It's time. Tell him it's okay."

After the long night, watching him suffer, I'm ready for him to move on.

I hold his hand, drawing all the calming energy I can muster through my feet from the earth below, and send it to Chuck through his withered hand. His freckles seem more pronounced, like little islands scattered across a sea of yellow skin.

It's okay, Chuck. Go be with Don.

I feel the energy in the room echoing Chuck's breath as it slows. He takes a last gasp of air. And then he dies.

Debbie rushes me out of the room to keep me safe from the contaminated blood that rushes up my brother's throat and out of his mouth. She stands with me in the hall, talking about Father Vincent and how nice the service will be. "Would you like to have family and friends gather here afterward?" I nod, unable to speak my gratitude.

After they change the sheets and clean up Chuck, I return to his side. He is lying peacefully with his hands on his abdomen.

Debbie says, "I'll call your mom so you can stay with Chuck."

I whisper, "Thanks."

I pull up a chair and sit next to Chuck's bed to study his lifeless form—how it's changed since last night. *Chuck is gone.*

What energy I have drains as I exhale. I stare at his things around the room. The framed cafe scene by Aldo Luongo that I'd given him hangs across from his bed. Next to it, a plaque with all the Star Trek Captains. *Chuck loved those shows.* Two Kachinas he'd purchased on a trip to the Southwest with Don, one with its arm broken, stand on the table below. A feathered Mardi Gras mask hangs next to the patio door near the woodcut of the old man. In all, they create a portrait of my brother.

He always wanted everything perfect, like keeping the closet door closed. It was open yesterday, so I closed it. When I returned to his bedside, he was talking to his angel.

It's time to honor my brother—to create a celebration of his life. Something that's beautiful, like every space he created in his home and the cabin. "Okay, Chuck, I need to get busy if I'm going to throw you a great party."

As I leave the room, a volunteer takes my place sitting with Chuck's body. That's when Dad walks through the front door. *Twenty minutes too late. I wouldn't wish that on anyone.*

With one look, Debbie figures out who the gray-haired man is. She steps ahead of me and directs him to a sofa in the common room.

I sit down next to him. "Chuck died a few minutes ago. You're too late."

His eyes open wide, his brow furrows. He bellows, "I would have made it on time if you had given me better directions. I've been driving in circles for an hour."

Sure, Dad. Blame me. "He's been here a month. If you'd come before, you would have easily found us."

"I did. They wouldn't let me see him." I look at Debbie, who shakes her head.

"Well, Dad, if that were true, why couldn't you find it today?" *Aha. Caught you. Let's see you wiggle out of that one.*

He huffs, about to walk away when I call after him. "Chuck is in his room if you want to spend time with him before they take him away."

Dad says, "No. It's too late." He shakes his head and walks away.

With little sleep, I have no patience for his bullshit. *I'm done with it…and you.*

I step into the hall near Chuck's room to check in with the staff. As I'm talking to a nurse, Dad slips into Chuck's room and closes the door. *I'm glad you found the courage.*

He's disappointed Chuck so many times. He will steep in the

karma for the hurt he's caused. I've earned my own with more regrets than I care to admit.

I walk into the dining room to call Mom and Aunt Dee. After I hang up, I call Father Vincent to confirm the date and time of the service. Next is the mortuary to arrange for cremation. With details set, I call Greg. "He died early this morning. We'll have a service at the Mission chapel."

"I wish I were there with you." I know he can't leave the horses.

"How are the animals?"

He says, "They are all fine. The dogs and especially Lance miss you. If only we knew someone we could trust to watch them." His voice is strained. *He loved my brother too.*

My heart thuds. "It's okay." I swallow hard. "I've got Aunt Dee and Mom. I'll be home as soon as I can."

When I walk toward the kitchen for another cup of coffee, Dad waylays me in the dining room. "You know about Chuck's insurance policy. How much money am I receiving?"

After all the disappointments Dad piled on, Chuck took him off as a beneficiary. But it's not my place to tell him.

"I don't know, Dad. Mom is in charge of Chuck's finances."

"Well, what did he tell you?"

"Chuck didn't share his decisions about money with me."

Dad's voice gets loud as his anger boils over, but I don't hear his words. He's disapproved of me all my life. I no longer care what he thinks, but I still feel the pain of it.

Debbie steps between us and tells Dad all that I had done for Chuck. "You should be thankful for such a caring daughter who travels a thousand miles to be with your son."

I bite my tongue. I won't let him get to me. Not today. I could tell him all the horrible things he's done, but that won't help anyone. And Chuck wouldn't want me to.

Dad continues to fume. I take his arm and walk him into the rose garden to inhale the peace and feel Chuck's presence.

"Isn't this beautiful? Chuck loved roses. He could see and smell them from his bed up to the moment he died. Isn't that wonderful, Dad?"

He doesn't answer, but his scowl softens. We sit together on a bench admiring the garden in silence, each of us lost in our own inner world.

When Debbie calls me to the phone, Dad slips out. I don't see him again until the day of the service, set for Labor Day so Chuck's friends will be off work and can come from LA. I look forward to seeing them again.

Mom is worried about recent scandals of people's ashes getting mixed up. I can't let that happen to Chuck, so I visit the crematorium to check on Chuck's remains.

I'm the only visitor in the voluminous facility. After identifying myself, I ask the technician to take me to Chuck and open the cardboard casket. It's only the empty shell of the brother I've loved all my life. I kiss his cheek, then watch the attendant roll him in and light the flames. The white firebrick structure with steel supports resembles the kilns at UCLA I used to fire my installation. *Another thread that weaves the blanket of my life.*

The tech walks me out and says to return for my brother's ashes the morning of the service.

"Why so long?"

"The kiln needs time to cool after it's fired before I can remove his ashes."

Okay, Chuck, I whisper as I walk to his Camaro. *Go be with Don. We'll talk later.* I'm sure he'll be back to see who attends his memorial.

I stop for cappuccino and chocolate, like in grad school, to steady my wobbly legs and bolster my energy, then toss the wrapper from a Snickers and an empty Styrofoam cup onto the passenger seat. I pulled into the agreed upon parking lot to meet a local ceramic artist. Dave, at UCLA, told me this friend of his creates beautiful vessels, perhaps one I could buy to use for my brother's ashes.

I lean against the fender of Chuck's Camaro as we swap stories about teachers and artists at UCLA we both know. He looks like a clay artist: tall and tanned, with lean muscles and long hair tied at his nape.

"Dave told me what you are looking for. My deepest sympathies."

I describe Chuck to him. Each time I talk about his death, it shatters the illusion of him smoking on the patio at the Sarah House, surrounded by nurses busting their guts.

He opens his hatchback and removes three raku pots to choose from for Chuck's ashes. I select an earthy blue and green lidded vessel with sparkling bronze accents. *Stunning!*

Fingering its cone-shaped bottom, I ask, "How is it supported?" He pulls out an eighteen-inch metal stand. This urn will carry Chuck to the afterlife with the beauty and grace he deserves.

I pay him with the bills I'd pulled out of a drive-up bank on my way. He re-wraps the vessel and places it in the trunk of Chuck's Camaro. We hug and part. As I drive away, I soak my face and shirt with tears.

Back at Mom's house, I go through stacks of photos of Chuck and Don. I show Mom the piece I'd written about Chuck's work with AIDS LA and about his laughter and all the joy he gave to friends and strangers alike. "I'm sending it to the Santa Barbara and LA papers."

"Don't send it to the papers, please. It's beautiful, but your father's friends don't know he had a gay son, let alone one who died of AIDS. They'll shame him if they learn his namesake was gay."

"Surely not," I say. Mom nods.

Dad clings to his conservative buddies at the Elks Club and VFW. After being divorced for twenty-five years, Mom is still protecting his secrets. *I can't fight anymore.*

As a compromise, she suggests I print my piece in a booklet with photos of Chuck to give people who attend the service to take home as a remembrance. I reluctantly agree, then pull together a veiled announcement for the newspapers announcing Chuck's death, giving the time and place for the service and the location of the reception.

"Try the computers at Kinko's," Mom suggests. She gives me directions.

Once I step inside the office services shop, I lose track of time, falling into a creative fog working at Kinko's computer until Aunt Dee shows up to check on me around midnight. She came from Florida to support Mom and me. She attaches photos to poster boards for the reception.

At three in the morning, I drive to the Sarah House to sleep. A new resident needed the empty room, so Debbie asks me to move to Chuck's room. "If you stay in his room, you'll have time to pack his things." It's better than putting up with Dick.

A resident helps me make my brother's bed with fresh linens. It's eerie yet comforting to be in the company of Chuck's Kachinas, the woodcut of the old man, and the people sipping coffee in the colorful cafe scene. Before I try to sleep, I shake the hand-rattle I packed to balance the room's energy.

Chuck comes to me in my dreams. He's with Don and Tawna in Yosemite, with a waterfall in the background. In the morning, I go over the service details with Father Vincent, finalize plans for the reception, then drive to Kinko's for a second night to finish the handouts and photo boards. I'm numb checking off items on my To Do List, with Chuck smiling down.

On the morning of Chuck's service, the technician at the crematorium leads me into his work area. "I have to finish preparing your brother's remains." He points to an orange molded chair. "Do you mind if I play some music? I usually listen when I'm here alone."

"Sure. What are you going to play?"

"My friend gave me his old eight-track system with a bunch of tapes. I hope you like 80s music." I nod. "Something slow? Or upbeat?" he asks.

"Upbeat. I'll dance with my brother's spirit to help me stay awake."

The technician must think I'm crazy, but he just smiles and resumes his work.

If I am crazy, I'm okay with that. I believe a loved one's spirit comes to help us when we need them. So, I talk to my brother. When I feel a chill across my shoulders or a tingle up my spine, I know he's talking to me. Chuck helped me stay calm when Dad showed up too late. When he blamed everyone else, Chuck gave me the strength to let go of my anger.

The music comes over the speakers. I kick off my shoes; my bare feet on the cold concrete floor feel like standing in the shallows of a lake when we were young, its silt squishy between my toes.

With the beat of Madonna singing "Holiday," I twirl and jive. Chuck and I danced to her songs to forget the bad times.

The twirling makes me dizzy, my head light from lack of sleep, but I don't care. *We're celebrating, right, Chuck? We're dancing…with Don, and Scotty too.*

I sit down, but when a Three Dog Night song comes on, I dance again—even freer. Their song played in 1969 when I got stoned for the first time with the girls from the telephone company in an apartment next to a police station in Burbank. Making cookies, they set the bowl in front of me, and said, "Mix it with your hands." As I did, they poured bags of chocolate chips over my fingers into the dough, the sensation like fireworks of light and color that exploded all around me.

Dancing to the music eases my pain and grief for a few precious moments. I throw up my arms and call out, "Celebrate, celebrate." My skin tingles with joy.

Chuck and I danced through our whiplash and body pain when we were injured in a car wreck. When we were younger, we danced with Mike and laughed through all the trauma Dad created with his promotions and dismissals, his gambling and lies—while the fire burned all around us, just as I dance now waiting for Chuck's ashes.

"One" by Three Dog Night blasts over the speaker. Fitting. As my family collapses in grief, I keep going to make everything beautiful.

Tears streak down my cheeks, but I keep dancing, afraid to stop, afraid I might collapse in a heap. Chuck turned forty-nine a few weeks before he died, his vibrant life snuffed out too soon, his joyful laugh silenced.

Next I hear "Try A Little Tenderness."

Dance, Deborah. Dance. Dance your way through the pain. Hear Chuck's laughter, hold on to its sound. It will never be heard in this world again.

Right now, I can't laugh. Not without him. *But I will again. Soon. I promise.*

When the music stops, the technician places a baggy of Chuck's ashes into the raku ceramic vessel, nestles it in its box, and carries it to the Camaro for safe transport to the service.

When I return to the Sarah House, Judy calls me. "Mike won't make it to Santa Barbara. Both his hands have swelled; his fingers are like fat hotdogs, and the doctors don't know why. First, his skin turned black then broke open, oozing a clear liquid."—I cringe— "They've prescribed medications, but nothing is working. The pain is unbearable."

Mike is powerless to save his brother. The loss is manifesting in his body.

Judy says, "I'm not coming either. Mike can't do anything without my help—not eat, open a door, or even wipe his butt."

Mike's illness is keeping him from facing the reality of Chuck's death. During his three tours in Vietnam, he faced more death than anyone should in one lifetime. Mike helped Chuck throughout his illness, when I couldn't. It's my turn. *Heal well, Mike.*

People enter the chapel who I haven't seen in years—members of Chuck's gay community. And Don's family too, though thankfully not Edith. The monk's deep voice resonates throughout the elegant chapel as he leads us in song. He opens the lectern to people to share stories about Chuck. Most are humorous, all touching. Debbie from the Sarah House spoke about Chuck talking to the angel.

I don't see Dad, but after everyone has left the chapel, Father Vincent finds me. "I saw an older, gray-haired man crying throughout the service. Was that your dad?"

"Probably."

"He's in a great deal of pain."

I shrug.

Dad finds me at the reception and gives me a tender hug. Then he ruins it. "There weren't enough flowers at the chapel. They should have been all roses."

If that is all you have to say, then I pity you. No one cares what you think. But I forgive you.

I turn away without speaking. I scan the room to verify everything is in place for the reception. Debbie and her staff brought the flowers from the chapel to the reception, including the exotic arrangements with birds of paradise Mom and I ordered. I placed Chuck's urn on a table in the entry with the modest bouquet of red roses from Dad. The volunteers distribute the rest throughout the community space as if Chuck had directed it all.

I swap stories with people I know when two girls, who I'd never met before, tell me they were on Chuck's bowling team, how he loved to bowl, and did for as long as he could. Chuck took them to a sex shop during a San Diego tournament. That sounds like my brother. We laugh out loud and everyone is staring at us. Chuck would have loved it. He loved making people laugh.

CHAPTER FORTY-FIVE

HOME TO HEAL 1995-1996

I claim a few of Chuck's things for myself, then divvy up the rest between Mom and the Sarah House residents. The framed woodcut print of the old man, two Kachinas with their broken off parts, and the feathered Mardi Gras mask I pack into my suitcase between layers of clothes, using newsprint as extra protection. Dee packs the urn with Chuck's ashes into a box, tapes it up, and ties it with string and a handle to carry it through the airport and place under my seat on the plane. My brother's remains stay with me. *No one can touch them.*

"What's in the box?" The uniformed lady at the security access point narrows her eyes.

"My brother. He died a week ago." I fight back the tears that haven't fallen.

"Do you have the paperwork to travel with remains?"

Oh, shit. "The funeral home put the papers in the lid of the urn. They didn't say when I would need them."

"Get them out. I must see them."

"The box is all wrapped up. If I open it, I'll never get it repackaged." I look at the long line forming behind me, people looking at watches, worried about making their flights. "Can't you just let me through?"

"You can go through, if you leave the package."

I stop breathing. "What?" My grief, pushing on my solar plexus, threatens to explode.

"It's illegal to transport remains without documentation." Her voice gets louder and sharper with every word. My control cracks.

"Are you crazy? I'm not leaving my brother's ashes behind." I'm yelling. She's getting mad. She crosses her arms and taps her foot. My voice escalates to a shriek. "He just died. Can't you give me a break?" My tears form a deluge, soaking my face and shirt. I grab short bursts of stale air to breathe.

"Calm down, Miss, or we'll restrain you."

My eyes, with red lines piercing the brown center, open wide. My fury rises. "What if this was your dead brother?" I'm about to blow up when a little voice in my head shouts a dire warning. *Stop, Deborah. Or you'll end up on the evening news.*

I can see it now. *Crazy lady arrested at airport over brother's ashes.*

With hands shaking, I tear away the wrapping, imagining how the box falls and breaks. *I'm sorry, Chuck.* My eyes flow like a broken tap.

I spread wrapping paper, bubble wrap, and scraps of tape across the security platform. Using both hands, I pull out Chuck's urn and twist the lid. *It won't open.*

Still more tape. Dee packed it well. If she only knew.

As the last piece of tape gives way, I lift the lid and find the papers inside. "Like I said." I hand them to the woman, but she pulls her hands away.

"Are there remains on them?"

She's kidding, right? I must be trapped in a Laurel and Hardy movie.

"No," I say too loud. "The remains are sealed in·a heavy plastic bag." I tipped the urn to show her inside. "See?" I open the papers and hand them to her. She looks them over, gives a nod to her partner, then hands them back.

"You need to move along now. People are waiting."

What? "When I repack this urn. If it breaks…" I stuff what packing I can into the box.

"Are you satisfied?"

Her look is steely. I face her, mine full of disgust. "You're not a very nice person." I wipe my eyes on my sleeve, my guts about to burst as I hold back my wrath, fearing she'll keep me from boarding if it seeps out.

With my brother cradled in my arms, the box at risk of coming undone, I turn to walk away. My purse swings from my arm as I mutter under my breath, "What a bitch!"

"What did you say?" she calls after me.

Without looking back, I hurry down the corridor to a row of empty seats near my gate. Kneeling on the floor, I repack the urn the best I can, all the while mumbling swear words. I can't leave the package to go into the ladies' room, can't set it on the floor to pee. So I wipe my tears on my sleeve, crunch my groin, and board the plane.

I tell Greg on the two-hour drive home from the airport about the wicked security guard, then recount my interactions with Dad. When we pull up to the house, he gives me a hug, then carries my bags inside, along with Chuck's ashes. "Go say hello to the horses."

I have longed to be with them, to smell them, and touch them.

Lance comes loping over to see me. He stops and drops his forehead onto my chest.

"Hi, son. I missed you too."

I rub behind his ears and down his neck, combing his mane with my fingers. He shifts, placing his shoulder in front of my face. I throw my arms across his withers, and the waterworks release.

My grief cuts a chasm of sorrow through my heart like the rain divided our drive in Kings Canyon. We filled that crevice with the help of friends. In time, I will heal this hole in me. Until then, I need to get busy creating our home—a safe place for me and Greg and all our animals.

Standing in the field with Lance, I feel a tingle at the nape of my neck. I gaze at a cerulean-blue sky above the red oak and shagbark hickory trees. The wind is gentle, the air a pleasant warmth on my skin. I hear Chuck's voice in the hawks soaring above and in the squawks of the blue jays. I picture him with his quirky brow arched, the corners of his mouth lifted in a half smile. With a deep breath, I work the knots in Lance's shoulder with the flat of my fist. Around me are holes in the barn roof, their mending past due, and weeds as tall as my head begging to be whacked.

We settle into life on the farm: learning, repairing, nurturing. Greg and I take what's here—leftover boards from house renovations and scrap stored in outbuildings—to build walls, windows, and doors in the barn, making stalls for the horses and a coop for chickens. We find pieces of sheet metal to patch the roof. After leveling mounds of earth to plant grass and make paths, I transplant the fragile roots and tubers of peonies and irises I rescued from a broken cement retainer wall and the house's limestone foundation, hidden from the previous owners' attempt to remove them all. We cultivate the earth to grow vegetables and berries, creating a landscape both functional and beautiful. Greg and I work as a team, sometimes arguing about different ways of solving problems, but end each day with love and laughter.

The raku vessel containing Chuck's ashes sits on his antique sideboard in our living room. On the first anniversary of his death, we find Wolfie, our sweet Australian shepherd, lying by the front door as if waiting for my brother to return. And in the dark of the night, he leaves us to be with Chuck. So we bury them together in the orchard.

I stand near their grave under a mulberry tree, where robins flutter to sample its fruit, and sink my bare feet into the tall grass. In this moment, I pledge to my brother and myself to remain on this farm, to heal as I heal this land, and work to realize my vision of this place for us and our animals. Here, amid this beauty, I will install my sacred space with its four horses and thirteen goddesses, for I am home.

ACKNOWLEDGMENTS

I have received encouragement and support from family, friends and professionals alike, in life and in writing this story, and I want to share my appreciation.

I must begin by thanking Ruth Ann Molyneaux for your friendship and guidance when I began my writing journey, for introducing me to the Celebration Gallery, the members of Art@Emmanuel, the Soul Journeyers book club, and for growing with me as an artist. To Mary Lamphere, who created and published the Word of Art books, and led the In Print prompt group where I received kind critiques of my early writing, your never-ending enthusiasm and encouragement have been beyond generous.

I am grateful for my critique partners and their valuable insight into my story: Judy DePue, Serena Phillips, and Kimberly Diaz. To my friend, Caryl Barnes, I appreciate your clarity, and keen eye in proofreading, along with your ongoing support. And a special thanks to Catherine Conroy, my dear friend, for your persistence, insight, and hard work. You are the best.

To Nancy McCroskey, an artist and friend, you helped me become a clay artist and succeed as director of Artlink and taught me everything about clay and life lessons that have served me beyond the studio, like patience and striving for excellence. My writing mentors, Jane Friedman, Jennie Nash, and Allison K. Williams, have been instrumental in shaping this story and me as a writer. To all the members of Cawfee Talk: Kim Reynolds, Stephen Woodfin, Kat Caldwell, Michaela von Schweinitz, Rebecca Dolence, Victoria Marie Lees, Susan Soesbe, Rebecca Grogan, and especially Sara Gentry, Angie Androit, and Amy

Bernstein, I am grateful for your continuous support and honored to be counted among you. My thanks to Christine Swanberg, Poet Laureate of Rockford, who taught me the joy of writing poetry, and to Christine de Smit, a gifted instructor, who encouraged me with her kind words in my early days of writing.

I send a big thank you to my fellow authors and book coaches, Joan Fernández, Mary Bernstein, Caroline Malloy, and Tricia O'Brien, who worked with me on *Dance*; to Elaine Schroller for her publishing expertise; and to my Memoir Bridge group, Susan Hurley, Cassie Blair, and Cindy Heusel, whose support never waivers.

I am grateful for my equine teachers and friends who taught us how to care for our horses: Shae Rooney sold me my horse and soulmate, Lance, and helped find Greg's horse Ben; Marge and Vern Diehl taught us how to talk to horses; and Ginger Stout brought Ruby into our lives, a sweet Thoroughbred mare, who gave us three foals—some of our best teachers. You've all given us so much. Thank you.

My appreciation goes to my dear friends who are a part of this story: Melanie Vuicich-Mallis, Lyda Prack, and Dian Planck. You came into my life when I needed your friendship.

To my family: Dee Kreager, Tom Estep, and Bob Lucas; you help anchor me. And Greg, whose love makes all things possible.

This book would not have been possible without the generosity and kindness from each of you. I am forever grateful.

YOU'RE INVITED...

...to please leave a review for my book on Amazon. Even a few
sentences will help other
like-minded readers discover

Dance While the Fire Burns:
Family, Identity, and Dreams, a memoir.

...to discover insider background
on this book and writings on my website
www.DeborahAnnLucas.com.

I hope to see you there!

ABOUT THE AUTHOR

Deborah Ann Lucas and her husband have lived on their twenty-acre farm in north-central Illinois for thirty years. Deborah earned an MFA in ceramics from UCLA, a certification as a Hellerwork practitioner, and as a memoir and fiction book coach. She's published on Brevity and JaneFriedman.com and at DeborahAnnLucas.substack.com.

She's currently working on her series of memoirs and horse novels for adults, along with stories and art inspired by her life down the long lane with their rescued animals, now including two retired racehorses, a German shepherd dog, and a slew of cats who have wandered into their sanctuary of loving care.

You can learn more at DeborahAnnLucas.com

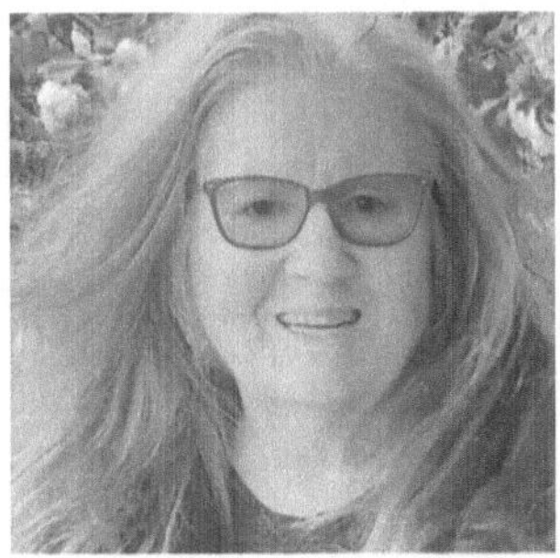

instagram.com/deborah_ann_lucas
facebook.com/DeborahAnnLucas
goodreads.com/22152619-deborah-lucas